A BEARD CUT SHORT

THE LIFE AND LESSONS OF A LEGENDARY PROFESSOR
CLIPPED BY A SLIP OF #MeToo

TODD NEFF

*Earthview*media

Published by Earthview Media
Denver, Colorado

Printed in the United States
First edition
ISBN-13: 978-0-9829583-7-7

Cover design by John Pendleton

This is a work of nonfiction. Any errors of fact will be corrected in subsequent editions.

For Pat

("She who suffers most")

Quid Pro Quo
for John

Tears welled,
and the profound poignancy of his bearded wisdom
 travelled through the whole of my body
and poked through my skin.
You can only play the hand you're dealt,
 he said,
grazing through the dreadful carrot sticks
whose very crunch inspired the strength of his eyes.
This putrefying fuel was followed by
 two Snickers bars,
and I smiled to consider the sinful balance of his soul.
This solitary creature,
 who thrusts his age at you without apology
 with the prominence of his facial grey,
is bigger than life.
His wife fatigued,
 but his empowering energy doesn't wane.
I ponder this:
 perhaps everyone is dealt a wild card,
        or four, or seven, or too many to count.
 And then, daily existence
        becomes a set of decisions—
 how will we play our chips?
He is choosing deliverance.
And thus, a helping of natural goodness and a little sweet
 divinity
        —the equilibrium of his ingestion—
 are precisely what emanate from him.
He is wise. And I am lucky.
 For adorning his chin is, distinctly, a crown.
        And indeed, I've been dealt a royal flush.

— "Ladybug," March 1999

Contents

Prologue

Denver, November 2018

Ars longa; vita brevis.[*]
— A favorite John
Rubadeau quote

I t's Wednesday, the week after Thanksgiving 2018. I sit at a kitchen table that got banged up during my wife's and my move from Boston to Denver seventeen years ago. We had kids soon after that, giving us an excuse to not replace the scarred kitchen table the girls would eventually trash anyway during some toddler—or, as time progressed, preschool, elementary school, middle school, or high school—project.

I'm a writer to a large degree because of the person sitting across the table from me. He is seated, right leg athwart left and wearing a shirt as shopworn as the table—gray on the outside, hunter's plaid inside—and glasses, though these are smaller than the ones he wore when, nearly thirty years ago, I first walked into his University of Michigan classroom.

And there's the beard.

Aside from the beard, John William Rubadeau looks nothing like Santa Claus. He was a lanky six-foot-five when I met him; seventy-eight-year-old spinal disks have reduced him to a lanky six-foot-three-and-three-quarters. He evokes more a vastly stretched-out elf escaped from the North Pole workshop. If there were another simple-yet-precise way to describe John's beard, I would use it. But it's a Santa

---

[*] Art is long; life is short.

Claus beard, one that he already had back when I was a sophomore in college. He was about as old then as I am now, and although his sideburns were still dark, the beard was already white.

Though not new to teaching, John had been in Ann Arbor for just two years as of early 1989, his classes full of freshmen and sophomores taking lower-level English courses such as the argumentative-writing class I had with him. That wouldn't last. Within a few years, word got out: there was this hyperactive, foul-mouthed master of the English language whose classes were some combination of a standup act, a motivational seminar, and a gathering of good friends. The English Department wisely moved him to upper-level courses, opening them to students across campus—future lawyers, doctors, businesspeople, engineers, and teachers in addition to those interested in the sciences and humanities. His English 325 class was called "Art of the Essay." His English 425 course went by "Advanced Essay Writing." They were the same thing, though: both focused on the basic elements of what he felt were the essentials of good writing, and both were really about much more than just writing.

By then, you had to be a senior (or an underclass athlete with godlike priority) to get in, and the class, and then the waitlist, filled overnight. He had won the 1990 Matthews Underclass Teaching Award for outstanding teaching of first- and second-year students; he would win, in 2005, the Golden Apple Award, recognizing a single University of Michigan professor for outstanding teaching; and he would also receive a 2016 nod from *College Magazine* as one of the "10 Best UMich Professors that Keep You On Your Toes." For three decades, he was, based on postcourse student assessments, among the University of Michigan's highest-rated teachers. His students would elevate him to second place overall in the university's RateMy-Professor.com rankings as that digital popularity contest took hold, and he was second because the first-place guy had more reviews, not better ones. John's students loved him to the point that, since two former students asked him to officiate at their wedding in 2004, he has married forty-five of them all over the country.

Those who won the Rubadeau lottery picked up a course pack whose front cover announced: "Grammar: the difference between

2

knowing your shit and knowing you're shit." A couple of pages into it, John described what was ahead:

> *This course will focus on (1) improving your vocabulary, (2) strengthening your grammatical, mechanical, semantical, and syntactical skills, and (3) helping you find your voice. I insist that you make the private public (ideally to illustrate a universal truth or a general principle) in order that you establish your authority to comment on the topic of your essay, that you pen an essay which is not generic, and, most importantly, that you write with a human voice (not dead, wooden prose written by an obscurantist majoring in philosophy [mea* culpa *to any philosophy major reading this course description]). Although this course is not difficult, it is perhaps the most labor-intensive course you will take.* Quid pro quo—*be prepared to bust ass for me, and, in the process, you'll learn much about writing.*

A couple of pages later, there was an opening note to his twenty-student classes, of which he taught three each term.

> *Having taught for forty-one years (the last thirty at the U-M), I realize full well that the first day of class generally (note CYAQ)* sets the tone for the remainder of the semester. With that acknowledgement made, I shall herewith commence this semester on a negative note.*
>
> *In 1987, I taught a truly horrible class here at Michigan (it was an Argumentative-Writing class, and the students mistakenly thought that the key to writing argumentatively was to be confrontational and to be*

---

* Cover-your-ass qualifier.

insulting to one another), and I immediately took steps to rectify the errors I had made. Since that horrible experience, I loved every class I taught—until the winter semester of 2003 when the computer fucked me once again and assigned to one of my 425 sections three of the worst grade grubbers and whiners ever assembled in one classroom setting . . . .

I am here to teach you about the intricacies and nuances of the English language not to coddle you or to support your conviction that you are the next Shakespeare. I expect that you bring to this class NO knowledge about writing; I shall teach you the knowledge that I know (note no CYAQ) you need to know in order to give you an edge over the competition (you will hear this phrase frequently during the semester), the competition against which you will be measured the rest of your life.

If you will be devastated because you receive less than an A in this course, drop the class this first day. The average grade in this class is a B+, and, in this select population, most of you are average. ("In the land of the blind, a one-eyed man is king."— Erasmus. In high school, you had one eye; the lion's share of your classmates was blind [Should I have used "were" in this context? I know for certain. Do you? I have no expectation that you would know.] At the University of Michigan, you all have one eye.) . . . .

I judge you no more severely than I would judge you were I your employer and were you representing my firm or were I your graduate dean in law school or med school or grad school and were you a representative example of the students my university was graduating.

If you want to learn about writing (or rather, "rewriting,") take this class; if you want to have a good *time while learning, take this class; if you want to make an impression on someone who can exercise a huge impact on your desire to pursue graduate studies or who can help you get your dream job, take this class. If you are willing to work hard to meet my demanding expectations (*quid pro quo*), take this class.*

Finally, if you were offended by my use of the word "fucked" [above], don't take this class. As I shall tell you three times today, "My idiolect is, at times, somewhat scatological." In words attributed to the great jurist Felix Frankfurter, "Obscenity, like beauty, is in the eye of the beholder." What may be obscene or vulgar in my eyes may not be in yours—and vice versa.

While all this helps explain what John Rubadeau's class was about, it sheds no light at all on why he's sitting at my beat-up kitchen table the Wednesday after Thanksgiving 2018. That story starts in 1957, with E. B. White.

White is famous today for his children's books—*Charlotte's Web, Stuart Little, The Trumpet of the Swan*. Back then, he was at least as well known for writing in the "Talk of the Town" pages each week for *The New Yorker*. In the July 27, 1957, edition of the magazine, White describes having received in the mail from a friend a short book that White had once owned. It was a self-published work of just forty-three pages. Its author was White's English professor at Cornell University, William Strunk, Jr., who self-published it in 1918. The "little book," as Strunk called it, had been required reading in Strunk's English 8 class that White had taken in 1919.

White lauded the little book, calling it Strunk's "attempt to cut the vast tangle of English rhetoric down to size and write its rules and principles on the head of a pin." White shared with *New Yorker* readers the little book's key dictums ("omit needless words," "use the active voice," "avoid a succession of loose sentences," et cetera) and quoted what would become perhaps the most famous few sentences in high-end English-language pedagogy: "Vigorous writing is concise. A sentence should contain no unnecessary words, a paragraph no un-necessary sentences, for the same reason that a drawing should have no unnecessary lines and a machine no unnecessary parts. This requires not that the writer make all his sentences short, or that he avoid all detail and treat his subjects only in outline, but that every word tell."

This little book was *The Elements of Style*. White, at the urging of Macmillan Publishing, expanded it into a longer, but still little, book of the same title. "Strunk & White," as it's also known, has sold some ten million copies since it appeared in 1959.

That's part of the story. The other part of the story is that John, who for decades told class after class that he loved teaching so much that he would sooner keel over dead at the chalkboard than retire, suddenly has time on his hands despite it being the Wednesday after Thanksgiving—a busy time in the fall semester back in Ann Arbor. John is available because, four months ago, he was fired.

Those familiar with academic hierarchies know that it takes extraordinary incompetence, gross misdeeds, or both for a tenured senior professor to get himself fired. But despite his long tenure, John had no tenure. John was a lecturer—a senior lecturer, but still an inhabitant of the lowest tier of the college-teaching hierarchy (grad-student teaching assistants aside). He remained an instructor because, as he told me years ago, he had no interest in writing "academic bullshit."

Rather, he had written three novels. The first was a gentle parody of the popular Harlequin romance novels, its cover featuring John wearing a dress at an ancient typewriter. The second was a satire of his misadventures raising pigs in the hollows near Harrogate, Tennessee. The third, which John called his magnum opus, was a satirical assault on the Roman Catholic Church. It was also a commentary on growing up in Madison, Wisconsin, in the years after the Second World War and on about everything else Americana 1940-1980. He worked on that book for thirty-five years, starting it while a Fulbright-Hays lecturer in Constanţa, Romania, and continuing through his eight years at Purdue University and through most of his time at Michigan. During the school year, he spent countless hours reading and grading student papers. In the summer months, he spent countless hours in his Ann Arbor basement, rewriting again and again what would become *A Sense of Shame: Born in a State of Sin.*

He published his magnum opus in 2014 under the nameplate of an extremely small publisher based in Denver, Colorado: Earthview Media, an S-corporation founded on the advice of my accountant. With help from another former student of John's, I had published my first book under its aegis four years earlier.

The magnum opus is 1,143 pages long, and that's not including a 292-page glossary in which thousands of terms—from *abattoir* to *zygote*—are defined. It took me three years of on-and-off reading to finish it. When I told him I'd wrapped it up, he informed me that I was, to his knowledge, the third person to have done so: John himself and John's doctor being the other two.

"My doctor told me, 'Either you're a genius or you're fuckin' crazy,'" John said.

Cut the "Either" and replace the "or" with an "and," and that sentence takes you a good way along the path to understanding John Rubadeau.

As far as the firing, the union representing the university's roughly 1,600 lecturers had taken up the case, as had a former student and now attorney helping John pro bono. (Several former students had offered to cover all his legal costs.) Everyone with a law degree told John to keep mum.

The *Ann Arbor News* and the student newspaper *The Michigan Daily* published stories mentioning #MeToo transgressions—that is, behavior amounting to sexual harassment or worse. The reporting relied on a union rep avoiding specifics and anonymous sources alluding to inappropriate behavior with respect to faculty colleagues. What little I had gleaned—for example, a female professor's interpreting John's repeated offerings of bone-shaped biscuits for her dog to be a sexist and/or racist power play—seemed a stretch. A nameless former graduate student viewed John's puppylike gregariousness as suspicious; so too John's inviting students to his and his wife's and dogs' home for dinners and get-togethers. Even John's walk-in photo album was deemed "creepy," as another teaching assistant put it. (His Angell

Hall office featured thousands of shots of him and his students, to the point that he had hung paddlewheel-like mobiles to deal with the ever-multiplying two-dimensional hordes.)

Suddenly, this linguistic craftsman, expert editor, and inveterate grammarian—this wildly enthusiastic teacher and life coach to generations of students—would not have the opportunity to keel over at the chalkboard. The thought of it saddened me. But it also got me to thinking.

Let's say John had been able to work until his contract ran out when he was 83, and that he would have then retired despite his desire to expire midsentence while propounding the perils of profuse alliteration. That would have added close to 500 students to the 3,000 or so he had already taught at the University of Michigan. Five hundred students is a healthy number. But at some point, Father Time would retain his perfect winning streak, and John would be gone.

For a few years I had considered asking John to collaborate on a book to share the alchemy of his teaching with the wider world. But he was either editing papers late into the night or rewriting his magnum opus. Then, when he finished *A Sense of Shame*, he declared that he would write no more books. I had doubts of my own, too: how would we approach such a project? Then one day I reached for Strunk & White for a quick reread. I'm not the only writer who does this as a reminder of the bad habits that creep into one's prose: entropy applies to arts and sciences alike.

It dawned on me that Strunk's relationship with White paralleled John's with me. Strunk had been White's teacher at a great university. White had become a journalist and writer of books, as had I. (That White wrote for *The New Yorker* and I wrote for the Boulder *Daily Camera*, and that *Charlotte's Web* has sold slightly better than my history of Ball Aerospace—let's not dwell upon.) Strunk was a great teacher with firm ideas about what works and doesn't in writing—same with John. The only notable incongruity, really, was that Strunk had died nine years before White received that copy of the little book in 1957. John remained very much alive. For the sake of parallelism, though, I figured I could always just terminate John.

I reached out to John and proposed the idea of collaborating on a foul-mouthed, funny book inspired by *The Elements of Style*, being careful not to mention the part about possibly having to kill him. The idea was to capture the man's grammar, writing, and life lessons to share with the sizable percentage of humanity who didn't make it to his class. My expectations were low, though buoyed slightly by an offhand sentence in an email he had sent me more than a decade earlier.

In the summer of 2008, I had brought my daughters, then ages 3 and 5, to see John and wife Pat at their home in Ann Arbor—one of thousands of visits by students and former students they had entertained over the years. This was, after all, a man who had written more than 2,500 letters of recommendation, more than one of them for me. The girls had gotten their "beard rubs" (in which John sweeps the distal regions of his facial hair back and forth across the face of a recipient who instinctively winces) and had been awed by the enormous Bear, a Giant Schnauzer the size of a llama. As the girls hesitantly pet the immense dog, John mentioned that recent eye surgery had made it hard for him to read the student papers at the heart of his stock-in-trade. In an email follow-up, I had mentioned that he could always teach indirectly.

"I have a sense that you're going to figure out a way to keep teaching until you're 97... but you could write the new Strunk & White instead, maybe," I had written.

He had responded: "97? Fuck you. 107! I've always hated far-far-too-prescriptive Strunk & White, and if I did write a grammar book, it would be full of salacious and obscene examples. At least it would make for interesting reading."

That I still had this email in my digital possession ten years later was as unlikely as my having retained various papers from my 1989 argumentative-writing class with John: my notes; John's handouts duplicated in the purple ink of that protocopier, the mimeograph; and my not-terribly-well-argued essays. This packet remains the only physical remnant of my undergraduate classwork.

In the fall of 2018, I forwarded that old email to John and suggested the idea again. To my surprise, this time he was interested in collaborating on what he would soon call our "dirty grammar book." Maybe it was the decade-old email; maybe it was his not knowing what to do with the all the time suddenly larding his days; maybe it was Pat's gentle coaxing in the interest of having a rare, quiet, John-free week. Whatever the case, we coordinated schedules and settled on a few days after Thanksgiving.

Now he's seated at this beat-up kitchen table with me. My notebook computer is open and aglow with an empty Word doc. A digital recorder with an afro-like windscreen points in John's direction, awaiting his wisdom. Grammar books, his and mine, clutter the scratched-up faux-wood Formica: *The American Heritage Book of English Usage; A Handbook to Literature; A Pocket Style Manual; The Gregg Reference Manual;* what he describes as his *vade mecum, The American Heritage College Dictionary* with its 343 usage notes; and, of course, *The Elements of Style.* The course pack from his final semester, spring 2018, lies open to page forty-seven, where John's distillation of English grammar awaits under the heading GRAMMAR REVIEW.[*]

We will indeed review grammar. What I don't yet realize, though, is that the answers to other questions that will strike me over these next few days in Denver will push grammar to the back of the book: Where does John's teaching persona end and the real person start? Who is this marvelous teacher, this improbable motivational guru, this mentor-turned-friend? Where did he come from? Why did he get fired? Did he deserve it?

It will take me months to amass—through Freedom of Information Act requests, interviews, and other means—enough background to grasp what this book really will be about. It will not so much be about grammar, dirty or otherwise. It will, rather, be about "a tragic life well-lived," as John describes his extraordinary personal history; about the life lessons he imparted in part because of that well-lived, tragic life; and then about a firing that should never have happened.

---

[*] Revised and updated at the end of this book.

1

Quid Pro Quo

Quid pro quo. One is rewarded commensurate with the effort one has put into the task. These three words should be your mantra for achieving success in any [yes, any] activity you participate in during your lifetime—be that activity vocational, avocational, social, emotional, philosophical, ethical, moral, or any "*-al*" you can suffix to any word.

— John Rubadeau

My notes are sparse, in pencil, on yellowed college-ruled spiral paper sliced from its helical moorings and haphazardly stapled together with other course materials. There's a date: 1/18/89, corresponding with my fifth class period with John Rubadeau in the winter semester of the year the Berlin Wall would fall. I know this because, stapled a couple of pages before my notes begin, a badly faded purple-mimeographed sheet is titled, "AN EXTREMELY FLEXIBLE SYLLABUS FOR JOHN RUBADEAU'S ENGLISH 225— WINTER '89." Why I took no notes on days one through four I can't recall, but it doesn't surprise me.

I was a sophomore in college and had recently wrapped up a fraternity hell week including, among other morsels, "continuous keg." Here, a dozen pledges had formed a looping line in the front room of a large, musty house whose first-floor windows had been temporarily newspapered over. At the head end of the line had been a keg of Goebel beer. A couple of "actives"—full-fledged frat boys—had taken turns pumping and pouring and never closing the valve at the end of the black-plastic line they moved from one big disposable plastic cup to the next. There had been a garbage can a bit past the keg because it was pretty much impossible for anyone who wasn't a bull elephant to down the equivalent of thirteen 12-ounce beers in a matter of minutes. The actives had made bets on which of us would hold out longest before resorting to the garbage can and getting back in line to continue this highly inefficient process of liquid transfer.

Up high on the first page of my 1/18/89 notes, I wrote: "TITLE PAGE" and "Paginate" (this underlined) and then "Read backwards."

John was not advocating reading magazines or books backwards. I now know that backwards reading was a standard Rubadeau self-editing technique, one he practiced with his own writing. Then below that came a bit of Latin.

quid pro quo

I had heard it before but didn't know what it meant. Next to it I wrote: "something for something—no free lunch." That's not far off *The American Heritage* definition: "An equal exchange or substitution." Typically, you use *quid pro quo* (italicized here as foreign words typically are) when you're talking about returning favors in the I'll-scratch-your-back-if-you-scratch-mine sense. Implicit in the term is a mild sense of corruption.

While John was well aware of the standard usage, he meant something else. He applied *quid pro quo* in the broadest sense of the original Latin's literal "something for something." He did this for two reasons. One, he was making clear his expectations and stoking our motivation to put in the hours he expected of us as we wrote our own papers and critiqued those of our classmates. Put in the effort, and you'll reap the rewards.

Two, he was telling us that, in general, you get out of about everything—your job, your relationships, your hobbies, your volunteer efforts—what you put into it. This was a deep life lesson disguised as a vocabulary booster. I don't know if I picked up on it then or not. Probably not. I had, after all, been randomly assigned to this required lower-level English class with a focus on writing argumentative essays. I wasn't looking for, or expecting, life lessons. I was looking for three credits and a decent grade which, I would guess, were universal sentiments among the twenty of us seated in a circle of chair desks John joined us in. I didn't know who this crazy bearded guy was. None of us did.

It was only his fourth semester at the University of Michigan. As was the case with all the teachers in my life to that point, it seemed as if he had beamed down into this Angell Hall classroom from the Starship Enterprise—fully formed but context-free beyond the narrow confines of the subject at hand—in his baggy flannel shirt, well-worn jeans, and hiking boots rather than a snug Starfleet uniform. His hair, dark and parted on the left side, merged into sideburns that bleached abruptly into a terrifically curly beard long enough to obscure his neck. This was a tall man with a tall man's slouch which I imagined had been ingrained from years of bending down to connect with people rather than lord over them imperiously.

His eyes sparkled through his glasses; he possessed the energy and enthusiasm of a middle-school boy out on a playground. An antsy dude, he often hopped up from our circle to pace about or scribble words such as "*quid pro quo*" or "After boiling for twelve minutes, the baby was given its bottle" on the chalkboard. Digressions were common enough that he assigned a student to remind him what he had been talking about before a tangent that could come from, and then lead to, just about anywhere. That day in January 1989, to demonstrate the ridiculousness of English spelling, and the diverse pronunciation of the consonant cluster *gh*, he hopped up and wrote on the chalkboard:

Though a rough cough and hiccough plough me through.

He proceeded to chalk a list of ten vocabulary words as dictated by a student who had been assigned the previous class period to collect them, the goal being to stump John: *salient, atavism, obsequious, encomium, spate, ubiquitous, iconoclastic, eponymous, perfidy, flummox*. Unflummoxed, John defined each without hesitation, as one would recite one's date of birth to a bureaucrat. The man commanded a vocabulary of untold legions.

13

John sat back down and launched into a digression he particularly relished given his somewhat-scatological idiolect. It had to do with the origins of the word *fuck*.

He asked us where the word came from. We responded by shifting uncomfortably in our seats. The notion of plumbing the origins of such a word in a classroom setting—even at the liberal bastion of the University of Michigan—pushed past edgy into mildly scandalous. Nineteen eighty-nine was not 1959, but *fuck* was definitely not something you'd read in polite publications. It was all quite exciting.

"Where does the word come from?" he asked us again.

"For Unlawful Carnal Knowledge?" someone piped up.

"A folk etymology!" John leaped to his feet. "So is 'Fornication Under Consent of the King'—that's another one. False acronym; ergo, false etymologies."

A couple of big steps and he was back at the chalkboard, asking us to turn to a "Table of Indo-European Sound Correspondences" that his mimeographing had rendered more or less illegible. (Copy machines were, for the record, widely available by 1989.) I had no idea what a sound correspondence was, much less why someone teaching a sophomore writing class would want to illustrate what a sound correspondence was. But despite my sense that John had been freshly beamed down from the Starship Enterprise, he had earned a PhD in linguistics. He proceeded to trace the word *fuck* back to Sanskrit and beyond—all the way back to a notional, 5,000-year-old Indo-European proto language.

On the chalkboard he wrote "*peig.*"

"That's a proto-Indo-European root," he said. "It comes to us from middle-Dutch *fokken,* which means 'to cut' or 'to mark by incision.' Look at your sound correspondences on the handout."

I looked at the handout and was unable to make sense of it.

"The Indo-European sound for *p* evolves into what when we get to Germanic and Old English?"

"An *f*," someone with extremely good eyes said.

"Right! It's no accident that the Latin *pisces* turned into the German *Fisch* and the English *fish*, or that our word *foot* comes from the

Latin root *pod* or *ped*, as in *podiatrist* and *pedestrian*," John explained. "Goddamn great! Now how about the *g*?"

Catching on, I ran a finger across the mimeographed table, from a purple splotch I took to be a *g* to what I took to be a *k*. A classmate got there first.

"*G* turns into a *k*," she said.

"Yes, yes!" John said. "Does anybody know the Latin word for *knee*?"

Silence.

"No? Okay, well, it's *genu*. As in *genuflect*, for you Catholics. The German *Knie* and English *knee* derive from *genu*. Same story with one of the Latin words for *cold*: *gelidus*, which is the root for the English *gelid*—which means . . . What do you think?"

"Cold?" someone said.

"Yes! Extremely cold, in fact. The *g* sound turned into a *k* or a hard *c*."

Put it together, he said, the Indo-European *peig* evolved into the Dutch *fokken*, which became the most popular bit of vulgar slang in the modern English language.

* * *

At the beginning of a given semester, most teachers tell students what they're going to learn. Some teachers tell students why they're going to learn it. Few teachers explain how they will facilitate the learning at the heart of their knowledge-imparting mandate. Students are generally as ignorant about a teacher's pedagogical strategies and approaches as a surgery patient is about the detailed preparation that happens in an operating room before a procedure. The strategies are left opaque because it doesn't really matter to the student or the patient.

John explained at least part of what he was up to. He told us that we would learn more about writing through the hours and hours of critiquing the work of our fellow students than we would learn from him.

Three decades later, I wonder if tracing the word *fuck* through Indo-European sound correspondences and explaining that *scatological* comes from the Greek word for *shit* were deliberate acts of barrier-busting. At my kitchen table in Denver, I suggest, "You're signaling to the class that you'll tolerate language and ideas that might otherwise be suppressed in the polite society that most of them came from and that your classroom is a place where people can open up, speak their minds, and not worry about saving face."

"Yeah," he says. "But, by the same token, I never want to alienate people. I never use racist or sexist language. I give them a heads-up that these are my boundaries."

"Such as?"

"I do test the limits of people's mores and taboos. For example, I say 'goddammit' all the time," John says. "Thou shalt not take the name of the Lord thy God in vain—I believe it's the third commandment. Well, I can't take the name of the Lord thy God in vain because I don't believe in God. So when I say 'goddamn,' it has nothing to do with God. It's just a figure of speech with me. Just like saying—one of my friends who's deeply religious says 'gollybum.' Gollybum? What the fuck? Just say 'goddammit'!"

He continues. "It goes back to euphemisms in general. I hate it when I see 'he fudged up' or 'he forked up' or 'the F-word.' Why do we use these? Every single person knows the actual word is behind it. Same with the 'N-word.' Everybody knows what it means, but 'nigger' has so much emotional baggage and tension to it that I think you should write it in the context it was used. Put it in quotes, of course, if someone said it. But assuming it's not being used as a mutually accepted colloquialism among African Americans, it shows a lack of knowledge, a lack of education, and absolute observable prejudice and bias. That's information a reader can use to understand context as well as content.

"And, of course, there's 'collateral damage,' which a lot of people don't know is a euphemism for killing civilians. Why don't you say, '150 kids were killed today in Yemen because of American bombs we sold to the Saudis, and 4,500 died of starvation because of our

16

materiel'? Do you know, by the way, the difference between *materiel* and *material*?"

"Yes," I say.

"Hm," he says, having lost an opening for a digression from the digression.

My daughter Lily, 15, happens by the kitchen table, something that's easy to do given the house's open layout and small footprint. Focusing on the mobile device in her hand, she accidentally knocks over the microphone I've set up. These things happen when your virtual environment outranks your physical one. John narrates: "Lily just knocked down the microphone. Thanks, Lily. She's very busy chatting on the phone with her friends."

"That's what they do," I say. "She's in high school."

"It's called 'Snapshot,'" John says. "She taught me about Snapshot today. I thought it was a hockey thing, and then I learned it has nothing to do with hockey."

"Snapchat," Lily corrects.

"Such an excellent conversational partner, isn't she? Does she speak English?"

Lily snort-laughs.

"And she laughs through her nose. What a trick. Fits perfectly with a freak family," John says.

Lily snort-laughs again and disappears back upstairs with the iPhone into which she packs all her friends. I steer us back to his class.

"What I'm trying to get at is, with this 'somewhat scatological idiolect' of yours and how you dress on the low end of casual, to put it charitably, and the way you had everybody move the rows of desks into a circle back when I had your class, you're sending a message," I say. "And the message—messages, I guess—is that here's a place where we're not putting on airs, where we're not judging, and where we're not going to worry about what society thinks about the word 'fuck,' "You create a place defined by expertise and . . ." and I can't find the right word.

"Empathy," John finishes.

Empathy: from the Greek prefix for "in" and suffix for "suffering," which a German guy turned, in the 1850s, into *Einfühlung*, and which later was translated into English that's much closer to the original Greek. It's the ability to put oneself in another person's shoes and treat him or her as you would like to be treated. Empathy is not normally an academic prerequisite. But then, most classes don't involve learning to write by delving into often deeply personal experiences and then, gently but honestly, critiquing the written expression of similarly personal experiences as conveyed by others you barely know. John well knew how central empathy is to something more vital than academic success at the University of Michigan or any other institution of higher learning. A person short on empathy is rarely a good person regardless of his or her worldly success. An empathetic person is usually a good person, worldly success be damned.

Empathy can be innate. But often, it's cultivated through one's own humbling experiences. Lord thy God knows, John Rubadeau had his share of them, starting at the very beginning.

2

Rough Start

It is only through indignity that man rises to dignity.
— Francis Bacon (paraphrased)

A s she prepared to deliver her second child at St. Mary's Hospital in Madison, Wisconsin, Florence Rubadeau had more than an inkling that she had not married well. Her father, a wealthy pharmacist and entrepreneur in the northern Wisconsin town of Antigo, had sent a son and four daughters to college in an era when a small minority of people were so educated. The family had a cook, a driver and service cars, servants—the whole bit. Florence's early years had been charmed, as the caption beneath her senior-class picture attested: "Dancing and playing through life I go/Never a thought for work or woe."

Florence began her university years at Rosary College (later to be renamed Dominican University) near Chicago before transferring to the University of Wisconsin—Madison. There, the young woman with expressive blue eyes and a resemblance to Snow White excelled in class, joined Alpha Xi Delta sorority, and was feted as one of a handful of campus "Badger Beauties" by the time she graduated in 1928.

Now in February 1940, Florence had been married for five years and was the mother of a four-year-old daughter named Joan. Her husband Ken's drinking, which had clouded their relationship for some time now, was about to precipitate a move from a three-bedroom house on a quiet street in Madison to a two-bedroom apartment on a busy one. It probably wasn't a coincidence that the new place was a two-minute walk up the street from Ken's favorite watering hole, the Laurel Tavern.

Ken hailed from the mining town of Highland about sixty miles west of Madison. His parents had been born there, too, but were of entirely different stock than Florence's. Ken's father Herbert had been first a mailman, then a laborer, and, eventually, a foreman in a local mine before moving the family of six to Madison when Ken was in grade school. There Herbert Rubado, as the name was spelled then, worked as an assembly-line foreman at the French Battery Company (which later became Rayovac) and at the Burgess Battery Company (which became part of Duracell). Still, the scraps of family lore had a rural flavor, such as the one about Ken and his brother spending their days off hunting in the woods and subsequently fighting over who got to suck the brains out of a felled squirrel.

"I come from very sophisticated stock," said John, the baby who Florence brought into the world on February 11, 1940.

Ken Rubadeau never finished high school. He briefly managed his friend and jazz trumpeter Bunny Berigan's career and sold insurance with North American Life in Madison. He was a popular guy, a slick-talking bon vivant, and a blast to party with.

Along the way, he met Florence, who was working at the local phone company. She was smitten by this handsome, dark-haired man's sharp mind and quick sense of humor. He seemed to know everyone in town, and everyone in town appeared to like him. Yes, he was drawn to drink, but that was nothing out of the ordinary for a businessman who entertained clients. Florence was not the first up-standing young woman to fall for a charming rogue.

Ken and Florence married on an early autumn Saturday in Chicago in 1934. A newspaper brief in the next day's *Wisconsin State Journal* mentions the event having taken place in the cavernous St. Clement Church. More likely they eloped and chose the church to maintain appearances; neither a wedding announcement nor photos exist, and they never mentioned the wedding to their children. Florence's family—as staid, respectable, and proper as Ken's were drunken, wild, and Irish—never forgave her for marrying so far beneath her station.

John's first decade of life coincided with his father's descent into rampant alcoholism. Florence knew better than to try to control Ken, and her staunch Catholicism meant leaving him was out of the question. A typical Sunday in the Rubadeaus' first-floor apartment at 2801 Monroe Street started with morning mass where John served as an altar boy and at which Ken was inevitably and supremely hung over. Upon returning home, Ken would pull the sports section from the *Chicago Tribune* and mix an enormous martini in a Mason jar, finish the drink shortly after midday, and repeat. The afternoon brought shots of Jim Beam with Miller High Life chasers (a two-stage boilermaker, the modern aficionado will recognize). By the evening, he had passed out on the living-room sofa.

The notion that Florence might dance and play through life became deeply ironic. This sensitive soul bottled up her burdens save for the occasional comment to her daughter that "I'm the horse. They put everything on me." Her family was right. She had made a mistake, and now she was forever trapped. Unhappiness filled the little apartment on Monroe Street.

By John's tenth year, Ken's employer—now National Guardian Life—had had enough of his drunkenness. Ken took a series of low-wage jobs: he did something or other in the basement at the Rentschler Floral Company whose owners were drinking buddies; he was a minder in the Henry Vilas Park Zoo; he washed dishes at a hotel. These jobs were interrupted by wicked benders during which he might disappear for days at a time. Friends who called him "Kenny" largely bankrolled his addiction, the favor he returned by being, as his son recalled, "of quicksilver mind and tongue and the funniest guy in Madison, Wisconsin."

"But they never had to live with the sonofabitch," John added.

The charming, witty man-about-town was, at home, largely distant, surly, and short-tempered. Neither he nor Florence saw the point of complimenting John or Joan on some good deed or job well done. Among Ken's preferred punishments for his young son's real or perceived transgressions included a belt to the bare behind and forcing the children to kneel on kitchen linoleum that the old man had strewn with uncooked rice. The grains embedded so deeply that the boy had to pick them out of his kneecaps.

Money had always been tight, but now Florence, en route home from her secretarial job, would get off the bus two stops early to save a nickel in fare. They fell behind on rent with regularity, saved from eviction only by a patient landlord. They started their weekly dinners with chili sprinkled with a pound of hamburger, a meal which they ate for a couple of days until Florence added noodles and called it "goulash." Canned fish and the occasional creamed codfish ball filled out the Friday menu. John's paternal grandmother broke the monotony on many Sundays with homemade macaroni and cheese, chicken dishes, and Irish specialties such as scrapple and custard pie. Florence's sister Peg, her husband Earl Wilke, and their son Tom came by on Sunday evenings with a pint of Lady Borden vanilla ice cream and Spanish peanuts. Florence made chocolate sauce, and the ice cream was divvied up for what was the weekly treat in the Rubadeau home. Wilke, a former University of Wisconsin football player and the revered football and basketball coach at the high school John would one day attend, had little respect for Ken Rubadeau, but it didn't much matter: by the time he got there on a Sunday eve, Ken had usually passed out on the couch.

Well after Ken's white-collar days had ended, Florence instructed her children to tell anyone who asked that he worked for the National Guardian Life Insurance Company.

"But he doesn't," Joan protested.

"I'm going to say it again," Florence told her. "If asked, you say Daddy works for the National Guardian Life Insurance Company."

To maintain appearances, Ken continued to wear a suit and dress shirts, the latter monogrammed with his initials "KWR," when he left the house for his menial jobs. He had the shirts laundered, starched, and pressed at the local Chinese laundry and generally sent John to pick them up. Usually without enough money to cover the bill, John told the proprietor that Ken would pay him later. The man handed over the shirts and later told Ken, "KWR! KWR! Tall boy always short!"

Ken's absences became more frequent over time. As John walked to school after his father hadn't come home, he sometimes spied him sitting at the end of a dock and fishing with a short bamboo pole whose line disappeared into the spring-fed waters of Lake Wingra.

The deep sense of insecurity that had always darkened the Rubadeau household became more pronounced. While Joan had found solace playing with her dolls under the apartment stairwell just outside the apartment door, John did what any self-respecting boy lacking adult supervision would do—he more or less went feral. He spent as little time at home as possible. He and his friends discovered a great venue for playing games of cops and robbers or cowboys and Indians in the catacomblike basement of the under-construction Temple Beth El, a synagogue conveniently located across from the backyard of the Rubadeau apartment building. Caught trespassing by the police, John found himself marched before the synagogue's rabbi, Manfred Swarsensky, a man who had no business being alive.

Antisemitic rioters had burned down Swarsensky's Berlin synagogue during Kristallnacht in November 1938, and he had been arrested and sent to the Sachsenhausen concentration camp. There he was subjected to torture, beatings, starvation, and hard labor prior to his release on the condition he leave the country. Why he was freed, he would never know. That was in early 1939; now, just over a decade later, the middle-aged rabbi suggested to this skinny, cropped-haired Catholic boy that playing in the future synagogue's basement was fine so long as he and his buddies didn't break anything and didn't get hurt.

Come late May, the boy would pay back the rabbi's kindness in carp, a gesture reciprocated with baked goods that congregants continually brought the rabbi. With a spear and a Wham-O crossbow he rigged with 100-pound-test fishing line and a modified beer can from which the line unspooled, John took advantage of spawning season and daily hauled a dozen or more of the whiskered mud-suckers out of Lake Wingra. He presented these to Rabbi Swarsensky who then gave them to the temple's poor to make gefilte fish.

* * *

"You know the joke about gefilte fish, don't you?" asks the boy who is an old man now.

We are at the kitchen table and have been discussing the grammatical applications of "that" versus "which" (which John insists are, in many cases, interchangeable, though not in this parenthetical instance) when Rabbi Swarsensky's name comes up. John is unsentimental about physical objects and saves few possessions, but his wife Pat has told me he still has the carp spear and the Wham-O crossbow.

"No," I said. I know I don't have to ask him to tell it.

"You catch a carp, then you scale it, gut it, cut off the head, cut off the tail, and then you let it soak in brine for two days," John says. He ornaments his jokes with improvised detail and delivers them matter-of-factly. Presently, he could just as easily be describing dish preparations to a cooking-show audience. "You take it out and pour some olive oil on it, add seasoning, and put it on a cedar plank. You put it in the oven for six hours at 250 degrees."

He pauses.

"And then you throw away the carp and eat the plank."

I laugh.

Rabbi Swarsensky has been gone since 1981. His fledgling congregation has grown to more than 600 families. The basement, like most synagogue basements, is bereft of goyish boys playing cowboys and Indians.

* * *

After spawning season ended, John maintained his habit of bringing the rabbi freshly impaled carp, though in smaller numbers. He delivered some of the larger specimens headless. John had decapitated them and used their heads as bait to catch snapping turtles with a trap he devised. He presented a captured snapper with a stick that the turtle bit down on and didn't have the good sense to let go of as John pulled it away. The stubborn reptile's neck stretched far enough out of its shell to provide a landing spot for a hatchet. John then sold the turtles to the local firehouse for use as turtle soup's essential ingredient. In 1950, he sold a fifty-five-pound snapper and received ten dollars for his efforts—a serious sum for a poverty-stricken ten-year-old.

Eventually, he earned steadier money as a caddy at the nearby Nakoma Golf Club and as a delivery runner for the florist where his dad worked. John needed money. But mostly he was saving up so he could adopt and support a dog. A great-aunt, who like virtually everyone on John's father's side of the family was of meager financial means, helped.

"Johnny, Johnny, come here, come here," she'd say in her heavy brogue, and, when he did, she'd give him a hug and sneak him a quarter, fifty cents, or sometimes even a dollar. "For the dog fund," she'd whisper as she released him again.

John soon saved enough to acquire a sleek boxer-lab mix from the pound. He named it Jughead, trained it diligently, and walked the animal straight past the synagogue's bemused secretary into Rabbi Swarsensky's office. Swarsensky also happened to love dogs—or he loved John so much he ignored the dog's presence.

Through his talks with John and from what the rabbi had surely gleaned from congregants, Swarsensky was well aware of the boy's home life. This spiritual man regularly spent a few minutes talking to the boy about life in Germany, about the importance of being kind to others, and about whatever happened to be on John's mind. Recalling these conversations many years later, John said he was too young to truly appreciate the man who had had the words "My house shall be a house of prayer for all peoples" etched into the new temple's concrete monument sign. John described Swarsensky as "a great man and the most influential spiritual man in my life in every aspect."

Ken Rubadeau's drinking got worse as John entered his teens. As age and alcohol withered the father, the son grew taller and stronger. By the time John was 14, their physical trendlines crossed, a fact which might have gone unnoticed had Ken not taken a swing at John after a verbal back-and-forth in the apartment. John was standing at the bathroom sink at the time and may well have deserved some punishment, but the boy swung back, connected hard, and knocked his dad out cold into the bathtub. Their relationship, distant anyway, wasn't any better or worse for it, though Ken knew better than to challenge John physically after that.

Around that time, John moved out of the room he shared with his sister (they had hung a sheet between their beds for a modicum of privacy) and slept on the dining-room floor. Next to his mattress lay a knife John had at the ready based on the delusion of an imminent break-in to a home containing little of value.

Around that time, his mother fell ill with an undiagnosed malady that gradually grew worse. She left her job at the phone company and spent more and more of her time in bed. John entered Edgewood High School of the Sacred Heart with a father lost to the bottle and a mother succumbing to crippling disease.

Even with John's earnings from delivering flowers, lugging golf bags, and massacring turtles, the family couldn't afford tuition at Edgewood, a private school. But to the devout-Catholic Rubadeaus, the idea of public school was anathema. John helped justify his attendance by serving as the basketball team's manager. He knew the coach well: it was the biology teacher—his uncle Earl Wilke.

Despite John being more than six feet tall—if rail-thin—as a freshman, his uncle put no more effort into fostering his nephew's basketball skills than he had in helping him along in life. The coach preferred that John sweep the floors and pick up wet towels in the locker room, tasks which John duly did. If this twist on the Cinderella story had a fairy-godmother equivalent, it would come in the form of a friend of John's, Jim Rasmussen, a basketball standout at nearby West High School. Jim's dad had affixed a basketball hoop to their garage and even installed outdoor lighting. Rasmussen worked on hoops skills with John into the night, and as John's body stretched to nearly six-foot-six, his skills expanded to include a hook shot, layups with both hands, some inside fakes, and a consistent free-throw stroke to earn points from the fouls the other moves would invite. The combination proved too much for his uncle to ignore. Although John continued to sweep floors and pick up towels, he was in the regular rotation by his junior year and was a starter as a senior.

He wasn't a star, and his size-13 feet caused problems that sometimes kept him off the court (Converse Chuck Taylors, the only basketball shoes there were, weren't quite up to modern Air Jordan standards). But he had some good games. After a 22-point effort in December 1957, the *Wisconsin State Journal* wrote, "The sharp shooting of John Rubadeau, lanky center, paced Edgewood High school's undefeated basketball team to its fourth victory, a 72-36 decision over Mayville Monday night in the Edgewood gymnasium.''

* * *

John and I walk into the Dick's Sporting Goods on South Havana Street in Aurora, Colorado. John is looking for something whose identity he refuses to disclose to me. We walk past skin-tight athletic clothing below massive images of impossibly fit people wearing such clothing, and stop in the back where the weights and exercise bikes and so forth are displayed. Whatever John seeks, he isn't finding it. He wants to inquire with a human being, but we note no obvious staff about the floor.

"You might want to step away for a minute," John says.

I look up at him with raised eyebrows. He nods.

"Okay," I say, and head over to the footwear zone. As I check out a paltry soccer-shoe selection, a hollering voice rings out from approximately the location I have just vacated and echoes throughout the massive store.

"Help!"

Really loud. I suppress a smile.

"Help! Help! Help!"

The smile bulls itself onto my cheeks. Out of the corner of my eye, I sense a sudden movement: a Dick's staffer. Where was he before?

I make my way back toward the source of disruption. John stands amid three alarmed and befuddled Dick's employees who have suddenly appeared is if from thin air. They have confirmed that he's OK and that they don't have the item he's looking for.

"Pat hates it when I do that," he says as we leave.

Pat later confirms this.

"Because he needs to be the center of attention, he does things that I really do find totally inappropriate, and I'm embarrassed for him. I can tell when he's going to raise a stink at a store," Pat says. "And I'll say, 'I'll meet you in the car. I've got my book.' If I support the person he's railing against, then I'm a horrible wife because I'm not agreeing with him. But I don't agree with him always. And I'm not compromising my principles for him. He can have his principles—I'm just getting out of the way."

A few days later, a Yes4All Premium Adjustable Slant Board for calf stretching arrives from Amazon—his gift to us for hosting.

* * *

The basketball writeup was the third time John had made the local paper in the past few months. His play had earned a mention the prior week; six months before that, his discovery of a body while out fishing had made the front page.

John went fishing every day the weather allowed—for large- and small-mouth bass, bluegill, sunfish—and between that and his carp-catching and turtle-hunting, he knew Lake Wingra intimately. He spotted something large under the surface and speared what he took to be a huge carp before he recognized that it wasn't a carp at all. The barbs didn't set, and he made no mention of his mistake in the subsequent interview with the police. A fellow fisherman, not much older than John, had apparently had a seizure sitting on the bank, fallen in, and drowned.

His senior year also brought John his first-ever girlfriend. His Catholic upbringing and its depiction of fundamental biological desires as "sins of the flesh" had contributed to his slow start. His physical appearance—nearly six-foot-six, rail-thin at 170 pounds, big ears, acne in full bloom—also may have played a role.

His basketball fairy godfather Jim Rasmussen was also behind John's meeting his first girlfriend. John and three buddies were playing basketball at the Rasmussens' when they got wind that John considered one Barbara Newton "the most beautiful girl who was ever born," as John put it later. When the group went inside for a break, two of them tackled John on the carpet while the third, a classmate of Barbara's at West High School, rotary-dialed Carson's department store on Capitol Square where Barbara had a part-time job. "There's a guy here who wants to ask you out," the friend explained, then reached the handset down close to the carpet where John's face was. As the friend did so, one of John's other pals gave him a solid punch to the gut.

"Barbara, hey, I'm John Rubadeau," he wheezed. "I'm a friend of theirs. Would you like to go out with me?"

To his surprise, she said yes.

28

3

Real World

I learned this at least, by my experiment; that if one advances confidently in the direction of his dreams, and endeavors to lead the life which he has imagined, he will meet with a success unexpected in common hours.

— Henry David Thoreau

They fell in love. In Barbara, John recognized a creative, musically inclined (she played piano), intelligent, sweet creature whose quiet demeanor complemented his gregarious, outgoing ways. In John, Barbara had found a tall, baby-faced, popular, witty guy who appeared to be motivated to improve his lot in life. They went on walks through the University of Wisconsin Arboretum with John's second dog, a German shepherd he had named Rebel and had trained so well that a leash was redundant; they went to movies; they watched *Gunsmoke* at her folks' place.

Barbara was a year behind John in school, but he had already planned on enrolling at the University of Wisconsin, so they'd still be together in Madison. His plan changed abruptly when the university admitted him on probation and deferred his admission for a full year.

In the eyes of admissions officials, John's lofty standardized-test scores hadn't quite compensated for his lowly grade-point average. Playing basketball, fishing, carp-spearing, turtle-hunting, training his dog, working various part-time jobs, and hanging out with friends held vastly more allure to John than doing homework did. His mom, increasingly ill, and his dad, increasingly intoxicated, could offer little in the way of guidance or long-term perspective. So now, in the summer of 1958, John had a year to kill.

An old friend of his father's, a contractor named John Cullinane, gave John a job on a road-construction crew that specialized in sidewalks, curbs, gutters, and sewers. The younger John worked with Sicilian immigrants whose command of their craft far eclipsed that of their spoken English. He became a dues-paying member of the International Hod Carriers' Building and Common Laborers of America union. He learned the finer points of mixing, pouring, leveling, and sweeping cement. The wages were nearly triple the federal minimum of $1 an hour. Cullinane boosted them further by ensuring that John learned how to finish cement, a skill that required him to stick around for a couple of hours after the rest of the crew had gone home. John waited for the gray slurry to set up and dry to the point that it lent itself to his smoothing and then sweeping in those fine parallel lines that make for better pedestrian traction. Those extra hours paid time-and-a-half, and Sunday work—inevitable if he poured cement late on Saturday—paid double time.

As the long Wisconsin winter approached, cement pouring ceased for the season. Playing hoops for the Middleton Plumbers in Madison's amateur Classic League filled some of the time he wasn't spending with Barbara, but John decided to look for work where the weather was warmer.

As a child, he had only gone as far as Green Bay to the northeast, where his mother's family had moved, and Chicago to the southeast, where he and his sister were sent by bus for week-long summer stays with his maternal aunt's family. The full script of his life so far had played out within a 125-mile radius. His unintended gap year presented an opportunity to change that and make some money. John decided to hitchhike to Florida with help from a sign that read, "I want to go home to Mom. Fort Lauderdale, Florida."

The fib worked nicely, though he had to deflect questions about the specifics of his mom's place of residence in that Florida beach community. Once there, he quickly found busboy work in the fine-dining restaurants of the Yankee Clipper, the Escape, and the Jolly Roger hotels. The pay wasn't what it had been on the concrete crew, but the weather was better. He worked until just before the holidays when he hitchhiked back to Madison and forth again to Fort

30

Lauderdale. When spring arrived, he returned as he came, writing up a sign that read, "I want to go home to Mom: Madison, Wisconsin." Another summer in cement followed, and in the fall, he started at the University of Wisconsin–Madison.

One might assume that the young John Rubadeau would devote himself to his studies—in his case premed, to pave the way for a future title of "Dr. John Rubadeau"—and thereby set himself upon the path to professional success and a life story Horatio Alger might have invented.

Not quite. John was much more interested in playing basketball in the "Red Gym," as the university armory-gymnasium was then called. He did this daily and at the expense of classes that he admitted later, "I really didn't go to very often."

* * *

At this point it's worth noting that, on page one of his Spring 2018 course pack, John led with this:

IMPORTANT NOTE

IF YOU WILL BE AWAY FROM CLASS THIS SEMESTER—INTERVIEWING AT NUMEROUS MED-ICAL SCHOOLS; VISITING SUNDRY FINANCIAL INSTITUTIONS; DOING SOMETHING THAT RE-QUIRIES YOU TO MISS MANY CLASSES—YOU MAY WANT TO THINK TWICE (OR THREE OR FOUR TIMES) ABOUT REGISTERING FOR MY CLASS. WHAT WE LEARN IS LEARNED INCREMENTALLY, AND YOU NEED TO BE IN CLASS FOR EACH CUMULATIVE INCREMENT OF THE SEMESTER. IF YOU MISS MORE THAN ONE OR TWO CLASSES, YOU WILL INCUR A TWOFOLD DISADVANTAGE: (1) YOUR ABSENCE WILL, OBVIOUSLY, EFFECT [SIC] YOUR GRADE; (2) MORE IMPORTANTLY, YOUR COMPREHENSION OF ALL THAT I AM TRY-ING TO IMPART TO YOU WILL LIKELY NOT BE AS EXTENSIVE OR AS THOROUGH AS IT MAY HAVE BEEN HAD YOU ATTENDED EVERY CLASS.

* * *

College seemed like a good idea in theory, but, in practice, it wasn't turning out to be something John was all that interested in. That ambivalence plus his preternatural aversion to authority showed through during ROTC training that was mandatory in those days. During one marching drill, John put his boots on the wrong feet for the visual effect. During another, in which the instructors unwisely positioned him on the left flank of several drill lines with a few marchers each, he turned right when ordered to go left. The rest of his line duly followed.

John's indifference to his studies became evident when grades came out at the end of his first semester. The young man who had been granted admission on academic probation in the first place was put on double probation. Finally recognizing the real risk of pouring concrete the rest of his life, he began actually attending class. He did quite well in his premed studies until he ran headlong into physics. John had absolutely no intuitive command of the subject, and, unable to afford a tutor, he failed the course. His medical career ended well before med school. John transitioned to studying business, which he did better at—though, over time, he realized he had no interest in it.

Meanwhile, John's relationship with Barbara was getting serious. Today they might have just moved in together; in 1960, such a thing was unheard of: cohabitation meant marriage, be it by volition or by shotgun. He floated the idea. Barbara's parents were skeptical—not because they had a problem with John in particular or because of some class schism (while the Newtons were better off than the Rubadeaus, Barbara's father worked a low-paying white-collar job at a hardware supplier), but rather because they were Presbyterian and John was Catholic. The Newtons sought out an impartial and respected spiritual man to consult about the propriety of such a sect-spanning marriage. They chose perhaps the most influential religious leader in Madison's theological community: Rabbi Manfred Swarsensky.

John and Barbara became engaged in March 1960 and married at Blessed Sacrament Catholic Church in January 1961 with Rabbi Swarsensky in attendance. John was 20; Barbara, a year younger.

They moved briefly into a house in the woods outside of Madison and then to an apartment in town. John continued his studies; Barbara worked as a clerk at the Metropolitan Life Insurance Company. They couldn't afford for them both to be students, so she made plans to go back and get her degree later. Barbara was already best friends with John's sister Joan who had been Barbara's maid of honor. She embraced her daughter-in-law duties, helping out around the Rubadeau family apartment, when Florence needed more and more help with housecleaning, laundry, and most other physical tasks.

In the spring of 1962, Barbara and John announced that Barbara was pregnant. Joan, who had moved to Wauwatosa, Wisconsin, came back for the baby shower and helped Barbara set up the nursery and fold tiny clothes. The baby, Richard John, arrived in August 1962, at the same St. Mary's Hospital where both his parents had been born. He came three weeks early, so his birth weight of five pounds, eight ounces came as no surprise. That he struggled for breath from his first gasp did.

Richard survived only two days. The cause of death was hyaline membrane disease, better known today as neonatal infant respiratory distress syndrome. Before Barbara came home, Joan and John did the heartbreaking work of boxing away the gifted baby clothes, taking down the crib, and returning the second bedroom to its earlier, emptier state.

John and Barbara mourned a loss made harder by the congratulations extended by those who had seen the birth announcement in the paper. This profound life change, one they had awaited with such joyful expectations, had ended in hours rather than decades. It was harder on Barbara—she had carried him, felt him kicking, brought him into the world, held him. But now life had to go on without her little boy. When she returned to work, and John returned to his studies, they were both a little older than their birthdates would have suggested.

Having realized he wasn't interested in studying business, John changed majors to zoology because he loved animals and then to sociology and psychology when he realized he didn't love animals quite enough to become a zoologist. He was also working the waning days of the cement-pouring season: despite the sidewalk-and-sewer business slowing as Madison's leaves flushed with color, John Cullinane kept John Rubadeau on the last crew into October so the young man's work year extended the six months needed to file for unemployment benefits. John also parlayed his canine-behavioral expertise into dog-training gigs which brought in more money and, just as importantly, kept him in close company with all sorts of hounds. Harold Rasmussen, John's high-school friend Jim's dad, also provided budgetary boosts as the weather cooled. The Rasmussen Fuel Company was right across the street from Camp Randall Stadium where the University of Wisconsin football team played. The elder Rasmussen gave John and a friend carte blanche to use the lot to sell parking spots to sports fans—and keep all proceeds. Rasmussen's extraordinary kindness cleared John more than $100 (about $900 in today's money) a half dozen times each fall.

John studied hard enough since digging his way out of double probation that he made the dean's list when he graduated in June 1963. Despite his various side jobs and the football-game windfalls, John owed $4,000 in student loans (that same nine-to-one inflation applies here, too) by the time he turned his tassel at his commencement.

Ken—who had, in recent years, been periodically committed to Mendota State Hospital (formerly Wisconsin State Hospital for the Insane) and who was presently a resident of that institution—was retrieved for the occasion. But with John on the field with his fellow graduates and his sister Joan minding Florence, Ken slipped away for a bender that went on for a solid month before he was finally corralled and hauled back to Mendota for another dry-out destined to fail.

Florence's health had deteriorated to the point that she now needed nursing-home care. She was moved to Dane County Hospital in nearby Verona, a public charity hospital formerly known as the Dane County Asylum for the Criminally Insane. The girl who had so gaily danced and played could, as a woman in her mid-fifties, no longer walk without help. Her strange neuromuscular malady, never properly diagnosed (doctors had told the family Parkinson's, but there were no tremors or other telltale symptoms), would soon render her semiconscious and unable to communicate beyond grunts and groans.

* * *

John and I are talking grammar at the kitchen table. John wonders if we should note that writers should try to keep a given paragraph in the same verb tense. John's phone barks (his ringtone). He doesn't recognize the number. Most of us have learned that unfamiliar caller-ID numbers will be spam calls and ignore them. John says, "Excuse me, I have to do this."

"Hello?" he says in a sort of French accent a half octave higher than his typical voice.

Anthony from Family Home Protection is on the line. "How you doin' today?" Anthony asks.

"Fuckin' great. How 'bout you?" John asks.

Anthony pauses and says, "Perfect. I'm calling to inform you about our brand-new program, in which you can prevent all kind of break-ins, fire, and all kind of medical emergencies." Anthony has an accent, probably from Southeast Asia where his call center is.

"Anthony, I think I . . . I want my mommy," John says. Then he yells: "Mommy! Mommy! I won a prize! I won a gift!"

I'm laughing now.

John continues, "Anthony, can you tell me: how much did I win? How much did I win, Anthony?" Then he yells, "Mom! Come and talk to Anthony. How much how much how much?"

Anthony is quiet. "Hello?" he ventures, just as John hangs up.

"Why do you answer that shit?" I ask.

"Because I have fun. It's fun," John says. He then explains how he routinely gets calls about penile implants "because this prick student of mine put me on a list to fuck with me." When these calls come in, he'll say something along the lines of, "It's so good that you called, because my problem—I almost split my wife in two yesterday. I mean, the cum was all over the place—even on the ceiling. She was just like a waterfall down there. God damn. Give me some help! Make it smaller!"

* * *

Not long before his graduation, John noticed a sign in a Bascom Hall hallway advertising jobs with the American Red Cross. Despite having no fixed notion of what he wanted to do with his life, this denizen of

35

Madison did know two things: he wanted to escape the city, and he wanted see the world. Although a dreamer, John was enough of a realist to recognize that he lacked the wherewithal to pay for either. The words "worldwide mobility" on the Red Cross poster caught his eye. He applied, interviewed, and was hired, but his position wouldn't open until the following summer. With another year to kill and debts to pay, John landed a job as the City of Madison's animal-control officer—more commonly known as the dogcatcher.

He drove around town in a police car or an animal-control truck chasing reports. When announcing his location to dispatch, he'd bark a couple of times and then relay his cross streets in English. John summarized his daily writeups in verse—combining, say, the capture of a skunk, the de-treeing of a cat, and the capture and disposition of a couple of dogs into a single rhyming missive. The police chief sometimes read these reports to assembled policemen during the department's morning briefings. Two incidents made the local paper. A July 7, 1964, *Wisconsin State Journal* story under the headline "3 Little Critters Prove to Be Cute (But Not in Snoot)" describes an incident in which John and a policeman flushed three baby skunks from a nest under a resident's front steps using a garden hose. "Although the men won, caging the tiny animals after a half-hour struggle, the skunks scored offensive victories against the men, the house, and a truck.

"'They're darn cute, but they smell,' John Rubadeau, dogcatcher, said hours later."

Their cuteness wouldn't save them. The skunk kits were subsequently shot, John explained to the reporter, because 85 percent of skunks carried rabies. (Note the use of passive voice; John actually did the shooting.)

Later that month, the *Capital Times* ran a short piece on John's saving a dog from Lake Monona. It had been a hot day. "Rubadeau reported that the dog, although it was near exhaustion, refused to leave the water until he forcibly removed it and took it to the City Humane Shelter," the story reads. "It developed that a resident residing in the area earlier had taken the dog from the lake, but it ran back into the water." The story's headline: "Dog Prefers Drowning to Braving Heat."

36

To the great loss of the dogs of Madison, John's career as an animal-control officer would be short-lived. In November 1964, John's Red Cross number came up. He was sent to Fort Sill, Oklahoma, for two months of training, leaving behind not only Barbara but also baby daughter Becky who had been born perfectly healthy in late April. Two months later, Barbara and Becky joined John in Albuquerque, New Mexico, where he started work as a Red Cross assistant field director at Kirtland Air Force Base. As a social worker, John spent his days informing soldiers of births and deaths in their families back home and helping arrange for leave and transportation, counseling enlisted men on family matters and financial problems, and helping soldiers returning from abroad reintegrate back home. He was in Albuquerque in March 1965 when his sister Joan called with word of a death in his own family: their mother Florence, in a vegetative state for many woeful months, had passed away in Verona.

Ken Rubadeau had been with her. His love for her had continued even if his devotion to drink had destroyed their relationship and imperiled their family. Ken had been with Florence because he had, true to form, somehow talked his way into being admitted to Dane County Hospital. Ken checked himself out again the day she died.

* * *

John sits across from me at the kitchen table. I have asked him to run through his family history. While he recognizes the value of history as far as past being prologue and those who forget it being condemned to repeat it, he has put little thought into his own. It's a habit he has cultivated since he lost that baby boy back in Madison so many years ago.

"I think the only way the heart heals is with time and dealing with reality," he tells me. "You can only live in the present. You can't live in the past; you can't live in the future. I grieved. But I didn't ponder over it. There was nothing I could do. You have to move on."

John is reasonably patient with me, but he would rather talk about writing and grammar. "Why do you need this for our dirty grammar book?" he asks. He takes a spoonful of low-fat Greek yogurt augmented with sliced-up strawberries and unsalted mixed nuts, a Costco concoction. John is enthusiastic about this breakfast staple of mine and will continue the tradition when he returns home to Ann Arbor, only to stop it again abruptly because, as Pat will tell me, it makes him mucousy.

"Context," I tell him. "The reader is more likely to bother with the writing and the grammar if they're interested in who you are."

His recall is shaky. He doesn't remember when his mom was born or died. He thinks his paternal grandparents were born in Ireland (they were born in Wisconsin). He thinks his grandfather left John's Grandma Jenny to gallivant around Milwaukee (he worked on battery-assembly line in Madison). Events and personalities do disappear in the fog of passing decades—that's what resources such as newspaperarchive.com and ancestry.com are there for. But while John may have misunderstood his roots, he took important lessons from them. Ken's lesson: John doesn't drink. Florence's lesson: John believes in euthanasia.

"Interestingly enough, *euthanasia* doesn't mean mercy killing," he says.

"No?" I say.

"*Eugenics* means good genes. *Euphoria* means good sounds. *Euthanasia* means good death," he explains, as he has, I'm guessing, to many, many classes during some tangent as important as the topic at hand. "I really believe in that. Euthanasia would have avoided all those years of my mother's suffering."

* * *

John's year in Albuquerque ended, and a year at Carswell Air Force Base in Fort Worth, Texas, commenced in 1965. Barbara enrolled at Texas Christian University and made the Dean's List during her first year. There wouldn't be a second year: John finally got his overseas assignment. Of the ten Red Cross assistant field directors sent to overseas military bases that quarter, nine went to Vietnam where the U.S. military presence had exploded from about 23,000 in 1964 to about 385,000 in 1966. John's destination would be the U.S. military base at Bad Kreuznach in southwestern West Germany. Barbara and Becky would accompany him.

Before leaving, John returned to Madison to visit his father. By then Ken had been reduced to a dishwashing job in the Park Hotel. But now he was back at Mendota State Hospital. There, John talked about life with his young family and about his plans to travel to Europe. He avoided asking about what his father had been up to. As John stood to leave, his dad told him, "I've given you a great gift."

John paused, assuming the gaunt old man in the hospital bed was kidding, but his father showed no sign of it. "Really?" John asked. "What gift would that have been?"

Ken Rubadeau considered his son for a long moment. "Poverty," he said.

"I don't know if that's a gift, but you've certainly given me a shitload of it."

His dad closed his eyes and was quiet for a long moment. "You'll see," he said.

4

Love Lost

Reality is too much for humankind to bear.
— T.S. Eliot

J ohn's voyage to Germany in 1966 began auspiciously: a clerical error identified him as the Red Cross equivalent of a rear admiral, an error which scored the young family a suite upstairs on the U.S.S. Geiger on the voyage from New York to Bremerhaven, Germany. In the cargo hold was a red-and-white VW Bus. John had joined the Red Cross to see the world; this would be his vehicle.

The base at Bad Kreuznach, not far from Mainz, had been a German installation during World War II. Its principal role now, as was the case with other American military bases in West Germany, was to deter the Soviets from directing their inherent expansionism into Western Europe. (Wisconsin native George Kennan, who had been the University of Wisconsin commencement speaker the day John had been down on the Camp Randall Stadium field, had first spelled out what became the U.S. Cold War containment policy in his 1947 "Long Telegram" from Moscow.)

Just as American military bases overseas mimicked the ones stateside, John's work in Bad Kreuznach paralleled the work he'd done in Texas. There were exceptions. For example, he recognized that the swimming pool in town could offer a nice escape for enlisted men and families on base during the summer. The question was how to get them there. He called over to the transportation division. A second lieutenant named Chris Poulos picked up. "I've got a favor to ask you—it's not for me," John said. "And I know you have a lot of influence."

Poulos did not have a lot of influence nor was carting kids and others to the local pool on his logistical to-do list. But with the base's school out for the summer, there were buses available, and, soon enough, the buses were running two morning and two afternoon trips back and forth to the local pool.

Sometime later, Poulos called John. "I've got a favor to ask you— it's not for me," Poulos said. "And I know you have a lot of influence." His wife Betty, fresh from college with a teaching degree, had no place to teach (the base's schools were staffed centrally by the Department of Defense). Poulos had heard that the Red Cross secretary had returned home. Betty wanted her spot.

"No fuckin' way," John said. "It needs to go to the wife of an enlisted man."

Poulous reminded him that most sergeants made more money than he did. Plus, Betty had just taken a course in shorthand. These facts seemed to soften John's stance.

"Is she offended by profanity or cigar smoke?" John asked. John used profanity; his boss smoked cigars.

She wasn't offended, and she got the job. Their boss, the Red Cross field director, was in his 40s and therefore ancient to these 20-somethings. Betty and John took care of business in the office to the point that they realized that there wasn't necessarily all that much business to take care of. The two shared a workload one of them could usually tackle. To better align workload with labor, John often invoked the excuse of the latrine.

"If somebody calls, tell them I'm in the latrine," John told Betty and then went to the gym to play basketball for hours. When the boss went away on vacation, John told her, "I'm talking half the time off, and you're taking the other half. If anybody calls tell them I'm in the latrine."

"John, I can't say you're in the latrine for four days," Betty protested.

While John was playing basketball in the latrine, he met a second lieutenant named Ron Pace. They were about the same age and as different politically and interpersonally as they were in appearance. Ron was a sturdy six-footer who spoke sparingly and poignantly and had never been heard to swear outside the walls of his brain. John was outspoken, foul-mouthed, and with "shoulders hunched over like Ichabod Crane and long legs swinging around and no ass on him at all," Pace recalled. There was, back then, no beard.

But they shared sharp senses of humor and recognized that, despite their differences, they had a lot in common. Ron's father had also been an alcoholic, and Ron had also been brought up poor—but a different kind of poor. Ron was born in a two-room log cabin with neither running water nor electricity amid the cottonfields of Gobler, Missouri (which Ron pronounced "Missourah"), in the state's boot-heel. His father and grandfather had been sharecroppers; Ron had, at the age of six, picked 100 pounds of cotton in a single day.

The Pace family made its own soap from the fat of hogs slaughtered at the first killing frost and the ashes from fires that had boiled laundry. They squeezed and condensed their own molasses from sorghum cane. They dried apples on the shack's roof and canned fruit and vegetables to sustain them through winter months when only turnip greens grew.

Ron's father left to fight in World War II. Upon return, to work in the steel mills of Indiana and Illinois. Ron's mother moved herself and her six kids—five daughters and Ron—back to her family in Waverly, Tennessee, where Ron learned the arts of woodsmanship from his maternal grandfather.

Ron didn't advertise his upbringing but, when asked, was happy to share stories of downing trees and, by manning the opposite handles of a crosscut saw with his granddad, reducing thick trunks into two-foot sections and then splitting enough of them to get through the winter. Ron once observed how his grandfather had care-fully extracted a squirrel from a hollow tree by using a switch of saw brier the old man had threaded into the tree's innards and twisted to snag the squirrel's furry tail. Fried squirrel and squirrel dumplings were on the menu in Waverly. The meat was a lot like the dark meat on a chicken, Ron told his tall friend, and a good-sized squirrel yielded about as much meat as a small chicken. The closest John could come to that was the story about his dad fighting with his brother over squirrel brains.

Ron's academic performance had also contrasted with John's. Ron was an A student, president of the student body, captain of the football team, and a guard on the basketball team at Waverly High. He paid his way through the University of Tennessee by working as a firefighter in California from June until December, graduated with a business degree in four years, and then enrolled in law school at Tennessee when, in his first semester, he ran out of money.

Rather than wait to be drafted, he enlisted and then enrolled in the Army's Officer Candidate School, where he finished as an honor graduate and, as a reward, could choose his destination. He chose an administrative role in Germany; all but three of his roughly 140 classmates ended up in Vietnam.

In Ron, John found a fellow traveler intent on seizing the opportunities their postings in the middle of Europe, rather than Vietnam, offered. They were the exceptions: many young officers preferred to stay on base where they counted the days until duty returned them stateside.

Another exception was James Moore, a military doctor who lived in the same apartment complex. Moore helped John outfit the VW Bus with screens on the windows and a wooden platform that consumed much of the of vehicle's interior (Moore had made similar modifications to his own VW Bus). Beneath the wooden platform was space for ten five-gallon jerrycans, food, luggage, and several cans of C-rations—the cigarettes in them being particularly useful as barter items should one need to jump the line at an auto-repair shop or elsewhere. A mattress rested on the wooden platform.

John filled the jerrycans with 20-cents-a-gallon gasoline from the commissary's gas tanks, a fraction of the price of filling up beyond the base's fencing. "Don't get in a wreck, or we'll blow ourselves up," Ron suggested when he first saw the setup. The cans' contents fueled many weekend and three-day trips together with wives both named Barbara.

Some trips went better than others. One road trip ended prematurely in Spain when the VW Bus's engine failed. John and Barbara, looking forward to a two-week excursion to Morocco and back, had set out with James Moore and his wife Madeleine. Moore, not just a doctor but also a skilled mechanic, determined that the air-cooled 1.5-liter engine's exhaust valves had crystallized and broken off, a fatal condition. They were in Madrid at the time and not far from the U.S. Torrejón Air Base to which the Moores towed the Rubadeaus' VW Bus behind theirs.

A Red Cross colleague John had met at a conference happened to be stationed there, and she was dating a colonel. In the dead of night, the colonel quietly had the car towed to the base's repair shop where mechanics swapped out the larger engine for a 1.2-liter motor from a wrecked VW Beetle. The Moores continued on to Morocco; John and Barbara drove slowly back to Germany, managing no more than about 30 miles per hour.

A trip to Vienna went smoothly from a mechanical standpoint. John pulled the VW Bus up in front of Schönbrunn Palace. John, a rigid tour scheduler with hangry tendencies, announced: "Jesus Christ, we're fuckin' late for lunch!"

He parked the VW Bus and stepped over one of those foot-high fences that are generally recognized as more polite and attractive means of expressing "KEEP OFF GRASS." Ron and the Barbaras observed as John set up a gas stove and a small pot into which he poured a couple of cans of Beanie Weenies right there on the Habsburgs' imperial lawn as Viennese strolled about in suits and dresses. "C'mon, get the fuck out of the car," John urged his mortified passengers. "Bring the Kool-Aid!"

In addition to being an inveterate tourist, John was an enthusiastic vacation planner, to the point that friends and colleagues recognized him as an informational trove on the topic of budget trips to Florence, Venice, Amsterdam, Copenhagen, Paris, Istanbul, and elsewhere—all destinations he had made a point of road-tripping to with Barbara and, on some trips, Becky (she stayed with a German couple, the Pohls, otherwise). The little girl with pigtails rode on her father's shoulders up the steps of the Leaning Tower of Pisa, the castle at Heidelberg, and the Eiffel Tower.

There were risks to following John's travel tips.

"I'd say, 'I'm going to Amsterdam for four, five days next month,' and he'd give you a laundry list of sights and things to do and say, 'Stay in this guesthouse on a canal—it's $2.75 with breakfast,'" Chris Poulos recalled. "He neglected to mention that there was no heat."

John's use of *fuck* cognates in mixed company, as he did in Vienna, was extraordinary for the day, it should be noted. One evening at a Bad Kreuznach officers'-club event (his Red Cross status made him the equivalent of a junior military officer) involving a dozen or so young officers and their wives, John said something to the effect of "I don't give a fuck" at a volume audible to all.

Fifty-three years later, Ron described the moment this way. "I recall to this day that as soon as the word came out of his mouth, there was a stunned silence. Almost like the blood draining out of your head from shock. Because you'd never hear anyone use that word with women present. He didn't care. It was just shocking to me, shocking to my wife, and to everyone in the room," he said. "That was my first introduction to John's cussing in polite or mixed company, and he continued to do it the rest of his life."

Ron's then-wife Barbara added, "I was 22 years old, and I don't think I'd heard someone say that in my whole life."

But there was, Ron recognized even then, more to the expletives than this new friend of his from Wisconsin simply not worrying about filtering his language to the degree his peers did. "John displays his emotions quite heavily, and John also likes shock value," Ron said. "And that gets him in trouble."

That night in the officers' club, as would be the case on many, many other occasions far into the future, it didn't. Perhaps it was John's energy and wit; perhaps it was his genuine interest in the lives and ambitions of these new friends; perhaps it was something as simple as their gratitude for the swimming-pool buses and travel advice; perhaps they appreciated the hook shot honed on the Rasmussen driveway. But the party ramped back up, and John continued to live in Bad Kreuznach without a scarlet letter *F* for verbal indiscretion sewn to his olive Red Cross uniform.

"I think the thing you admire is how easy it is for him to express his feelings and emotions," said Nanci Milam, a friend from that era.

45

"He's a talker, and he can talk about anything. And he is interested in people. He would always ask me things about my life and about what was going on in my life and my experiences and stuff like that, which was nice."

* * *

"Have you ever heard of the word, *uxorious*?" John asks at the kitchen table.

"I've seen it, but I forget the definition," I say.

"It's from the Latin *uxor*, which is *wife*, and *uxorious* means excessively devoted to your wife," John says. "I've been married three times, and the key is being excessively devoted towards your wife."

"The key to being married three times?" I ask.

"Ha," John says. "I'll tell Carol, so she's aware of it."

"I appreciate that," I say.

We're talking about student essays. He says he's saved several of his favorites from recent years. I say I'd like to see them. John picks up his iPhone and holds it like a slice of pizza he's about to bite into. "Hey Siri! Call Pat's cell!" he hollers.

"Calling Pat's cell, mobile," Siri says. John has called his wife Pat probably five times a day in his practice of uxoriousness. Typically, the calls have been triggered by a question that pops into his head that he knows Pat, who was John's Siri before there was Siri, can address.

Pat answers her cell. He asks if she could email the student essays from his computer. She'll have to go downstairs, she says. She'll call right back. A minute later, she does. She asks him his computer password.

"Hmmm," John says.

"The hint is 'coitus,'" Pat says.

"Coitus interruptus?" John wonders.

Pat types. "Doesn't work."

"Fuck you?"

Pat types again. "No," she says.

"*Quid pro quo*?"

"No."

"Let me call Yubadeau," he says. "Hang on."

"Yubadeau" is Elise Yu, a former student and typist and now attorney in Ann Arbor. She and husband Carl helped John set up the computer. Siri connects them.

"Hello?" Yubadeau says. She sounds groggy.

"Hi, darling. How're you doing? You sound like you're fuckin' dead. Where's Carl?"

"He's right here," she says and notes that they've been napping.

John asks if she remembers his computer password.

She gives him the password; he thanks her and tells her to go back to sleep. He calls Pat back.

"Guess what?" he tells Pat, uxoriously. "What an idiot I am. It's 'fuck': like 'If you see Kay' in James Joyce's *Ulysses*." And off goes a man who has told me for three decades how much he hates Joyce: "That book is an unalloyed absolute piece of shit. It stinks worse than a skunk's bunghole. I'm really serious." He turns to me. "Don't ever read it."

* * *

These were exciting times for a poor boy from Madison. John was making a decent salary working overseas and spending whatever was left over after the family's living expenses and his student-loan payments to travel to some of the world's great destinations with a beautiful wife and daughter. He was making great new friends. He was getting along famously with a massive white-gray Irish wolfhound he had picked up in Ireland—a dog so giant it could reach up and rest its paws on the tall man's shoulders when both stood. Adding to the novelty and energy of the times was the blessing of Barbara's third pregnancy.

Daughter Becky's health had sanded away the sharp edges of concern about her future sibling. But, like the baby who would have been his older brother, Roland Patrick came weeks early and lived for just two days before neonatal respiratory distress syndrome took him too.

Prior experience builds no callouses when it comes to losing babies. Barbara once again was devastated, and John mourned, too, before approaching this tragedy as he had the first: he willed himself to not live in the past and to move on with his life.

Willpower has its limits, though. The death of his first baby boy had left fissures in his Catholic faith. They cracked wider now. The providential God who was supposed to answer prayers had taken not

47

one but two of his sons. A Catholic indoctrination as ingrained as John's was hard to shed, but, as much to get even with God as anything else, he became what he would later describe as agnostic: "I was so pissed off at God for losing these two babies that I said, 'I'm gonna doubt Your existence.'"

Before long, Barbara and John took a leap of faith and tried again. By the spring of 1967, Barbara became pregnant for the fourth time. Military doctors took no chances this time: Barbara was put on bed rest for two months before Nick was born full-term and healthy in January 1968. Not long after that, John's assignment in Germany ended, and the Red Cross assigned him to Lackland Air Force Base in San Antonio, Texas, again as an assistant field director. This was a short-term posting: his boss told him he'd be going to Vietnam. The U.S. had more than 500,000 soldiers in Southeast Asia by then, and there was a tremendous need for Red Cross workers.

John was morally opposed to the Vietnam War, so, unlike a soldier, he could refuse the assignment. Doing so would end his Red Cross career, but he didn't actually care too much about that career. He had done his work, when not "in the latrine," with skill and empathy, but he had joined the Red Cross to have someone else pay for him to escape Madison and see the world. He had taken full advantage of the opportunity, piling 120,000 miles on that VW Bus over the past three years.

While leaving the Red Cross would expose him to the military draft, the combination of his age (he was 28 now), marital status, and his two children would probably protect him, John figured. He quit, though not before lining up a very different job.

John and Ron had taken the U.S. foreign-service exam. This would be, for John, about seeing still more of the world on someone else's dime. He could be diplomatic—as he was when interacting with the soldiers he consulted at military bases in the United States and Germany. His affinity for slinging the word "fuck" and various other undiplomatic terms in mixed company was not the trait that would hamper him most in the diplomatic corps. Rather, it was his deep distaste for heeding whatever he deemed to be misguided authority. U.S. State Department employees were charged with advancing the

U.S. national interest as interpreted by whomever happened to be leading the government at the time. In the late 1960s, the people leading the government considered the successful prosecution of the Vietnam War to be in the U.S. national interest.

It didn't matter anyway. Ron passed the written exam; John did not (the pass rate was only about 10 percent). John's days overseas were, for now, over. Fortunately, his backup plan panned out. He, Barbara, Becky, baby Nick, and their Irish wolfhound moved to Beloit, Wisconsin, a town on the Illinois state line just an hour southeast of Madison. There John took a job as coordinator of student activities and director of the Student Union at Beloit College, a liberal-arts school overlooking the Rock River and rows of factories on its western flank. Especially given the two little ones, it was good to be back in Wisconsin and close to family again. Like other institutions, Beloit College, with its enrollment of about 1,300, was being swept into the antiwar, women's-rights, civil-rights, and other establishment-questioning movements, all of it antimatter to a military-base's matter. John reveled in it.

In the summer of 1968, the family moved into a 1,200-square-foot college-owned house on Church Street across from a campus green and the small college's dormitories. John's proximity to work meant that he could stop back by the house and lead the giant dog—and, sometimes, his small children—over to the green to get some exercise. Dave Matthews, a Beloit student and dormitory resident at the time, recalled that the dog conferred upon the new coordinator of student activities "a sense of presence that he wouldn't have had otherwise. And it scared the shit out of people."

* * *

John joins me when I walk Oscar, the family puggle. He has not been able to ride our exercise bike as he does his own at home because ours is a recumbent, and the seat's adjustability fails to account for his spindly legs. He has, though, been able to use the spring-loaded grip exerciser he carries in his pocket. He has for years squeezed it 100 times, three times a day, after each set holding it closed for a minute, the excruciating pain

49

begetting a sort of yelp-grunt when he finally releases. When he handed the grip exerciser to me, I managed one set of fifty squeezes before giving up.

Oscar is a spry 11, and the half beagle in him leads him to sniff everything a dog has ever urinated on—which is, around the local park, everything. The topic of money comes up, and then the topic of our spending five grand on the girls' braces. Oscar stops to mark a tree; John says, "Check out this molar," and opens his mouth.

I note a big golden tooth in the lower-left quadrant of his primary headhole.

"Pat's first husband was a dentist. He made her a wedding ring with dental gold. They divorced. Anyway, I had to have a root canal, and it was going to be ridiculously expensive. I called a pal from the dental school. I said, 'We need to save money. I've got this ring—it's 100-percent pure dental gold. Could you melt down the ring, use it for the crown, and charge me less?'"

"You're serious," I say.

"Oh, fuck yeah," John says. "It was Pat's idea, actually."

"That's Pat's ring? In your mouth?"

"It was like $400 cheaper."

Oscar moves on, and we follow. John mentions that he's got something called an arachnoid cyst. I imagine a spidery-looking thing maybe on his elbow. No: it's in his brain, he says.

"What?"

He explains that, a few years back, he was feeling mentally sluggish. A hearing test yielded some strange results. He ended up visiting a neurosurgeon at the University of Michigan hospital. They did a scan and found that the part of his brain typically responsible for speech and language processing had, at one point, been replaced by a fluid-filled cyst. The neurosurgeon, John says, told him, "Theoretically, you should hardly be able to communicate. But I've never seen anybody that's got a vocabulary like yours."

Later, I call the neurosurgeon, Dr. Shawn Hervey-Jumper, who has moved on to the University of California, San Francisco. Hervey-Jumper recalls that, while these sorts of appointments are typically one-and-done, "I think he just kind of liked coming in, and I kind of liked talking to him, so we actually saw each other every six months for a while."

John has a good-sized cyst located around the Sylvian fissure by the front parietal and temporal lobes, Hervey-Jumper tells me. "That's where most of your language is organized."

"And his temporal lobe with that arachnoid cyst—some of the area where he would normally be processing language

50

would not be there. It's shocking when you see that—clearly, it's somewhere. But not where it is with most other people," the neurosurgeon says. "For him, not only is it not there, but it's how he makes his living. Really remarkable."

Pat will tell me later that John is "quite proud of his cyst, and he uses it as an excuse quite frequently."

* * *

As coordinator of student activities, John helped Beloit College student groups organize dances and other social events. His work demanded attention during evenings, weekends, and odd hours. Foremost among these preparations involved helping students organize what would become America's first-ever all-blues weekend festival. John approached the creation of the Wisconsin Delta Blues Festival with what his future students would recognize as a familiar degree of passion: by the time the festival opened in late March of 1970, the stage was set for the likes of Roosevelt Sykes, Son House, Johnny Shines, the Rev. Robert Wilkins, Mance Lipscomb, Mississippi Fred McDowell, and B.B. King. The music writer Andy Schwartz, then a Beloit freshman, later described McDowell having set up a table at the student union, "his bottleneck slide riffs ringing out as the smoke curled from a cigarette stuck in the headstock of his guitar. J.B. Hutto wore a double-breasted suit the color of an orange traffic cone and a guitar strap of butcher's twine . . . . Friday and Saturday night were devoted to formal concerts, if 'formal' can describe a crowd of mostly stoned college kids sitting cross-legged on a gym floor."

John flourished in the campus environment. He made friends as easily as ever and started hanging out with a cadre of young professors. This left Barbara with much of the parenting and household burdens even as she took classes toward her bachelor's degree—a degree she was as determined to earn as she had been in Texas four years earlier.

At home as well as abroad, John could be tough to live with. The poor boy had become a minimally earning man whose only real way to maintain financial equilibrium was to ruthlessly manage expenses. In Germany, he had scolded Barbara for smoking—not so much because of health concerns (which had still been largely suppressed, obfuscated, and denied by tobacco companies) but, rather, because of the cost. The price of a babysitter was generally too high to justify the two of them going out. An extra dollar spent at the grocery store could ignite his temper and trigger a rant.

John was never physically abusive, and friends saw that he truly loved his wife. The same friends chalked up such behavior to two factors. The first was that, as Ron put it, John was so cheap that "he gets mad at a penny because it's not a nickel." The second was that, as Ron's ex-wife Barbara explained, "He had no one to emulate. His dad was an alcoholic."

She added: "When John was good, he was very good, and when John was ugly, he was very ugly."

Barbara, a quiet, equanimous soul, seemed well-suited to maintaining balance through her husband's behavior swings: he was, after all, a witty and interesting guy. But charismatic people can be hard to live with—in part because their charm tends to shine brightest on outsiders. In this regard, perhaps, he had something in common with his father.

Barbara generally took a Zen approach to her husband, bending malleably with the occasional rant rather than breaking into open conflict by asserting herself and fighting back. With classes to study for, a six-year-old, a toddler, a giant dog, and a husband off establishing himself in what might or might not lead to a fruitful career in academic administration, she was certainly stressed out and sleep-deprived. She was most likely unhappy. She may have even, as she had confided in a friend, been thinking about leaving John.

John got home late from a student event the night of June 18, 1970. He wasn't surprised to see the lights still on: Barbara, having put the kids to bed, was surely up studying. The family was going camping that weekend with some young professors and their families, so she had to get her work done beforehand. The giant wolfhound greeted him as he entered, as excited to see him as if it had been months rather than hours since he had left the house. John went to the kitchen to see if Barbara were at the table where she often spread out her books and notebooks. She wasn't there. He was about to call out her name but stopped himself: the kids were sleeping.

John stepped out of the kitchen, walked past the dog now curled up on a rug, and made his way up stairs that groaned with each step. The upstairs hallway lights were also on—strange. He cracked open the door to the kids' room to check on them. They were both asleep. He closed the door, twisting the knob as he did. He walked to his and Barbara's bedroom.

The lights were on here, too, and it seemed terribly bright. The bed was still made and empty.

Then he saw her.

She lay on the floor next to the bed, face-down, her body strangely twisted. Her head rested on what seemed to be a big crimson pillow.

"Barbara?"

John then saw the crimson pillow for what it really was: the carpet, soaked in blood.

5

Flight, New Life

Das Leben is wie eine Hühnerleiter: kurz und beschissen.[*]
— A favorite Rubadeau quote

Why a brilliant, beautiful, twenty-nine-year-old woman with two small children she dearly loved would view a bullet as a solution to whatever troubled her would forever remain a mystery. The *Wisconsin State Journal* reported it simply: "Rock County Coroner Richard McCaul said police found a .38-caliber revolver under Mrs. Rubadeau's body. She had been shot once in the head."

It had been simple. The hoisting of the gun John had used as a dogcatcher, the pressing of its cool tip against her temple, the contracting of a forearm muscle that, through a short, efficient kinetic chain, pushed her index finger forcefully against the trigger. It had been over in a few seconds.

It wasn't at all simple for those she left behind. John's sister Joan stepped in as she had when Barbara had lost her first baby nearly a decade earlier—this time to clean out Barbara's closet so John wouldn't have to. John and the kids stayed the weekend they should have been camping at the family home of the classics professor, Art Robson. Joan minded Becky and Nick. Nick was too young to grasp what had happened. Becky wasn't. In the Robson backyard, she said, "Aunt Joanie, Daddy said that Mama's not coming back."

---

[*] Life is like a chicken ladder: short and shitty.

"Daddy's right, Sweetheart," Joan told the child. "Mama's not coming back because she's got other things to do with God."

John's mother had been gone five years. His father had died eighteen months ago, in late 1968, of accrued damage from decades of drinking. John had buried two babies. He had formulated and lived a major tenet of his still-developing life philosophy: living in the present—not in the past; not in the future. The present was suddenly a catastrophe: his wife of nine years, the love of his life, the mother of his children, lay in the morgue by her own hand. All presupposition of his future had involved Barbara.

The classics professor saw to it that a succession of friends kept John company for a couple of days. John spent much of that time in a small parlor off the Robson living room. Sometimes he was catatonic; sometimes he wondered how his own life could go on and how he would possibly manage things with his kids; sometimes he spoke as if nothing had happened at all. Dave Matthews, the student and friend of John's who at Robson's request spent hours with John, recalled that he, Robson, and others convinced John that it would be best, at least for a little while, for Joan to take care of the kids. She and her husband Roland had a daughter and a son about the same ages as Becky and Nick. Also, Joan and Barbara had made a pact that if something were to happen to one of them, the other would raise the deceased's children.

John resisted at first but ultimately agreed, and off Becky and Nick went to the Milwaukee suburbs. John soon recognized that he, too, had to get out of Beloit. Besides the job, there was nothing there for him. Everyone knew of his wife's suicide, and everyone felt sorry for him. As John put it later, "I didn't need that shit. It was awful."

Barbara's family was entirely unsympathetic, blaming John for their daughter's apparent unhappiness and, therefore, her suicide. He decided to get away—far away. He first considered finding a cargo-ship berth to Australia; when that didn't pan out, he settled upon returning to Germany, this time to Hamburg.

* * *

John wonders if a former student and now friend of his, Jake Butt, might come over for dinner one night. Of course, Carol and I say. For the occasion, John insists on buying the pork loin that a crock pot will transform into pulled pork. Jake arrives with a single crutch under his right armpit, one capable of supporting 300 pounds, which Jake's mass comes within about 40 pounds of.

A succession of Michigan football players had taken John's class over his last couple of years. Jake was among them. He was, his senior year, the nation's top tight end. Then he tore his left ACL in the Orange Bowl, an injury which dropped him to the fifth round of the 2017 NFL draft where the Denver Broncos selected him. He sat out the 2017 season, rehabbed, played well in three games three months ago, and then tore his right ACL during practice. Jake is now a few weeks out of reconstructive surgery and has just started to put weight on the repaired leg.

John is perhaps the only human being who calls Jake "Jonathan," his legal name. They have talked on the phone now and again over the past couple of days. When John calls Jake, Jake always answers, "It is I," just as John does in his cell-phone voice mail intro: "You have reached the home of John Rubadeau. It is I. I was just using the predicate nominative or subjective complement in order to impress."

Having lived in Michigan's South Quad dormitory, I am familiar with high-end football physiques. Lily and Maya have not come across a six-foot-six, 260-pound individual, much less a lean one. Such morphology does not generally exist in civilian life. They are clearly awed, though I'm not sure how much of that awe has to do with how handsome he also happens to be.

It's soon clear that John hasn't befriended Jake because he is an NFL player with 80,000 Instagram followers. He likes Jake because Jake is self-effacing, engaging, intelligent, and funny.

When the topic turns to sports, a subject which Jake and I are enthusiastic about, John tunes out or exhibits an unfamiliarity as deep as Jake's and mine would be were the topic Thomas Wolfe or Nikos Kazantzakis. "Why don't you ask the Broncos bosses if you can't go play with Hog?" John wonders. "Hog" is Ryan Glasgow, a former student and good friend of both John's and Jake's who plays for the Cincinnati Bengals. Jake and I chuckle at the idea of Jake knocking on the office door of Broncos Hall-of-Fame quarterback and current General Manager John Elway and asking, "Um, Mr. Elway, can I go play with Hog?"

Later, John admits to knowing more about sports than he lets on. "Feigned ignorance gets me into some really interesting conversations. I often play the fool just to see people's reactions," he says.

I ask Jake why he took John's class. He was referred to it through the football team's academic center, Jake says. He had his doubts the first day of class, though.

"There's this crazy old man yelling at all of us," Jake says. "I'm like, 'What did I get myself into? This guy's insane!' And to be brutally honest, I think this is important to say: I hate English."

"Same!" Lily interjects.

"You never told me that, and I told you for years I hate football," John says. He hates it because, as Pat puts it, "he finds it stupid and boring"—but more so because he doesn't want to see his friends getting hurt, which they invariably do. John has suggested that Jake quit; Jake has reminded John of "Scratch your itch"—a guiding principle which, along with *quid pro quo*, is one of John's most-repeated life mantras.

"Well, I know you're sensitive," Jake says. "I hate English, and I think part of that . . ."

"Why?" I ask. "Why do you hate English?"

"I hate English because it's stupid," Lily offers.

"Thank you, Lily," I say.

"For me, it's just the way my brain works," Jake says. "I like math because I can get an answer multiple different ways, and I can check whether or not my answer's right. Whereas with English—I just never know if what I'm doing is right."

"Just call, ask me, and I'll tell you what's right," John interjects.

"Is it uncertainty with, like, spelling and grammar? Or whether you're putting the ideas out there the right way?" I ask.

"A little bit of everything," Jake says. "Just the uncertainty in general where I just didn't know: is this going to get me an A, B, C, or D? I'd turn in a paper, and I had no idea. But I'd heard that in John's class, you're allowed to write about whatever you want to write about."

"Make the private public," John says.

Jake's essay was about growing up in Pickerington, Ohio, as an Ohio State Buckeye fan, dreaming of playing for Ohio State and winning a national championship with Ohio State—yet going on and playing for Ohio State's biggest rival. His classmates "got to see a little piece of my life. That's what makes the class so special: everybody's sharing a little bit of themselves, and you just get to know all these people that, otherwise, had it been a normal English class, I would have never talked to any of them."

57

"You may disagree with me," John says, "but I think you kids learned more from each other than you did from me. When are you going to get a chance to write something deeply personal and then share it with people you don't even know?"

John stands and walks to the kitchen to chat with Carol. I mention to Jake how, in the few days he's been with us in Denver, probably a dozen former students have called, often asking him for advice about family, significant others, or life direction.

"I had a girl—I didn't know what to do, didn't really know where to go," Jake says. "He just gave me advice. And you don't get that. He's the only teacher I've ever had that I've formed this kind of a friendship with. Even coaches that I spend every single day with, who recruited me since I was 16 years old—I don't talk to 'em, you know?" He nods in John's direction. "But we talk every week almost."

* * *

John had never been to Hamburg, but Beloit College ran a semester-abroad exchange program there led by Hans Peter Ahlers, a professor of German. Ahlers and his wife Jeanne suggested that John come along with the group of eighteen Beloit students who would leave for Hamburg in late summer 1970. He could stay with the Ahlers in their apartment on the Rothenbaumchaussee until he got settled. John had fond memories of his time with the Red Cross in Bad Kreuznach, an experience that had deepened his long-standing interest in Germany—in particular, the paradox of the country's rich intellectual history in music, literature, and science counterposed with the darkness of Nazism. He packed a single duffel bag and off he flew.

The group hadn't been in Hamburg long when Ahlers pulled aside Beloit student Gray Currier. Currier had grown up in New York City and had joined the merchant marine as a teenager and later the U.S. Army's airborne infantry. With the Army, Currier had been sent to Mainz, Germany, to join the 8th Infantry Division which was head-quartered in Bad Kreuznach where John had been stationed with the Red Cross. Currier had landed in the Mannheim stockade for his views on the Vietnam War. John had, back in Beloit, gotten wind of this unconventional student's background and introduced himself. Now

Ahlers told Currier about Barbara's suicide and John's interest in catching up with Currier.

They caught up, and it soon became apparent that John needed a place to stay. Currier approached the German woman to whom Beloit was paying a small sum to host him for a semester's homestay. Inge Eden was in her fifties with two grown daughters and a son who was about Currier's age. Her husband had been killed on the Russian front.

"Frau Eden," Currier began, "I have this friend whose wife committed suicide and, much to my surprise, here he is in Germany. I don't really know him very well, but I'm sure he's a fine fellow, and it would be a great favor if you had room in the house to put him up."

The widow took the widower into her three-story home and refused to accept payment for her hospitality. They had breakfast together, sharing tea and fresh bakery bread—sometimes blackened by an overzealous toaster—with butter and jam for breakfast, cold cuts for dinner, and schnapps as they watched TV in the evening. Each morning, John and Currier rode the train from the suburb of Bergedorf into downtown Hamburg. Currier went to his classes; John looked for work and otherwise passed the time exploring the city. They sometimes met for lunch at a university cafeteria. Here they gorged on the main meal of the day at a steep discount. Currier got to know John well and saw a man who had been knocked down hard and was looking to get his feet back underneath him. He also came to see what most of John's friends and acquaintances, saturated as they were with the man's charm, sense of humor, and speed of thought, really couldn't. There's a sadness in him, Currier recognized. "Some of our greatest comedians are people who are very unhappy about certain things in their lives, but they're able to turn it to good effect with their humor," he said.

Of course, Currier grasped John's sadness at an especially sad time, one complicated by John's renewed questioning of what was left of his Catholic faith. That faith had already been broken into an angry agnosticism with the loss of his baby boys. Barbara's death had now swept its remnants into full-blown, unabashed atheism. This was, as his agnosticism had been, an emotional sort of atheism, one fueled by a quiet fury toward a God who would treat a particular, faithful

59

Catholic from Madison, Wisconsin, with such blatant disregard. Also, though, Currier was old enough to recognize a pervasive undercurrent of dissatisfaction in his older friend, one that manifested most obviously in an impatience and an impulsiveness that could set him off on a different mental or physical tack at any moment.

John was not the type to stay in bed and brood about such things. One day, he was walking around town near Hamburg University when he came across a bearded guy hitting a tennis ball against a wall. John struck up a conversation and soon found himself opposite a tennis net from the younger man, who quickly recognized that the American interloper's excellent range and quickness could in no way compensate for his grossly deficient tennis skills. Bernd Munderloh did have the presence of mind, though, to ask John if he played basketball.

Bernd played basketball for the Eimsbütteler Turnverband, or ETV. The quality of German basketball at that time was such that, when John joined Bernd and teammates on the ETV hardwood, it was quite clear that they had landed a whale.

John soon found a job at the American Express travel agency in town, so, within a couple of months of parachuting in with his duffel bag, he was earning some money, playing basketball with his new friends at ETV, hanging out at the bar afterwards drinking beer and (in John's case) apple juice, and bedding women in the oft-vacant apartment of Hans Peter Ahlers and wife Jeanne, for which he had retained a key. Having established his footing in the German city, John thanked Frau Eden profusely for her kindness and generosity and presented her with a new toaster as a parting gift before moving into a Hamburg commune with his basketball buddies.

Given that this was Cold War-era West Germany—with communist and expansionist East Germany being geostrategically contained maybe thirty miles down the Elbe River to the east—the authorities frowned upon communists (which many of John's basketball buddies happened to be) and their commie communes. Understanding this, the basketball players had cleverly named their commune Ingenieurbüro Maren. Maren, a common female name, was in this case a mashup of "Marx" and "Engels." *Ingenieurbüro* means "engineering firm." John's tiny room had towering ceilings, but he could touch both walls with outstretched arms. The company was pleasant, though, and the price was right: John doesn't recall having paid rent—which is fitting, really. Didn't Karl Marx himself say, "From each according to his ability, to each according to his needs"?

At the American Express travel agency, John did office work and, more interestingly, served as a guide on package tours to Russia and the United States, his role being to herd groups of thirty or forty American Express tourists from Switzerland and Germany onto and off buses and make sure they didn't miss planes from Leningrad to Moscow and such. The trips to the United States gave him the opportunity to visit his kids who had, at John's behest, moved from Joan's home near Milwaukee to that of Barbara's brother and his wife in Alexandria, Virginia. Before such trips, he saved up to present Steiff teddy bears and other toys to two small children who wondered when their daddy was coming home.

John had been in Germany for about a year when he stayed in America after an American Express U.S. tour to see his friends Ron and Barbara Pace who now lived in Memphis, Tennessee. Ron had come home from Bad Kreuznach and, in September 1968, had left the service as a captain. While working his way through a glacial recruitment process for the diplomatic corps, he earned an MBA at the University of Tennessee by the end of the following year and entertained a bevy of job offers ranging from banking to the airline industry to Alcoa, the aluminum giant. He chose what he described as "probably the least desirable," in part because he didn't want to take a fast-track job at a powerhouse company only to leave it in six months or whenever the diplomatic corps finally came calling.

That job was at Cosco, a company that made baby furniture, strollers, and other products for infants. Even at Cosco, the bosses recognized Ron as a rising star and suggested he take the plum position of assistant to the company president doing special projects. Ron suggested instead that he take a sales territory out in the field. As with the banks and the airlines and Alcoa, he didn't want to take some coveted role and then abandon it and leave the company in the lurch months later.

But then, despite being among the top 1% of applicants and weathering a four-hour grilling by a handful of diplomats in a final interview that had happened to fall on the day after his second son was born (Ron had taken a red-eye to Washington D.C.), he wasn't selected. The chairman of the selection committee came out into the hallway and broke the news. "We've never had anyone who did so well who didn't make it," the man confided. But the vote had to be unanimous, and one of the senior diplomats had blackballed him for reasons Ron would never learn.

And so, as John arrived in Memphis, "the best-laid plans of mice and men having gone awry, here I was selling baby furniture on the road," Ron said.

John joined Ron on his sales route from Memphis to New Orleans. For 400 miles straight south on Interstate 55, they caught up and got to the crux of what was tormenting John. He wanted to raise his children—but he also wanted what was best for his children. Would raising them himself be best for them? Would they be better off with Barbara's brother and his wife in Alexandria where they were settled in and were doing well in an upper-middle-class life that John might never be able to provide? Should he just give them up? With Ron mostly listening, John worked his way to the conclusion that the dilemma was unanswerable. What was certain was that Becky and Nick were John and Barbara's children and that John wanted them back.

After Ron took orders for baby furniture in the Big Easy, the two men drove back to Memphis. John then flew to New York and then back to Germany, knowing that, however wonderful his year in Hamburg had been, he had to leave.

* * *

It's lunchtime on Saturday. We're at the kitchen table talking grammar and writing. John declines lunch for now but does make himself a bowl of Talenti Mediterranean mint-chocolate-chip gelato, which he has microwaved for fifteen seconds, "to where you just see the melting starting around the edges."

"How does that change it?" I ask.

62

"To me, it just changes the entire taste," John says.

Lily and Carol are off to the western suburbs to see if Lily's new, $800 Edea skating boots, which are tearing up her feet, can't be adjusted into something more like functional figure skates and less like overpriced medieval torture implements. Maya has come downstairs, finally, grabbed a handful of pretzels, and fled back upstairs.

"Is that breakfast?" I ask as the she ascends. "Pretzels?"

"Yes," Maya yells as her door thumps shut.

"I want to tell you something now," John says. "In about two years, or maybe in about a year, or maybe in two months, some guy's gonna discover Lily, and she might lose interest in skating. And the next three-four years are gonna be horrible for both of 'em, because they're so goddamn beautiful"—he's referring to Maya also now—"because boys will discover 'em, or they'll discover boys. And you know what boys want."

"Yeah."

"A hard dick has no conscience," John says. "You've gotta have a sex talk with 'em, in my opinion. You've gotta tell 'em, 'A hard dick has no conscience.'"

"Yeah," I say. I come from a long line of repressed WASPs, so this advice sounds to me something like, "You've got to scale El Capitan without ropes."

"You need to tell 'em that their hormones are gonna start kickin' in. You need to tell 'em that they're gonna have desires that they've never had before and that they have to learn how to control their desires—that's what makes us human beings and not animals," John says.

"Um hmm," I say.

"And then you really have to talk seriously about birth control and about condoms."

"Yeah. For me it's like STDs—very bad. Not good. But pregnancy . . . ."

"Yes. You don't want to scare them about sex. With my children I said, look, you can't drive, right? I did this when they were fourteen—my three daughters. There are certain things in life that you have to be old enough to do. You have to be sixteen to drive; you have to be eighteen to vote. You have to be twenty-one to drink. I have a nice example of virginity in *The Passionate Papers of Fiona Pilgrim*—when the father tells the daughter, 'Treat your virginity like a valuable gift—which it is. Don't give it away to someone you don't really love because it's a gift that can only be given away once.' So make sure you give it to someone worthy of you—not to some nameless drunk after a night at the local watering hole," John says.

63

"It is important that they understand guys' motives," I say.

"There's nothing better than 'a hard dick has no conscience,' in my opinion."

"Yeah, no, it's pretty much boiled down there."

* * *

News that John's brother-in-law intended to adopt his children made going home all the more pressing. One complication was that John had no home. He decided to land where his friends Ron and Barbara lived. By the time John packed his duffel bag for the return trip, the baby-furniture company had transferred Ron to Atlanta. John resettled there, immediately rented the apartment above the Paces', and, a few days later, flew to Washington, D.C. with Ron accompanying him.

Their first stop was a Virginia courthouse where Barbara's brother and his wife's case for adoption came before a judge. Ron served as a character witness. He told the court that, based on what he had seen back in Bad Kreuznach, he considered John a good father. He had observed John doting on Becky, taking her on walks in the woods near the base, and bringing her along on trips around Germany and beyond. John's lawyer added the following: "If someone's claim that they would be a better parent were justification enough, no child would be safe in her mother's arms."

John would keep his kids. He and Ron left the courtroom, drove straight to Barbara's brother's house, and fetched Becky and Nick. On the plane back to Atlanta, Becky sat on Ron's lap and cried, distraught because her cat had run off somewhere and couldn't be corralled in time for the flight.

It was 1971. John was 31 with two kids to feed and clothe, rent to pay, and no job. The monthly Social Security benefits Becky and Nick received after losing their mother provided a vital infusion of cash. John found work teaching basic math and English to patients at a halfway house for those discharged from mental institutions. These lessons often devolved into adult babysitting. He also found a nanny for the kids, and Barbara Pace was there to help as she stayed home raising her boys, Kevin and Derek. The families grew close, with Uncle

John viewing the Pace boys as if they were his own sons and Uncle Ron and Aunt Barbara doing the same with Becky and Nick.

The halfway-house job was, once again, just a job for John. For the first time in his life, though, he had a long-term plan in mind. He intended to earn a master's degree in English and then return to Germany, this time with his kids, to teach high-school-aged students.

While he had trained many dogs, John's experience with the formal instruction of human beings had been limited to his couple of months working with mentally unstable adults who might, at any given moment, drop to the floor and start whooping. And while he had taken all of the required English classes at the University of Wisconsin, English hadn't been a particular focus. The casual observer might have rightly considered this new direction an odd choice.

To Ron, though, the idea of John pursuing English as an academic focus made perfect sense. From the time he had met John in Bad Kreuznach, the gregarious Red Cross man had shown an uncanny curiosity about words. This interest was most obvious in John's ongoing study of the language in a publication not generally a focus of intense study among scholars of English: *Time Magazine* which John pored over like some madrasa inductee with the Koran. He often pointed out interesting words and turns of phrases to Ron, ultimately convincing his new Army-officer friend to subscribe to the publication himself. John's independent studies extended beyond Henry Luce's weekly news roundup, too, and so his application to the Master's in English program at Georgia State University in Atlanta was at least somewhat less out of the blue than it otherwise seemed.

The Georgia State English Department people were at first skeptical. John's knowledge of the English canon was not so sparse that he believed Rosencrantz and Guildenstern to be cofounders of a New York law firm, but he certainly lacked the depth he would need as a specialist in the field. Yet his vocabulary seemed boundless: while he couldn't go into depth on the themes of Shakespeare's plays, he knew about every word in them.

John was accepted at Georgia State on the condition that he take six undergraduate English classes to erect the infrastructure and scaffolding for his master's-level classes. In the fall of 1971, he started what would become a master's degree in English and linguistics with an emphasis on teaching English as a second language—precisely the background he would need to teach at a German high school.

He went to school part-time while cutting back on his halfway-house hours but picking up part-time evening work with the Red Cross. His father's pronouncement of a "gift of poverty" had gone, in his mind, from fanciful to Kafkaesque as he struggled to keep his spending in line with his meager earnings and his kids' Social Security lifelines.

At one point, a fellow resident in the apartment complex told Ron about lucrative work he had found selling lifetime photo-development services. For $200, the buyer received a photo album and the opportunity to fill it and infinite successors with photos forever and ever. Just as $200 sounds like less than it actually was (roughly $1,200 in today's dollars), the idea of prepaying for lifetime of photo processing was less crazy than it seemed. Images had always been and, presumably, forevermore would be captured on strips of plastic coated with light-sensitive emulsions, and, back then, it cost perhaps $5.00 to develop a roll of thirty-six shots.

Ron told John about it. John trained on the art of door-to-door salesmanship for a day or two and set off to knock on doors with a demo photo album under his arm. One could knock on doors at any time, but evenings when people were home tended to be best, John had been told. Ron and Barbara wished him good luck and saw him off. The Paces kept an eye on all four kids for a couple of hours until John returned. His body language implied defeat.

"Fuck," he said. "I knocked on 283 doors, and I didn't get a foot in one."

John kept it up for a couple of weeks and met with uncannily consistent futility until one evening he was on the brink of a sale to a young Black woman with two little kids. He could all but feel the crispness of the $20 bill his commission would yield when the woman said, wisely, "I can't do this yet—I've got to get my husband's opinion."

John said, "Don't be silly. He couldn't possibly be that niggardly about photos of these beautiful children of yours, could he?"

Right word; wrong context.

John fared better in school, and he soon got a job in the Georgia State English Department's office in Sparks Hall in addition to the Red Cross and halfway-house gigs. By June 1972, things were improving, but money was still tight, and he needed help with the kids. He wrote a letter to his German basketball buddy Bernd Munderloh in June 1972 on the back of a photocopied page he had typewritten, copied, and sent to several German friends in search of an au pair. ". . . I will have very little money and MUST get an au pair girl," John explained. "I don't want someone to sleep with (I have enough of that here in America and quite honestly am getting sick of that type of relationship) but someone to love my children while I am working & going to school."

Meanwhile, John often hitchhiked the twelve miles from the apartment on Ashford Dunwoody Road in the suburb of Brookhaven into Georgia State's campus in downtown Atlanta. Other days, Ron gave him a ride. John's stock wardrobe included faded jeans and his old Red Cross jacket. Sometimes before heading to town he escorted Becky to school. She recalled the tall man with the short beard smoking his pipe as he walked her into her second-grade classroom and then performed his stock gag for those under the age of about 18. This involved employing minimal sleight-of-hand skills with which he pretended to detach his thumb. Some of her classmates hid behind the curtains.

John never would get that German nanny. He had prefaced his typewritten au pair emergency call with "Let me say at this point that I am not the least bit interested in marriage, but what I need is a mature (between 19 and 25), responsible woman who will take care of my children and give them the love and affection they so desperately need from a woman." He would soon find someone who fit that mold much closer to home.

One day not long after John wrote those words, a young woman who had just graduated from Winthrop College in South Carolina showed up to interview for a job at the halfway house. Nancy was petite, quiet, religious, and musically gifted on the piano—that is, more or less the diametric opposite of John on all obvious fronts (John claimed to be tone-deaf). John was aware of only the first two of these

67

features when he chatted her up, at which point he discovered the lovely southern lilt from her upbringing in Atlanta. Nancy didn't end up getting the job, but John ended up with her phone number.

They started dating. She had never traveled and, being a decade younger than John, was charmed by this tall, worldly, larger-than-life intellectual who was seemingly enamored of her. Barbara Pace recognized the dynamic immediately. "She was one of those girls in college who would love these intellectual giants and be so taken by their charismatic ways and personalities that they couldn't see anything else," she said.

By October 1972, John wrote his German friend Bernd Munderloh a four-page letter that mixed lexically solid if grammatically suspect German with English. He repeated that, by January, he really needed a "mother's helper" au pair. He and Nancy were together almost every day, he continued, and he confided that he was in love. He described a weekend getaway in the mountains with just the two of them as *sagenhaft, tadellos, ausgezeichnet* (fabulous, perfect, outstanding). He also noted that "Nancy and I had arguments which one has with a person whom he is getting to know (Don't worry about the syntax and grammar of the foregoing sentence—I'm not a purist.). She does have serious doubts about: (i) my desire to live in Germany the rest of my life . . . .

"(ii) The fact, I'm sure, that she is only 22 and I already have a daughter almost nine—but you are only as young as you feel and act. I'm 32 going on 21—yet she may be too young to make this commitment. However, she loves the children, and they love her. But you are absolutely right: they desperately need a mother.

"(iii) I don't know—as I get to know her better—if she's like most materialistic American bitchy women. I would say now she is really an exception—a wonderful exception and [my current and foreseeable lack of] money will cause no problems."

There was other news in this letter with direct impact on John's plans to spend the rest of his life in Germany. He would, he told Munderloh, probably spend another couple of years in the United States to earn his doctorate. John had impressed his major professors in his master's program and had been offered a spot in the PhD program, complete with a stipend. For a dissertation topic, he chose to examine Black English from a linguistic perspective and how English teachers' attitudes changed with respect to Black-English speakers once those teachers had been educated in its underlying logic. As the token white guy on the Middleton Plumbers and other basketball teams back in Madison, as well as while working with Black servicemen during his Red Cross days, he sensed that, while Black English might have sounded wholly different than that spoken by the Queen of England, it was structurally just as solid. This was a radical idea.

Nancy and John married in December 1972, six months after they had met. She wasn't terribly interested in living in Germany, but that wasn't the big hurdle. John's PhD would price him out of work at a German high school. Upon graduating in 1975, he looked for work stateside in what was clearly a buyer's market for English PhDs. John came across a job posting for a position at Lincoln Memorial University in Harrogate, Tennessee, and assumed that hundreds of PhDs with fancier academic qualifications than his would swarm to it.

To stand out in this crowd, he went with an unconventional cover letter, unfortunately lost to history. He introduced himself as a paraplegic Vietnam veteran. His mother, he continued, was black; his father, a Choctaw Indian with a lisp; his wife, a full-blooded Cherokee with a chakra deficiency. His hobbies included playing slave hymns on his digeridoo, writing haikus inspired by the women's liberation movement, and, on occasion, slipping into Victorian dresses he collected for moments when the urge to cross-dress struck him.

While he played it straight with his academic credentials, the rest of his application was intended to catch the eye of someone with a sense of humor and the capacity to recognize that this applicant from Georgia State was poking fun at what would soon become known as the political-correctness movement.

Douglas Gordon, a professor of English at the little college on a hill above the hollows where Kentucky, Tennessee, and Virginia met, was just such a person.

6

At the Cumberland Gap

Ah, but a man's reach should exceed his grasp,
Or what's heaven for?
                        — Robert Browning

D oug Gordon had been hired at Lincoln Memorial University the year before, having just earned his PhD at the University of Tennessee at Knoxville. Gordon was now the English Department chair of this remote school of fewer than a thousand students.

The place had an interesting history. LMU came to be thanks largely to the impetus of Oliver O. Howard, the man a more famous institution of higher education, Howard University, was named after. Howard was a Civil War general who led the Union's Army of the Tennessee. Years later, he recalled during a lecture tour that brought him to the Cumberland Gap region, that Lincoln himself had remarked to him about the loyalty to the Union of the hill people of East Tennessee despite the state having been Confederate.

Howard took up the cause of establishing a university in the region to reward that loyalty. He raised money to buy property that had once been an enormous, 700-room hotel and resort complex that speculators had believed would thrive as the region blossomed into an industrial hub on the order of Pittsburgh. A financial crash had ended that dream in 1895.

Two years later, LMU came to be, and seventy-eight years after that, John's cover letter piqued Gordon's interest. It didn't hurt that a Georgia State administrator who happened to know LMU's academic dean highly recommended John. John, now 35, landed his first faculty job: he was now an assistant professor. He went to work teaching freshman-level writing courses to the children of tobacco farmers, coal miners, and others making their hardscrabble livings in the surrounding hill country. There were exceptions, but, in general, these classes consisted of about thirty students whose shaky command of written English—nothing out of the ordinary for incoming college students—was made wobblier yet by the deep imprints of the local dialect. John was, in many cases, teaching English as a second language as he had envisioned he would—just not to Germans. Despite the red ink bleeding from his pen, John found that he loved the work and his students. The culture was interesting too, what with banjo pickin', hootenannies, molasses stiroffs, and ample moonshine.

Nancy and the kids were happy, too. This region of steeply wooded hills and tight valleys was a welcome change from urban Atlanta. Their new Irish wolfhound took to the scenery and augmented John's persona as its predecessor had in Beloit. The family and hound lived in a dorm that housed student athletes, among others—John served as a faculty advisor in residence. Becky, now 13, was particularly enthusiastic about that sort of scenery.

They would move from the dorm after about a year. The back-to-the-land movement was in full flower, propelled by disillusionment with the Vietnam War, urban decay, pollution, the energy crisis, consumerism, and corporatism. Publications such as Stewart Brand's *The Whole Earth Catalog* and Eliot Wigginton's *Foxfire* series of books served up motivation as well as instructions on how to get back to nature. John and Nancy enlisted a real estate agent and visited a 120-acre farm—half of it in Tennessee, half in Virginia—on a winding dirt road cut into steep hillsides about fifteen miles east of town. In *Farming Circe's Acres*, the novel he later wrote based on the experience, John describes his first impressions.

> *The green trough of the valley was laced by a sparkling blue-and-silver sliver of a river that snaked its serpentine course through the middle of the advertised pasture of fescue, orchard grass, and alfalfa. At*

71

> *points along its meandering flow, the water either*
> *lapped soothingly over boulders or rifled and eddied*
> *raucously where the banks of the brook converged to*
> *form a narrows . . . .*
>
> *An ambrosial essence of honeysuckle, Russian*
> *olive, and mint—wafted across the meadows by the*
> *weakest whisper of a breeze—delicately scented the*
> *air . . . .*
>
> *The pastures were bejeweled at this time of year*
> *with solid patches of yellow and white daisies; varie-*
> *gated smatterings of purple and white violets, the last*
> *dying remnants of the growing season; and thousands*
> *of clusters of billowing, crimson clover, each sprig*
> *nodding its scarlet crown in rhythmic unison with it*
> *neighbor's bowing in obeisance to Aeolus, the god of the*
> *winds. The flowers flourished against a luxurious*
> *background of shamrock-green grass.*

In addition to the bucolic setting, the three-bedroom farmhouse painted white with red trim, the barn and other outbuildings, and the 3,000-pound tobacco allotment all served as further enticements to purchase the property. John had read Thoreau and envisioned his future in Tennessee Hill Country: "I was gonna work as a professor at Lincoln Memorial University, come home, sit on the porch swing and rock back and forth, admire nature, and have great moments of self-discovery."

He embarked on his second school year at LMU as an English professor-gentleman farmer. The Rubadeaus hadn't set down roots in rural Appalachia for long before it became clear to him that all was not well at the tiny university. The university's president had something to do with that.

Frank Welch was about the same age as John and had been at Lincoln Memorial University for two years when John arrived. Welch had shaken some things up for the better: reorganizing various small departments into eight large divisions, adding evening classes, backing student internships to help them get real-world experience, and creating new associate degrees as well as a bachelor's degree in nursing. Enrollment was on track to more than double from an alarming low of 385 students when Welch had arrived in 1973. He had also courted and convinced Col. Harland Sanders of Kentucky Fried Chicken fame to donate a substantial sum for the creation of the Abraham Lincoln Library and Museum on campus, a center of research and learning that had recently broken ground. The growing collection included thousands of documents and artifacts such as the cane Lincoln carried on the night of his assassination.

But Welch had an abrasive dictatorial streak and some curious tendencies. Right after he arrived, he fired the entire faculty and forced those who wanted to continue to interview for their jobs again—at the time a radical move for a small business much less a small college. He replaced the receptionist's desk in his office suite with a shiny white version made of some mystery material, and he remodeled the president's office with silver-and-gold, diagonally striped wallpaper. His aesthetic tastes also applied to his sartorial choices. He wore a thick, black wig not unlike Elvis Presley's late-life coif. He dressed in three-piece suits but also in polyester leisure suits—Gordon recalled one having been canary yellow and another baby blue, the same blue as Welch had the auditorium painted. Faculty who didn't get along with him were not invited to the faculty Christmas party.

"Anybody who was sensitive to seriousness in higher education could not see this otherwise than some sort of con game," Gordon said later.

Welch pursued the protection and fortification of his authority with Machiavellian zeal. John, sensing this at one point in a meeting with Welch and Gordon, told the university president, "Frank, I just want to say this one thing: you don't have to be concerned about Doug or about me because we have no ambition at all."

As Gordon put it later, "I cracked up. I couldn't believe he'd said that, but there was a sense in which he was right on target. Because we wouldn't have been there but just for a love of teaching and supporting students. If we would have had any ambition, we wouldn't have been at Lincoln Memorial University."

Welch stood maybe five-foot-eight; Gordon was tall like John, about six-foot-five. (The two professors were so similar in size that Gordon passed on to John all of his old clothes and shoes—fine articles because Gordon's stepfather owned a couple of high-end men's-clothing stores in Virginia). The two young English professors joked that, should Welch send them packing, they could cite "too tall" as the justification for their firing. But in general, they were so busy with teaching and inking up student papers that academic politics were typically a minor annoyance.

* * *

At the kitchen table, John tells a grammar joke.

"There's a traveling salesman, and, every four or five months, his route would take him by Boston," he begins. "One time he's there, and he stops into his favorite fish restaurant where he always orders scrod—you know, the young cod or halibut served in Boston restaurants. Well, this time, for the first time in the many years he's gone there, they don't have scrod. So he orders something else. When he leaves again, he hails a cab. The cabbie, a loquacious sort, asks him if he had a good time. The salesman says, 'Yes, I love Boston, but I didn't have such a good time this time.'"

"'Why?' the cabbie asks."

"'Well, this was the first time I'd been to Boston that I hadn't gotten scrod,' the salesman tells him."

"The cabbie flicks on his turn signal and says, 'My, that's an unusual usage of the passive pluperfect.'"

John is a PhD linguist and loves grammar as a mathematician loves equations. I recognize the need for proper grammar, spelling, and orthography. But with the exception of pointing out funny mistakes on signage, the study of linguistic mechanics does not float my boat as it does John's. We have, in the effort to capture a wide swath of his teaching, been covering a lot of grammar over the last couple of days. Having exhausted that conversation, the topic turns to the big-picture writing lessons he has imparted over the years. As is the case with his mantra for living the right life ("quid quo pro; scratch your itch"), they are simple.

(1) Audience and purpose. A sports column reads differently than an obituary reads differently than an energy-drink advertisement reads differently than a mutual-fund prospectus.

People magazine reads differently than *The Atlantic* reads differently than *National Geographic Kids.* They have different audiences and different purposes. The same holds true for about every form of written communication.

Sometimes hits and misses can be subtle. John describes the case of a former student who was a third-year medical student applying for pediatric oncology residencies. The student asked John to review his application essay. The young doctor wasted precious words giving background on medicines and procedures his specialist audience well understood. By the same token, had the former student been giving a talk about pediatric oncology to a lay audience, explaining what "pediatric oncology" was (the field of medicine dedicated to treating childhood cancers) would have been advised.

(2) The dumb reader. Closely related to the above, writers for a general audience should think hard about the audience's familiarity with the topic they are trying to convey. John boils this down to, "Think about the 'dumb reader.'" The dumb reader is not actually dumb—she's just not steeped in the topic and may need some background.

(3) The secret to writing is rewriting. John calls his and everyone else's first drafts "shit drafts." The less-scatological writer John McPhee calls his first drafts "unreadable things." Good writing is a multistep process, and rarely do you nail it on the first go-around. You've got to get the ideas down on paper. Then you edit, which is shorthand for asking a lot of questions: "Is the copy clean?" "Is this accurate?" "Is it saying what I want to say to the audience I'm trying to reach?" "Is it well-organized?" "Is there something that needs adding"—or, more importantly, "What can I cut?" and "Is there a better, more succinct way to say this?" because drafts tend to be bloated, and, in our digital era, attention spans are short. I print out my drafts and pencil edit them and invariably spot problems I'd missed on the screen. John reads aloud, from the last sentence of the essay or other written work to the first sentence. This backwards reading forces the author to see what he or she has actually written as opposed to the words imprinted in the writer's mind. Whatever your approach, assume that, regardless of your literary brilliance, your first draft is indeed a "shit draft."

(4) Synergism. A street with litter here and there seems normal enough; one that's strewn with trash darkens our opinion of the place. So too with writing. "A misplaced comma is no big deal, and the misuse of a dash is no big deal, and a misspelled word is no big deal, and an uppercase word that you lowercase is no big deal," John says. "But the combined effect

of all the 'small' errors makes you look illiterate and undermines your credibility. In writing, the whole really is greater than the sum of its parts."

* * *

In addition to a heavy teaching load at Lincoln Memorial University, John also had the farm to contend with. There was a big garden—the aim being back-to-the-land self-sufficiency in the realm of vegetables—that Becky, 13, and Nick, 9, were charged with maintaining. Nick fed the roosters and chickens; Becky was responsible for her horse, Misty. Nancy was responsible for Pace, a baby boy born in June 1976 whom they had named after John's best friend Ron.

The actual farming involved a cash crop. John now owned enough land to grow a government allotment of 3,000 pounds of tobacco and a barn big enough to hang it all for curing. He also had the good fortune of having a neighbor interested in doing the actual tobacco farming. John would buy all the necessary supplies and, come the end of the harvest, split the proceeds with this man John described as "the nicest guy in the world. He had like twelve kids, and he'd married his first cousin, not the sharpest thing in the world to do, but anyway." In return, the neighbor and some subset of his many offspring would supply the know-how, the insecticides, the weed killer, the farming equipment, and the backbreaking labor.

A different neighbor, one outfitted in bib overalls stained with Red Man tobacco juice and other dusky foreign substances, suggested John could make a lot of money raising pigs. Ernie Estep, whom everyone in the hollow called "Goobie," was in his late twenties and had not himself ever raised pigs—he had just heard it was an easy way to make some money. Nor had, John would later learn, any other neighbors in the hollow. John, forever short of cash, subsisting on a starting professor's salary, and now with another mouth to feed, was enthusiastic. How hard could it be? Feed them for a year. Take them to market. Rake in bacon for bacon. Repeat.

John hired a neighbor to bulldoze out a pig wallow near the tobacco barn which would do double duty as swine shelter. John cut holes in the barn's exterior wall for each of four pigpens. He ran ¾-inch PVC pipe from the spring high above the pig lot and gravity flowed water into the wallow. The pipe would provide drinking water and a cool place for the pigs which, John learned, lacked sweat glands. He fenced the whole thing in with metal stakes that he had to bash into the hard ground with a sixteen-pound sledgehammer. Nick had the dubious honor of steadying each stake. The task so tore up the English professor's hands that he ended up in the county-hospital emergency room and had to hire out the rest of the job.

With the preparations done, John bought three piglet sows and a young boar. He soon came to understand that the cliché "eat like a pig" had not been coined indiscriminately. Corn feed prices seemed to rise in concert with the piglets' appetites to the point that the family pork-production budget approached one-third of the family food budget even with Nancy's diligent coupon-clipping. John supplemented the pigs' trough with two five-gallon buckets of slop from Lincoln Memorial University cafeteria scrapings and leftovers that he daily schlepped back to the Rubadeau farm in the nose of his old VW Beetle.

The four piglets' cuteness—doelike brown eyes, curly tails, wiggly energy—wore off quickly as they constantly escaped their pens and raided neighbors' vegetable gardens. After weeks of chasing them around Appalachia, John learned that nose-piercing the little rascals with circular rings through their septums would halt these incessant prison breaks. It's known, in the hog-raising business John was learning the hard way, as "ringing." Becky fetched the first piglet; Nancy agreed to hold it. With the crunch of a metallic C becoming an O through the flesh of a snout, the piglet screeched out one end and shat out the other—all over Nancy. This marked the end of her pig-raising career.

The challenge of running a farm with no agricultural or, more generally, rural-life experience didn't stop with the pigs. The rooster ambled away and kept impregnating a neighbor's chickens until the neighbor finally shot it. The Irish wolfhound gathered fleas from the wild and shared them throughout the household. The awesome hay-bale "fort" the kids had discovered in the barn turned out to be infested with chicken lice from chickens who had previously found it a perfect nesting place. Tufts, and then clumps, of Becky's and Nick's hair fell out. Treatment cleared it, but the kids had to endure baldness made worse by crusty scabs.

With winter's arrival, the pipe from spring to wallow froze, and John began his days by filling two five-gallon jerry cans with water from the sink and lugging them down to the trough, a task he repeated each evening. The farmhouse's water supply, gravity fed through plastic piping from a spring uphill from the farmhouse, froze repeatedly, each time sending John out to shake the tubing and pound on the pond's surface ice to restore flow. He fought incessantly with the VW Beetle's tire chains, without which he couldn't make it through the unplowed stretches of dirt road between his house and his university job. He often showed up covered with dirt and wet from snow. A vicious winter blizzard socked the family in for a good two weeks at one point.

With time and the spring thaw, Nancy sought sanity with increasingly frequent trips to Knoxville, about an hour away. With baby Pace, she browsed suburban malls, garage sales, flea markets, and rummage sales—as much for a taste of civilization as a need for cloth-ing and household items. She found herself marooned at home with her baby boy as John, Becky, and Nick were off at their respective schools.

Also by spring, the boar had done its job and thirty-two piglets came into the world. John then had the pleasure of castrating the baby boars with a razor blade ("You know Rocky Mountain oysters? These were Rocky Mountain peas. Completely useless."), clipping all the piglets' needle-sharp teeth, cutting their tails off, and giving them iron shots. With his scruffy beard, his Montgomery Ward bib overalls, and his hobnail boots, he looked like a farmer. But he was learning everything as he went, either from the occasional advice of neighbors or from the local U.S. Department of Agriculture extension agent, the man who had noted the need for castrations, teeth clipping, and the iron shots.

In May, it was time to bring his pork-to-be to market. Goobie, who had suggested in the first place that John raise pigs, agreed to haul thirty-one of them to the feeder-pig market in Cookeville, about 175 miles away, in exchange for meals and gassing up his pickup truck. He,

John, and Nick drove off in a pickup with the squealing litters. The thirty-second pig, the runt of runts, John gave to the neighbor as a token of goodwill.

In Cookeville, John had been expecting a quiet affair of a couple dozen pig breeders. He was surprised to find ten times as many and thousands of animals. He noted also that the pigs here were enormous—maybe he had come on the wrong day when they were selling finished hogs for slaughter. At about 2 p.m., John, Nick, and their drift of pigs shuffled into the first receiving pen. The whispers among the crowd of farmers and pig buyers and onlookers with apparently nothing better to do on a sunny day in Cookeville ignited into open laughter. It was as if this tall man with the beard were introducing an entirely new species of pygmy pigs.

The biggest of them weighed less than half the fifty-two-pound average that day, the smallest about one-third as much. Neither his neighbors nor the agricultural extension agent had mentioned that he should have avoided insemination at the first estrus, that he should have weaned the piglets earlier and given them higher-protein food, or that he should have treated them for the worms they all had. These should-haves added up to John attempting to sell the smallest pigs in the market's sixty-year history. He was paid accordingly, and he didn't need a calculator to understand that he had lost a fortune on these goddamn swine—enough to completely cancel out his windfall from the previous year's tobacco allotment.

Somehow, despite all the distractions of what he had imagined would be a blissful Arcadian existence, John's teaching was going well: students chose him as Lincoln Memorial University's top teacher in this, his second year at the institution. It would also be his last.

* * *

It is Sunday, and John and I head to the mountains—to Breckenridge, where another former student and friend, Emily Higgins, lives. I stop at the Conoco at Eighth Avenue and Colorado Boulevard to fill up. John goes inside to buy gum. He returns and declares that he has had a great conversation with the attendant.

"You should buy gas here all the time," he says.

We drive out Interstate 70 into the mountains. I point out the herd of bison just past the Genesee overlook and, beyond Idaho Springs, the abandoned mines on the slopes above. Their tailings have long polluted Clear Creek whose ancient path the highway follows. I teach my teacher that gray tailing piles are from silver mines and yellow ones are from gold mines and that you can still see them all over the hillsides a century later because they're caustic to plant life.

Though it's only the first Sunday in December, dots of distant skiers wend their way down Breck's bright slopes. We meet Emily at Flip Burger on the town's main drag. Since taking John's class in 2015, she has been referred to by the bearded man as "E-Higgs." I ask her how a biopsychology major ended up in John's class. She needed to satisfy an upper-level writing requirement, she says. A roommate of hers had taken the class and had talked about it.

John elaborates, "She bonded with this guy in class, Kyle Kalis. He weighs 300 pounds. Plays for the Cleveland Indians now."

"The Cleveland Browns, I suspect," I say.

"Whatever," John says.

Kalis is also known as "Picasso," because, in addition to playing guard at a second-team All-American level, he is a talented visual artist and musician.

"My roommate was a voice major. She and Picasso wrote a song together which they sang in John's class, and they practiced at our house," E-Higgs says. She is sharp, self-effacing, engaging, and funny—like Jake, but a foot shorter, 130 pounds lighter, and blonde. She's applying to graduate schools and working for the Breckenridge Outdoor Education Center, which gives people with all sorts of disabilities a chance to experience slopes, trails, and rivers.

We talk about her having absorbed John's approach, as she put it, "of encouraging that brain barf—don't stop writing; get it out there. And then the emphasis on editing and revision, not only with your own writing, but also when you look through someone else's writing and critique it and learn."

"The secret to good writing is?" John says.

"Rewriting!" E-Higgs says.

"If you hadn't gotten that one, it wouldn't have gone well," I say.

"He would have been so mad," E-Higgs says.

She talks about the background of the essay she wrote for John's class. "I had a huge crush on this boy in college. I thought we'd be perfect together. Why doesn't he see it? This went on for like a year. And we sat down and I was ready to be really mad at him: 'You treated me poorly! This is not OK! This is not what I want! And I'm ready to yell at him and he goes: 'I think I'm gay.' That just totally changed the direction of the conversation."

The essay's title: "My Boyfriend is Gay."

We have eaten our burgers. E-Higgs notes, as Jake did, that John is the only Michigan professor she's kept up with.

"Yeah, because you're so goddamn funny," he says.

"Yeah," she says, "but it's nice just to have this connection and have someone recognize that I am funny and intelligent—and modest!—and I can use commas. It's nice to feel noticed at a big school like Michigan, and I think it's another reason that your class feels really special. I think you make a big effort to get to know people and learn something about them. That's probably another reason why people feel comfortable to talk about things in that classroom setting. It's a special space."

John smiles. "We didn't learn shit, but we sure had fun, no?"

* * *

John was a popular teacher at Lincoln Memorial University. His interactions with a student named Marty Cosby help illustrate why. Cosby's family farmed tobacco and hay and raised cattle a few miles from the Rubadeau tract. John saw Cosby as a smart kid but one who lacked focus and didn't seem to be taking John's exhaustive essay comments to heart—if he were reading the comments at all. John made a habit back then of adding his signature to the end of his essay corrections. He tested his theory on Cosby by signing "Sid Luckman" rather than "John Rubadeau" at the end of one of Cosby's marked-up essays—Luckman being the famous Chicago Bears quarterback of John's childhood. Later, John asked Cosby if he had read the corrections.

"Yes, of course, Dr. Rubadeau," Cosby said.

"Really," John said. "Then do you recall the name I signed it with at the end?"

"John Rubadeau?" Cosby asked.

Essays and their signatures weren't foremost on Cosby's mind, John soon learned. Cosby had real questions about whether he was cut out for college. His friends were off working and making good money in the coal mines and factories. Cosby had his eye on quitting and doing construction work. John would have none of it.

"No no no no no," John said. "You don't want to do that all your life. You need to stay here and get your education. You'll be miserable." He added: "If you drop out of this school, I'll never talk to you again."

Cosby stayed. He graduated with a degree in education and met his future wife along the way. He became a special education teacher at Forge Ridge School, the Harrogate K-12 where he had once been a pupil. He went on to become the school's principal and earned PhDs in education and theology along the way. Cosby had definitely been cut out for college.

"You knew, as a student, that he cared about you. He was not there just to be getting a paycheck. He was there to make a difference," Cosby said many years later. "You knew it. You felt it. He encouraged me to stay, and I'm very thankful for that."

There was, however, a growing disconnect between John's impact as a professor and his physical and behavioral presentation on campus. During the winter, he often arrived with his jacket and jeans dirty from farm chores or from having to fight with the VW Beetle's tire chains on the commute in. He swore liberally, as always, and was known to spice up faculty meetings "because you never knew when he might stand up and say something outrageous," Gordon said. What did John in was standing up for Gordon.

In April 1977, it rained six inches in a matter of hours, and the floodwaters that periodically inundated this region's narrow valleys rose again. The Rubadeau farmhouse, high on a hill, stayed dry. Down closer to the creek, though, Nick swore he watched as wild turkeys held their mouths open wide to the sky until they drowned (this in accordance with Appalachian folklore). After the floodwaters receded, Gordon organized a food and clothing drive for the families of the many local students whose homes had been washed out by the deluge. Gordon did it because he felt he was in a position to help, and it was the right thing to do.

His colleagues took note. Sometime later, the university president Welch appointed John to head the committee selecting the recipient of something called the Algernon Sidney Sullivan Award; it was to be conferred during the college's graduation ceremonies. The committee selected Doug Gordon for his flood-recovery efforts and informed Welch. That the only dissenting vote had been that of Welch's wife, a business professor, served as a hint of what was to come.

When the graduation program was published in early June, to the surprise of John and others, the Algernon Sidney Sullivan award recipient was neither Doug Gordon nor anyone else. At the commencement ceremony on June 5, there was no mention of the award at all. That night, John called the chairman of the executive committee of the university's board of trustees, a businessman named Samuel A. Mars Jr., to ask for an explanation. Why hadn't Gordon received the award which he so deserved? Mars said he'd look into it. A couple of days later, a faculty member stopped by and told John that he and several others were upset about the Sullivan award as well as other issues related to Welch's leadership. John called Mars again, this time asking him for a meeting with faculty. Mars agreed, but only if Welch were present. This was an odd demand from a man leading the board charged with overseeing the university's president, but Welch clearly had the board of trustees on his leash.

Presidents of tiny universities often enjoy imperial power. That was certainly the case at LMU, and Welch regaled on his throne, large and in charge. With the threat of Welch's presence, the willingness of John's colleagues to air their concerns wilted in the heat of imperiled job security. John was faced with the prospect of going it alone or letting it go. He had a young family and a farm, and pig-fiasco debts, to pay for and would have been forgiven for stepping back as his colleagues had done. It was just a silly award, after all, and Gordon, while annoyed with the whole thing, was looking for another job anyway. Most people would have simply let it go. John could not.

There were two reasons. First, Doug Gordon was his friend, and John took friendships very seriously. He may have served in the Red Cross, but he would have been the one who belly-flopped on the live grenade in the foxhole to save a comrade.

Second, John bristled at authority in general but viscerally despised capricious abuses of power and the injustices they invariably engendered. Welch was, in John's mind, abusing power. True, it was just a silly award. But it was also about right and wrong. That the potential costs to John incalculably outweighed any possible benefits (those being, in essence, zero) seemed not to register with him at all. He did recognize the risk of speaking out, though, and talked it over with Nancy. She told him he should do what he felt was right but to be sure to keep his composure.

Welch scheduled the meeting for June 9. As John entered Welch's Duke Hall office, he had only Gordon's unawarded award on his mind. Welch was considering something else entirely: Mars had wasted no time in alerting Welch to John's phone calls which Welch considered as "seeking to undermine my position as president and to eliminate my position of authority and leadership."

Welch wore a three-piece suit with lapels that would have lofted him in a stiff breeze; John arrived "with about three days of beard growth on his face" and "with blue jeans that looked like he had been feeding the hogs in them for the last week," as Welch would later describe it. He had told John before that it wasn't the university's fault that he had bought a farm and couldn't find a way to dress appropriately. The English professor sat down in one of two chairs facing Welch's desk. There was a tap at the door. Gary Burchett, Welch's deputy, entered. Welch had called him and told him to sit in on the meeting; this request came to no surprise to Burchett as Welch had, on occasion, ordered him to do so when Welch felt he needed a witness.

Burchett sat down in the other chair. He and John were on good terms, so perhaps this was a good omen. Burchett proceeded to witness what he later described as a measured discussion regarding the Sidney Algernon Sullivan Award that bordered, as he put it, on a "philosophical debate." Rubadeau explained the committee's role and Gordon having deserved the recognition. Welch explained that he respected the committee's opinion, but that he, as president, was vested with the ultimate authority on every decision made at Lincoln Memorial University.

"Well, that's not fair," John said.

"That doesn't make a difference," Welch said.

"Yeah, but the university bylaws say that you can't overrule the decisions of the selection committee. The selection committee chose Doug. I'm the chair of that committee."

"And I'm the president," Welch said.

Burchett said nothing but saw what was coming. He had watched Welch's and Rubadeau's relationship rot like wet tobacco over the past two years. They had had a great start: when John flew out for the interview, he had worn a suit, was nicely groomed, and was freshly shaven. John had stayed with Welch, his wife Cynthia, and the three Welch boys, in fact. But no sooner had John shown up that first summer all scraggly in his old Red Cross fatigues at the university picnic in Democrat Hollow than did Welch, for whom style was at least as important as substance, darken on his new hire. John, for whom substance was everything and style meant little, increasingly felt the same way about Welch.

"Their personalities were oil and water," Burchett said.

Welch continued casually, as if ordering lunch. "The reason that I called this meeting is that we don't feel you are the appropriate person to be employed by this university," Welch said, using the royal "we." "I'm giving you notice that you're being terminated immediately."

John uncrossed his legs and leaned forward. "On what grounds?"

"It's just not a compatible relationship," Welch said. He stood, walked around his desk past John to the door, opened it, and held the knob. Burchett stayed where he was. John stood and walked to the open door, where he towered over the short man. What John said next was out of his mouth before his mind could have winched it back in, had he wanted to, which he didn't anyway: "Well you arrogant little Napoleonic-complex fuck," John said. "You can't do this."

"Yes, I can," the president said. "And you're fired."

7

Constanţa and Atlanta

A man needs a little madness or else—he never dares cut the
rope and be free.

— Nikos Kazantzakis (from *Zorba the Greek*)

Word got out that Frank Welch had fired John. John's friend
and neighbor Ernie Estep came by the farmhouse a couple
of days later.

"John, we need to have a serious talk," Estep said through the
screen door.

John stepped onto the porch; the door smacked shut behind him.
"Goobie, what's wrong?"

"I heard you done got fired."

"Oh," John said. "Yeah, I did."

Estep had served two tours in Vietnam and had earned a Bronze
Star. "Do you want me to kill the sonofabitch?"

John searched his friend's face for some sign that he was kidding.
None presented itself.

"No no—please," John said. "I think that's a tad extreme. It's not
that serious."

It was serious, though. John was a 37-year-old, unemployed English professor with just two years' experience at a tiny Appalachian
university. He had little in the bank, but he did have three kids, four
adult pigs, an exhausted and disillusioned wife, and a farm that had
greened back up into the Arcadian paradise that had so disguised its
brutal essence a year before. He did his best not to dwell on all this.

Don't live in the past! Plus: the firing meant he could get out from under the farm—yes! But only if he found a job far from Harrogate.

To this end, he did what PhDs looking for faculty jobs did: he turned to the *Chronicle of Higher Education* classifieds. His search would probably prove fruitless as these sorts of jobs generally filled many months in advance, and, with it now being June 1977, fall semesters would start again in less than two months. Still, he was paging through a back issue when he noted an ad for Fulbright lecturers. These lecturers were part of a U.S. State Department program that sent a variety of U.S. professors overseas to teach and do research.

He should have applied nine months earlier. Nonetheless, he put together a cover letter and sent it to the Fulbright offices at 11 DuPont Circle in Washington D.C. Then he did what he made a point of doing when he applied for—or asked for—anything: he assumed he wouldn't get it, and he more or less forgot about it. That way he didn't get his hopes up for something that was out of his control. By so doing, he reasoned, it saved him from being disappointed when things didn't work out, an outcome more common than any of us like to think about.

John took the same approach with this letter as he had with the missive that had piqued Doug Gordon's interest at Lincoln Memorial University two years earlier: the paraplegic Vietnam veteran bit, the Black-and-Native-American-with-a-lisp parents bit, the politically incorrect or politically too-correct avocations bit, the cross-dressing in Victorian dresses bit, and so on. It was another exercise in what someone not named John Rubadeau would view as casual recklessness toward a high-stakes proposition. He was "attacking every single sacred cow that could have been gored," as he described it later. "And the person who got it would either just think that 'This man is either insane, eccentric, or a racist bigot' or that the individual might just think, 'This guy's fuckin' hilarious.'"

Being "fuckin' hilarious" may or may not have been a qualification prized by the Fulbright people, but John's timing was perfect. His letter arrived on the desk of the Fulbright program's equivalent of a college admissions officer the very day that the office had been informed that the U.S. Fulbright lecturer slated to spend a year in Gdansk, Poland, had died. The Fulbright lecturer who had been assigned to Constanța, Romania, happened to have had Polish roots; when he found out about the sudden opening in Gdansk, the man asked for, and received, a lateral transfer to Gdansk. That left the position in Constanța open.

"And my letter came that very day," John said later. "And they all thought it was hilarious. And so they called me. I talked to them on the phone, I bullshitted with them, they invited me for an interview, I bullshitted with them again, and they offered me the job. And I had to leave within like six weeks."

Having just spent a year cooped up on a godforsaken, swine-stricken farm in backwater Appalachia, Nancy had no interest in spending a year cooped up in some boxy, gray apartment building in communist Romania. Their marriage was fraying anyway, and raising a baby and elementary-school- and middle-school-aged children was hard enough without a language barrier in a distant, xenophobic land behind the Iron Curtain. John could go; she would stay; she would care for the children—their biological son Pace as well as the stepchildren she had adopted before the family had moved to Tennessee. She picked out an apartment in the northern reaches of Atlanta. Her family was there and so were Ron and Barbara Pace who lived nearby. Ron would make a point of stopping by on the way home from business trips which he took almost every week.

John flew to Germany and stopped off in Hamburg. As long as the U.S. government was flying him back to Europe, why not rekindle the dream of finding a job and settling down, now with Nancy and three kids, in Northern Germany? He met with officials from the University of Hamburg's English department, an international school, and the city's education department. When it was time to head to Romania, he would do so courtesy of his friend Bernd Munderloh and other old basketball friends from Ingenieurbüro Maren. They had bought John a used red VW Beetle, tuned it up, and outfitted it with new tires. In September 1977, John drove it the 1,400 miles through Germany, Czechoslovakia, Hungary, and Romania to the coastal city of Constanța.

If one had to spend a year in the Eastern Bloc, Constanța wasn't a bad place to do it. Its history dated back 2,500 years to long before the

Roman poet Ovid was banished there in 8 CE. Depressed about his exile and pining for the warmth and company of Rome, Ovid wrote of the city then called Tomis: "A more dismal land than this lies not under either Pole."

When John arrived in 1977, the Black Sea port was a combination shipping hub, industrial center, and tourist destination with an eight-mile-long beach. John's apartment was no gray box but, rather, a corner unit with high ceilings and a balcony overlooking the seafront promenade on a Black Sea that was as blue as any other. It was one of the most fashionable areas in town, a short walk from the grand seaside casino since repurposed into a "House of Culture" dispensing dollops of communist propaganda. The place was pleasing to other senses, too. In through the open windows came "the sounds and the smell of Constanţa: the laving murmur of the Black Sea breaking in whitecaps over the embankments; the cawing bleat of gulls and the screeching caterwauling of the cats; the incessant haggling of gypsy rag pickers and bottle collectors, old women shrilly practicing their centuries-old trade and voicing the start of their evening rounds; and the sea scent, pervasive and pleasant," as he described it all later in his book, *The Passionate Papers of Fiona Pilgrim: An Epistolary Novel of Love and Lust.*

If the city had ever held a grudge against the poet for his harsh assessment, it had faded by the time it named an institution of higher learning after him in 1961. John's students at Ovidius Pedagogical Institute were quite different from those he had taught at the Cumberland Gap. These were graduate students from various fields for whom the *curs practic* course John taught served as a means of getting English-language certification to teach high school. Two months after his arrival, he wrote Munderloh that of the ninety students, all in their mid-twenties, eighty-seven were women. The gender disparity, John learned, was because most of the young men were off learning how to be engineers. The feminine scenery seemed not to be helping a mood seemingly inherited from Ovid himself: "I'm still so depressed, and when I write to you . . . I get even more depressed," he wrote Munderloh. The fact that the VW Beetle had blown a cylinder and set him back the modern equivalent of $1,700 for a fix "not worth a damn" had not helped.

This European experience would differ from that of a decade earlier. Back in Bad Kreuznach, when he wasn't working, he was traveling, often on the wings of three-day weekends he had earned with previous weekend duty. Here he taught twelve hours a week and had three-day weekends as a matter of course. Yet despite having the gift VW Beetle in hand and the "Romanian Riviera" and the rest of Eastern Europe at his doorstep, he more or less stayed put. John loved to travel; John did not love to travel alone.

He did travel the three-hour drive to Bucharest, the Romanian capital, several times. At the American Embassy, he answered questions first from Romanian police and then U.S. Marines before checking in with his State Department cultural affairs officer and rounding up black-metal canisters in which 16-millimeter American films had been tightly coiled in wait of projection. Sometimes he brought back cartons of Marlboros, too, the packs from which he could sell at great profit—though with some risk—to acquaintances.

In Constanța, he had a brief, passionate interest in a young woman named Rodika, but he broke it off after a couple of dates: John had been told that, should Rodika be romantically linked to a married American Fulbright interloper, the profession listed on her identity card would be changed from "teacher" to "prostitute." Whether this were true or not, he didn't want such a thing to happen. The absence of female or family companionship, plus his not having stumbled onto a local basketball team (he was no longer in his prime, but he could still play, as he had done in pickup games in Harrogate), meant that John had a lot of time and repressed energy on his hands. He channeled that energy into his writing.

John started not one but three novels. The first was a gentle parody of the popular Harlequin romance novels; the second was a satire based on his misadventures raising pigs in the hollows beyond Harrogate. He made less progress on these than on the third and most ambitious of them, a novel that would fictionalize his own troubled upbringing and the role the Roman Catholic Church had played in it.

It would be satire, but, like all good satire, it would be built upon a foundation of truths.

The plot was straightforward enough—a chronological story of a boy with an alcoholic father and a mother just trying to cope, a boy whose worldview had been shaped but ultimately twisted by the world's most powerful religious organization. The structure was anything but straightforward: John the author created a fictitious alter-ego author named Patrick Fitzpatrick who was writing from an asylum. Fitzpatrick in turn had created a fictional author name Joseph Patrick Kelly who was telling the story of his upbringing. Running concurrent to all this was a back-and-forth between the first-order fictitious author Fitzpatrick and the fictitious editor Clyde MacHound who, in long footnotes, generally assailed Fitzpatrick's writing, judgment, and intelligence. Fitzpatrick responded, in footnotes to the footnotes, with expletive-laden vitriol directed back at MacHound. As the novel got rolling, MacHound's fictitious son, the recovering substance abuser Clyde MacHound, Jr., emerged as a character in the footnoted conversations, generally more supportive of the fictional Fitzpatrick than his father was and often telling dirty jokes the story reminded him of.

The novel was, in short, nuts.

John pursued the project with a focus starkly contradicting his general impulsiveness, impatience, restlessness, and low frustration tolerance. He could sit for hours at a table in his Constanța apartment penciling words in his suspect cursive script. Occasional sharpening whittled down his pencils to stubs too short for a hand that could once palm a basketball. Legal pad after legal pad stacked up. Even had he wanted to use a typewriter, John had never learned how to type. For that, he enlisted his new friend Lucian Leon, one of four Romanians teaching English at Ovidius. John dictated; Leon keystroked together a first legible draft over what Leon recalled as "many hours, days, and weeks."

"He occasionally consulted me about spelling. One night he called me to ask about the spelling of specific words he was concerned about: 'scimitar, yataghan,'" Leon recalled. "It probably kept nagging him, ravishing his night dreams."

Leon, for his part, appreciated what he later described as John's "nonconformist attitude, colorful spontaneity (He often unexpectedly stood up from the lunch table muttering 'I gotta go, I gotta go,' and gone he was!), lively manner of speaking, dirty American English along with his attitudinal sensitivity, boundless humor, deep sense of brotherhood and identity of feelings, then the great sentiments of friendship and spiritual attachment reciprocally growing between him and my entire family, Granny included, whom John adored returning her love for him. We very often lunched together with Granny making cakes he much liked."

One can only write for so long before the brain goes gelatinous. John took long walks along the seashore or through town, preoccupied with what might come next in whatever he was writing. Even after sending money home to Nancy, his expenses were low enough and the dollar-Romanian lei exchange rate favorable enough that, from John's perspective, he had "tons of money" and not many ways to spend it. One product which caught his fancy, despite his teetotaling ways, was banana liqueur from Cuba, Romania's Caribbean comrade in communism. It satisfied his sweet tooth as well as his desire to, as he put it, "dull the terrors of the day," a justification that would have rung familiar to his deceased father. Five or six shots of the stuff and the Fulbright professor with an alcohol tolerance inversely proportional to his physical stature was completely looped. More than once, he would take out what was left of the day's terrors on a light bulb.

The light bulb hung high in his apartment's main quarters. From the time John had arrived, the bulb had not only gone dark at a rate of about once a week but had done so with a small, nerve-jangling explosion. He made a point of bringing it up with his friend Leon. One previous visit, they had been talking out on John's balcony when a seagull alighted on the railing. Leon, who had often chatted with John on this balcony, said, "See anything unusual about that seagull, Johnny?"

"It looks like every other seagull in the world," John said.

Leon shook his head. "It's the same seagull that's been here before—every day when we have lunch, it comes here to listen to our conversations."

"Lucian, I think it's just a seagull."

"That's not a seagull," Leon said. "It's a CIAgull."

Now John brought up the matter of the exploding light bulbs.

"Lucian, these fuckin' light bulbs keep scaring the shit out of me," John said. "I think I need to get some Western ones because they keep popping—especially this one." John motioned up to the bulb in question.

Leon considered the bulb for a quiet moment. "Why don't we go for a walk," he suggested.

They walked out, down a flight of stairs, and across Bulevardul Regina Elisabeta to the boardwalk on the sea. As they walked toward the old casino, Leon said, just as casually as if he were describing a sale at the local supermarket, "Now Johnny Dear"—Leon always referred to John this way—"what happens there is that when they were bugging your apartment, they had a loose connection, and the microphone's shorting out the circuit."

And so, late at night, crocked on Cuban banana liqueur, John dragged a chair directly below the offending light bulb—glowing unassumingly now—and yelled things like "[Romanian leader] Nicolae Ceausescu is a prick!" and "Communism is a vice that should be thrown down!" and "Long live the United States!"

Nothing ever came of these banana-boozed outbursts that would have landed a Romanian in the gulag, but a different episode made clear that he was indeed being surveilled.

Coming home late one night from the university, he parked in the gravel lot behind his apartment building. John unfolded his long frame from the little VW Beetle, locked the car door, and walked toward the door. He heard footsteps behind him.

John walked a bit faster. The footsteps behind him followed suit. He couldn't tell how many pursuers there were. He picked up the pace again; so did those behind him. He was close to the apartment house's back door, but they were close to him, too. Had the door been unlocked, he might have made it in. But it was always locked, and there was no way he could fumble with the keys, insert the right one, turn, pull open, and slam shut the door fast enough to save himself. As he reached the door, he turned to face his predators—there were three of them, Romanian gypsies—at the very moment they themselves became prey. Their pleading and howling in a language John didn't understand weakened into grunts and groans as a group of four men with obvious skills in beating the living shit out of people beat the living shit out of them and, in short order, hauled them off. These poor muggers had been as oblivious as was John to the secret police who, quite secretly, tracked his every move.

By June 1978, John's Fulbright fellowship had run its course, and he wouldn't be coming back to Europe anytime soon: his job search in Hamburg had come to nothing and, with that, as he wrote his friend Munderloh, "So much for the dream."

* * *

John has decided to join me in picking up Lily and taking her to a skating rink. Lily is a competitive figure skater. She must, five days a week, be driven from Denver East High School, where she's a sophomore, to the Ice Centre at Promenade in Westminster, about seventeen miles northwest. On previous weekdays, John has stayed back at the house, typically watching MSNBC or CNN, which keeps him appropriately incensed at the behavior of Donald Trump. We pick up Lily at the high school that looks like a statehouse, drive out to the rink, and drop her off with plans to return once she's on the ice. In the meantime, we visit the nearby Butterfly Pavilion.

I have not been here since the girls were very young. Despite my having emphasized that butterflies lack mouths and stingers, the kids feared these flutterers. I remember the humidity and the tropical plants and the damp pebbly concrete.

John walks ahead in his faded orange corduroy shirt and khakis with zip-away pantlegs, admiring the owl butterflies with their alien-blue wing tops (and owl-like wing bottoms), among hordes of others. I observe as John asks a volunteer about the pupation process and then a staffer about where the butterflies lay their eggs. She tells him, and me, that butterflies lay eggs on specific plants, of which the Butterfly Pavilion has few that match the varying habitats of the dozens of butterfly species brought here from all over the world. If they do lay eggs and the horticulturalists find a cocoon, they bring the cocoon to the display case where hundreds of these chrysalises hang, some occasionally jiggling of their own accord. We watch for a while in hopes of catching a hatching, then John walks along the winding paths again, slowly. His curiosity is all-encompassing, it seems, and it strikes me that being curious is the same thing as being young, mentally speaking—and that the opposite also holds true.

"Pat would love this," he says of his wife who will never see this.

I talked to her about coming out to visit and told her that you see lots of oxygen tanks in Denver. She had researched it, though, and the mile-high elevation combined with her lofty oxygen needs would render her homebound here. John has told me that her lung function is now failing at a rate of about 3% a year. He figures she'll make it another two, three years. Then he will suffer another great loss.

Pat, for her part, has told me that she intends to outlive him.

"He won't be okay alone," she said.

John and I return to the rink and watch Lily and her teenage competitive-skating cohort zoom around the ice, spin, dance, and leap. They occasionally fall or pop jumps, but there's an overarching sense of ease that comes with mastery. I recall her wobbling with each glideless step when she started eleven years ago and wonder if there's a better example of how radically a young human mind-body develops.

"These kids can really skate," John says. "Wow."

"That's what five, six days a week for years on end buys you," I say.

We leave after a little while. On the drive home, John says we should stop at an Italian specialty store to buy torrone nougat-almond candy for Pat—her Christmas present. I tell him I'm not familiar with Italian specialty stores in the area. The purchase of torrone nougat-almond candy for Pat *right now*, though, becomes a pressing priority. This happens whenever John gets an idea in his head. John holds the butt of his phone to his mouth and shouts, "Hey Siri, where's an Italian specialty store?"

Siri suggests Target. He asks again; Siri comes up with a destination a few miles out of the way. I head that way and follow Siri's directions to a residential street where Siri has chosen an apparently random house at which she declares us to have arrived at our destination. Two subsequent grocery-store stops yield nothing. Later, we buy torrones on Amazon.

* * *

After his return to Atlanta in the summer of 1978, John, his family, and their Irish wolfhound piled into their VW Bus and embarked on a westward swing. They spent time with friends in Colorado and then rolled into the town of Lebanon, Indiana, about thirty miles northwest of Indianapolis where old Bad Kreuznach buddies of John's, David Milam and his wife Nanci, now lived. While the Rubadeaus' love for one another had faded, they both fell in love with the small town. John soon informed his old friend Ron Pace that the family was moving to Lebanon.

With help from the Milams and an FHA loan with extremely favorable terms (these were subsidized based on income, of which John had none), the Rubadeaus bought a century-old, three-bedroom house near the center of town. School was about to start, and the house wasn't available yet, so Nick and Becky moved in with the Milams where they would stay as Becky started her freshman year in high school and Nick, the fifth grade. It was the fifth school in as many years for both of them.

Once resettled, John worked on his magnum opus and set about looking for work with the same sort of sacred-cow-attacking cover letter that had, against all odds and in contradiction of good sense, worked for him twice before. But the choice he had made in uprooting to Lebanon first and starting an academic job search second limited his options. English-instructor jobs at the region's colleges had been locked up for at least the semester. There were dozens of universities in Indiana, many of them within a long commute of Lebanon. If the lack of re-sponse was any indication, though, none of John's inquiries found English departments interested in a mixed-race, disabled Vietnam vet with an occasional cross-dressing habit—or the sense of humor required to take a chance on the tall white guy from Madison, Wisconsin, who wrote such things. Or maybe it was simply that no untimely deaths played out to his benefit.

What is certain is that Ron Pace was supporting the family. In late 1978, John wrote Munderloh a letter with the salutation *"Na du blöde Sau"* ("Well you stupid pig"). He continued: "So my novel's going well, and I'm making a lot of progress. You know that Ron is giving me $1,000 a month ($3,800 in today's money) in exchange for the potential of 10% of sales. But it's very hard to find a publisher. Still, I think the book is excellent (though it could be a real piece of shit, too)." At bottom, he added, "p.s. How do you spell '*kenicklefickef*' rabbit fucker *auf Deutsch*."

For the record, it is spelled "*Kaninchenficker.*"

For Nancy, the burdens John imposed had long outweighed the balance of his charms. She divorced him before the leaves turned gold in 1979. John's take on the reasoning, again in a letter to his German friend was that "it has to do with many things: money; creative time to myself; the fact that I'm such an asshole; etc." One of Nancy's first acts of her new, post-John life would be familiar enough: she would take in Becky and Nick for the better part of a year (Pace, just 3, lived with her full-time anyway). John moved out of the neat brick house they had just bought together and, in September 1979, he moved in with Ron in Atlanta.

Ron and his wife Barbara had recently divorced, and Ron was living solo in a big new house in Marietta, Georgia, about twenty miles north of Atlanta. While John's and Ron's marital lives had collapsed roughly in parallel, Ron's economic fortunes had moved inversely to John's. Ron had done well in his new territory for the baby-furniture manufacturer he worked for, but he had gotten bored. In 1973, he had left his job as a sales rep to work for a big bank in Atlanta that was planning to open a new branch in London. Ron was to manage it, but the OPEC oil embargo had derailed that plan.

Ron had then enrolled in an international-business PhD program at Georgia State, and, for much of the time John was earning his English PhD, they had both been students. But Ron had started and grown a side business as a manufacturer's representative for baby-furniture makers. The work had been similar to that he had done as a Cosco employee. The pay was not: he earned around five percent of sales. By the time Ron had finished his classwork and started interviewing for business-professor jobs (At John's urging, he had met with Frank Welch at Lincoln Memorial University. Welch had told Ron, "You and John are two of the most different people I've ever met. I can't believe you're friends."), he was earning several times what he would make in academia. Ron had left the program, never to finish his dissertation. This led John to tease him with the moniker "Mr. ABD," (All-But-Dissertation), the cursed distinction of an almost PhD.

All that's to say that, by late 1979, Ron could afford to play Medici to John's would-be literary Michelangelo. It was nice to have the company, Ron figured, and he was away on business much of each week anyway. The house was hardly furnished. As ever, John wrote in pencil on yellow legal pads at the dining-room table. He focused on two of the three novels he had started: the Harlequin parody and the magnum opus. His schedule reflected his obsession with the project: being downstairs at 6 a.m. and writing until close to midnight, fifteen- to eighteen-hour days, one after the next. Ron recalls legal-pad pages full of John's cursive taped to walls and scattered around the table.

When Ron retuned from business trips, the tall, scraggly bearded writer made a habit of putting on a bathrobe and walking out to the front porch, opening his arms wide and greeting his friend and benefactor with shouts of "Honey! You're home! I missed you so much!" If John happened to notice a neighbor—or, ideally, several— out walking or working in the nearby yards, he would turn up the volume and go all-in on the effeminate mannerisms. This was, keep in mind, a wealthy, conservative Atlanta suburb. On more than one occasion, Ron backed the car out the driveway and left again.

Occasionally Ron was able to pull John away from his pencils and legal pads. One night, Ron suggested going out to a place called Charlie's. They sat down at the bar next to a couple of women Ron guessed might not be entirely disinterested in two divorcees on the doorstep of 40. Ron ordered a beer, said hello, and struck up a conversation. John ordered a milkshake. As Ron recalled, "He's holding this milkshake with both hands like a squirrel, slurping on it. I'm doing my best to try to impress these girls, and he's there working on this milkshake. I'm thinking: 'You are the least-cool guy that I know.'"

John returned to Lebanon for the holidays and, before returning to Atlanta, spent an eventful day at the Chancery Court for Claiborne County in Tazewell, Tennessee. He had filed a wrongful-termination lawsuit shortly before he had left for Romania in 1977. On January 10, 1980, the case of John W. Rubadeau, plaintiff, v. Lincoln Memorial University and Frank W. Welch, defendants, finally proceeded. John and his attorney John Lockridge wrote that the firing was "arbitrary and capricious, and without cause as defined in the defendants' rules and regulations, and constitutes a breach of contract." John sought $100,000 in damages from LMU and $50,818.18 from Frank Welch himself (about $500,000 today, all told).

John's deposition was all about the Algernon Sidney Sullivan Award; Welch's was about John's deserving to be fired for other reasons. A couple of months before he was fired, Welch said he had called John into his office. "I indicated to him at that time that there were three basic elements that had to be cleared up in his conduct," Welch said. "One was his body. He had to start taking baths and wearing clean clothes. He had to clean up his mouth and cut out the filthy talk which he was using in class and on campus, and that he had to develop a positive attitude toward the institution and toward being a part of it, and I indicated to him at that time that under no circumstances would there be any further employment if those basic three areas were not modified . . . ."

John argued that the meeting never happened.

Welch also recalled from that final conversation in his office the day he fired the English professor that John had said, after Welch canned him, "You can't fire me. I will do as I damn well please. So, you can just forget it. I am going to do as I please, and you have nothing to say about my conduct, my appearance, or anything." While the precise language may have differed from Welch's recollection, John did believe that his success as a teacher and his popularity with students would protect him.

When John's lawyer asked Welch if John had been a competent instructor, Welch responded, "That is highly questionable."

A letter that James Caraway, the academic dean under whom John had worked, contradicted that in a letter "To Whom It May Concern" among LMU administrators, which Caraway had written the day after John had been fired:

> *I write in reference to Dr. John Rubadeau,*
> *Assistant Professor of English, Lincoln Memorial*
> *University. I have worked with John for two years*

*during which I have served as his Academic Dean and
as Professor of Humanities in the division in which he
works. I have found John to be a highly competent,
intelligent, sensitive, and industrious colleague. His
concern for his academic discipline and his concern for
and rapport with his students is excellent. In addition
to teaching fifteen hours each quarter, he has worked
individually with students and has published material
in major journals as well as presenting papers at major
professional meetings. Of major import is the fact that
he is keenly aware of the needs of his students, both
academically and personally, and he continually
evidences concern for them and for his colleagues as
persons.*

During the trial, John's attorney highlighted Welch's alleged
misdeeds and the fact that, just because LMU's board of trustees had
apparently bequeathed upon its president the power of Zeus, breach
of contract remained fair game in civil litigation. The university's
lawyer responded in kind, bringing up, among other things, John
having mooned, through the window of a closed classroom door, a
buttoned-up history-professor buddy (students taking in the professor's lecture could not see John's exposed ass, which John had duly
wiggled around).

The Honorable Billy Joe White took all this in with some
bemusement and, after mulling it over, issued his decision in April. He
ruled that the university had violated John's employment contract—
but that Welch, "having been clothed with the authority to hire and
fire personnel did not unlawfully precipitate or cause the breach between LMU and Rubadeau." The university was ordered to pay John
$1,900 ($6,300 today) and cover John's legal fees. It wasn't one hundred fifty grand, but he had made his point, and he certainly needed
the money.

By May 1980, it was time for John to go back home to Lebanon.
He moved into a two-bedroom apartment, half a duplex his friends
the Milams owned, a five-minute walk from the house he and Nancy

had bought and where she still lived. He continued to apply for academic positions, but he was considering other options, too. He wrote his friend Munderloh, "I'm looking now for a job in either sales or advertising in Indianapolis, but my prospects are not all that good what with the recession and changing careers at 40. Nonetheless, I remain optimistic." He had forgotten his optimism a couple of paragraphs later, though. "I'm still depressed about my divorce and my failure to find an agent or editor who thinks I'm the genius I think I am. Well this has been a difficult time for me, old friend. My life doesn't seem to be getting any easier as I grow older; but enough of this shit."

In the second week of July, in a note to Munderloh that led with the salutation "Hey *Arschloch*," (German for "asshole"), John wrote, "I'm sorry I haven't written much, but I've been busting my butt putting the finishing touches on my magnum opus."

A few lines down, John apologized for not having the money to visit Munderloh during his German friend's planned visit to Massachusetts.

"I hate to keep apologizing for my financial situation but *C'est la vie* (*d.h. So ist das leben*). I took the road not taken (a Robert Frost poem) and pursued (perhaps, in retrospect, it was a mistake) my art, such as it is. In short, I can't afford to come to Mass.; I hope you can come here."

"Still no luck with a job," John continued. "Things are bleak here in America."

"Things"—a word whose vagueness John Rubadeau the teacher bristled at—would soon turn around.

8

Nobody Eats Parsley

Carpe diem; carpe rosam.[*]
— A Rubadeau favorite

John had never intended to follow in his father's footsteps, but by the time he received the thumbs down from DePauw University, economic desperation had led him to eat-what-you-kill work as a Farm Bureau Insurance agent selling to small businesses. He viewed the job as requiring, as a character in his Harlequin romance parody put it, "absolutely no background, no training, no intellect, no aptitude, and no morals . . . ." The character in question happened to be a struggling writer who had been relegated to selling insurance to make ends meet.

The news from DePauw was mixed. The positive was that someone in the English department at the small school about an hour's drive from Lebanon had a sense of humor. The negative was that the only job they had open was for a romanticist. John was not a romanticist.

But as happens so often, someone at DePauw knew someone at Purdue, and, in the fall of 1980, John started as an English lecturer at the Big Ten institution in West Lafayette. He taught freshman English at first, and, within a semester or two, business writing. His workspace—a cubicle on the third floor of Heavilon Hall—reflected his status at the bottom of the department's teaching hierarchy: high

---

[*] Seize the day before it is spent; gather the flowers before they lose their bloom.

above were tenured faculty; below them untenured faculty; then graduate students (offering them part-time teaching jobs was a way to attract and support them); and then, finally, lecturers like John who were brought in to fill in the gaps.

The cubicle didn't bother John at all. This was a man who cared little about status or outward appearances as typically perceived. He still occasionally received boxes of hand-me-down clothing from his friend and former Lincoln Memorial University colleague Douglas Gordon. Gordon had handed Frank Welch his resignation about the same time John had been fired and was now at Christopher Newport University in Virginia. John wore the clothing proudly.

Through perfectly flat corn-and-soybean country, John drove the forty-five minutes from Lebanon to West Lafayette in a 1964 Volvo 122. It, too, was a hand-me-down from an old friend. Five years earlier, he had called Gray Currier, the Beloit student who had arranged for the impromptu Hamburg homestay with Frau Eden, just to catch up. The conversation had turned to transportation, and it had become clear that John and Nancy could use a car besides John's VW Beetle. Currier, now a civil engineer in Fort Collins, Colorado, had suggested to his wife Mary Jean that they really didn't need two cars given that Gray rode his bike to work anyway. Mary Jean, whose Volvo it technically was—it had been in her family since it had rolled off the line in Sweden—had agreed. John flew to Colorado and drove her red Volvo back to Harrogate.

This all is not to be mistaken with John lacking ego or ambition. It was just that he fed his ego and pursued his ambitions on his own terms—terms which overlapped little with the traditional American goals of accumulating wealth, power, and professional titles as ends in themselves or as escalators to social standing. Those who had earned PhDs often liked being addressed with the honorific "Dr."; John went with "John." He had spoken the truth when, back in Harrogate, he told Frank Welch that he and his tall colleague whose old clothes John was probably wearing at the time lacked ambition. But that applied only to the narrow version of ambition John knew Welch lived and breathed and demonstrated in those bad toupees and canary-yellow leisure suits. On those occasions when John's ambition overlapped with those of others, his internal fires blasted forth as if from the open door of a kiln. He believed himself to be a brilliant writer; he played basketball with intensity and a serious will to win. But generally, his ambition differed enough from those of the mainstream as to camouflage itself from all but his closest friends. He later described in a letter to his German friend Bernd Munderloh what he saw as—and, in his novels, satirized—"the American's overweening concern with acceptance, with doing things 'right' according to the expectations of experts and authority figures, with the idea that the façade is much more important than the infrastructure."

In other words, despite all the freedoms enshrined in the Bill of Rights, America remained highly conformist—particularly with respect to the worship of wealth and its ornaments. John had little interest in conforming. But at Purdue, as a new hire at a school known for educating engineers in the heart of conservative Indiana, he made a point of behaving and wearing sport coats, button-down shirts, and ties.

No, John didn't mind the cubicle or the fact that he was, at age 40, in an entry-level job teaching 100-level classes for low pay and no job security. He preferred to focus on his excitement about getting back into the classroom, and he poured himself into his teaching. Besides, the focus of his ambition and self-esteem now resided outside the classroom in the unfinished novels he was preoccupied with. Case in point: he drove the thirty-five miles up and back down Interstate 65 without the distraction of a radio so as to better cogitate on some plot point, turn of phrase, or character development. These details he occasionally scribbled on his arm or a yellow legal pad riding shotgun.

His starting instructor's salary couldn't cover expenses and child support, so he kept the insurance job—the Farm Bureau Insurance people were fine with that, seeing as it was entirely commission-based anyway. John, like his father, was somehow able to connect with all sorts of people—rich, poor, white, Black, and everything in between—from the instant he met them. His charisma would have been good for business (as it had been for his father until alcoholism derailed his career) had he liked the business. As it was, he made just enough money to justify the time away from his kids and his writing. His insurance work did, however, acquaint him with the former Patrice Prahin in the spring of 1982.

John met her at a party. He was there because he was sleeping with the woman hosting the party; Pat was there because the woman John was sleeping with was a friend of hers. Pat, for her part, was dating John's ex-girlfriend's ex-boyfriend, and the ex-girlfriend was also at the party.

So it was weird.

It might have been weirder had John realized how beautiful a creature this 31-year-old woman was—dark-brown hair, delicate features, big brown eyes that invited contact—and then found his attraction at odds with Pat's not finding him terribly handsome. Given that John was in a clean-shaven phase, Pat could note his thin neck, around which one could easily button a 13.5-inch shirt collar, made his helmetlike bowl of hair (epoxied in place with hairspray) and his bay-window glasses look even bigger. John was, perhaps fortunately, oblivious to Pat's obvious feminine magnetism for two reasons: (1) he was sleeping with the party's hostess and (2) he was a part-time small-business insurance salesman who had been told that Pat owned a small business—a custom picture-framing shop in Zionsville, about fifteen miles from Lebanon. She was a potential client.

How Pat came to own a frame shop in Zionsville, Indiana, is worth recounting. She was born and raised in Willowick, Ohio, a small town on Lake Erie northeast of Cleveland. Her dad was an appliance salesman; her mom worked at a Hallmark gift-and-card store. After graduation, Pat went to Miami University in Ohio and majored in Russian.

She was good at it but wouldn't study it for long. To the consternation of her Russian professor, she dropped out after the first semester of her sophomore year and married Jay whom the Navy ROTC had put through school. They moved to California—San Diego; then Long Beach, where daughter Heather was born; then Alameda— then to Great Lakes, Illinois, and then to Speedway, Indiana, for Jay to start dental school at nearby Indiana University. Their second daughter Alexis was born soon after Jay began classes. He was gone a lot and was the kind of person who, if Pat asked him to look after their daughters, would say, "I don't babysit."

They divorced. Pat, who had gone to dental-assistant school back in California, found work with a dentist who attempted suicide five times in less than a year. After the fifth time, Pat decided it was time to look elsewhere to support herself and daughters Heather and Lexi. She made a list of things she liked to do. Framing pictures was on it— she had done one at a do-it-yourself frame shop not too long ago. The frame-shop manager remembered her and had her do another one as a test. She got the job.

Pat met Bob, who managed a children's theater, and they began dating. Pat enjoyed picture-framing to the point that she was considering opening her own frame shop. Bob asked his friend Joani, who did numerology and read tarot cards, to do a reading (it was the '70s, after all). Joani asked, "What the hell are you planning? It's going to make money!"

A small Zionsville strip mall had an empty storefront, a three-minute walk from Pat's apartment and a two-minute walk from the babysitter. Bob's long experience constructing theater sets came in handy in erecting showroom walls. The owner of the do-it-yourself frame shop sold Pat used equipment he had bought from a competitor who had gone out of business. The guillotine chopper, the glass cutter, the mat cutter, and all the rest maxed out her credit cards and devoured the $500 she had borrowed from her parents. In 1978, Pat opened the Corner Vise Frame Shop.

"I did not know that businesses failed," she later confided.

This one wouldn't.

John stopped by the Monday after the party to pitch Pat business insurance. He wasn't teaching at Purdue during the quiet summer semester.

Pat, annoyed that John had used the party of the woman he was sleeping with as a pretext for lead generation, already had an insurance guy she liked and politely told John as much. He didn't seem to take it personally and left, the bells on the shop door ringing behind him. That seemed to be that.

But a couple of days later, the bells dangling on the doorknob rang again. Pat was in the back working on a job; a colleague up front came back and said a man was at the door. It was a Thursday, which was when the molding salesman typically came through. Pat regularly bought "chops"—frames cut to size—and ten-to-fifteen-foot-long strips of molding of different colors and profiles to be cut into frames. But instead of the molding salesman, there stood John again. He noted Pat's surprise and asked if she was okay. She was just expecting a salesman, she explained.

"I was just in the neighborhood selling insurance, so I thought I'd drop by," he said. "You see, I'm writing a book and need a woman's opinion on something."

Pat had forgotten that her friend had mentioned John being a writer.

In his Harlequin romance parody, he continued, his heroine is putting her clothes on one morning, "and I want to say she puts on a chemise—because I like the sound of that word—but I don't really know what a chemise is, and the definition in my *American Heritage College Dictionary* isn't that clear to me. So what's a chemise?"

This seemed at once an interesting question and the strangest come-on Pat had ever encountered. As a single mom (she and Bob had married soon after the frame shop opened but had soon separated) who could only afford cotton briefs and Playtex Cross Your Heart bras, she wasn't highly qualified to answer it, either—but she wasn't about to admit that to the tall interloper.

"I think," she said, "It's kind of like a slip, but a short one."

This fit nicely with the *American Heritage College Dictionary*'s definition that John had memorized.

"Will you go to lunch with me?" he asked.

"I thought you just came in to ask about chemises."

"Well, I did, but I just got the greatest idea. We could go to lunch, and I could poll the waitresses in the restaurant to see how they define 'chemise.' But if I'm alone, they'll all think I'm making the moves on them or harassing them and I won't find out a thing," he said. "C'mon, we're friends. You would really be helping me."

107

Pat's friend had also mentioned John being cheap. "Are you buying?"

"Only if I have to to get you to come with me."

"You have to," Pat said.

At lunch, John polled an impromptu usage panel of lunch-shift waitresses on the meaning of "chemise," thereby putting as much time and energy into the definition of this single item of clothing as had been devoted to any word in any novel in the history of English literature. Pat saw both a playfulness and a sincerity in his inquiries, and how engaged he was in these conversations with strangers. Maybe this insurance salesman wasn't such a jerk after all.

He continued to talk about this Harlequin romance parody he had been feverishly working on. In *The Passionate Papers of Fiona Pilgrim*, the main character is an English professor who has quit a tenured position to focus on writing literary novels. These find no audience, so he ends up having to sell insurance to get by. He comes up with a scheme to write a pulp romance set in Romania, *Tempestuous Summer: The Hottest Season*, and, using the persona of Fiona Pilgrim, an Indiana housewife with a husband and three kids, strikes up a correspondence with a famous British pulp-romance author.

The Passionate Papers unfolds entirely in written correspondence between the main character and the famous British author as well as in letters from the main character to an English professor friend of his (named Gordon Douglas, a wink at Douglas Gordon, his old friend from Lincoln Memorial University) who once spent a fictional Fulbright in Constanța, Romania. All the while, *Tempestuous Summer* progresses in installments sent to the famous British author. In the novel-within-the-novel, a young female American Ovid scholar finds love on the Romanian Riviera, a romance conveyed through an abundance of purposely hackneyed style: "Possessed of an innocent and naturally beautiful face with the most sensuous lips, Amanda West would not have looked at all out of place were she strolling down the Boardwalk at Atlantic City representing her native state of Wisconsin in the Miss America Pageant rather than elbowing her way through the bustling crowd of travelers at the *Gara de Nord*."

John made a habit of stopping by the Corner Vise Frame Shop when insurance-sales calls brought him anywhere near Zionsville. He commented on the pictures of the little-league team the little shop sponsored and played with the puppy a friend had given Pat before Pat realized the friend was sleeping with Bob. Then John was off to call on the next prospect. Often, these farmers—with whom John could converse as a peer, thanks to his Harrogate experience—only had time for him after sundown, so he and Pat went Dutch at the local salad-bar restaurant after Pat closed up shop. Pat welcomed the company: daughters Heather and Lexi, now 9 and 6, were in California for the summer with Pat's first husband.

If an insurance pitch wasn't in the offing, John hustled back to Lebanon to work on his romance-novel satire: he was pushing to wrap up the draft before the start of the fall semester at Purdue and then revise it the following summer. With the time and energy he put into teaching during the school year, there would be no chance to write.

John had gathered, during one of his visits, that Pat's birthday was coming up. He asked her to dinner to celebrate but conditioned the date on going Dutch. She declined. John did some quick mental arithmetic that yielded a negative number. Despite this, John asked if she'd go if he paid. She said she'd be delighted to.

Upon arriving at Pat's, he freaked out her daughters Heather and Lexi by collapsing to the floor, rolling about, and declaring, "I'm starving!" in a deeply misguided attempt at breaking the ice. John drove Pat to Chi-Chi's (think Applebee's with enchiladas) in the red Volvo. He was on the Scarsdale Medical Diet, he told her, and then proceeded to ignore it during an allegedly Mexican dinner with margaritas and a fried-ice-cream capstone. He told stories; she told stories—they both had stories, Lord knows. Apropos of nothing, he told Pat a joke for the first time. He had waited because all his jokes were dirty.

"What's the difference between parsley and pussy?" he asked.

Pat reached for a margarita glass reminiscent of a fish bowl. "I don't know."

"Nobody eats parsley," John said.

She laughed so hard she had to put the glass back down.

Then, as the check arrived, and John asked her if she had enjoyed her meal.

"Yes," she said.

"Good," he said, "because you ate like a pig."

Maybe it was the darkness cast by the bottom line of a restaurant tab that would alarm few highly educated forty-two-year-old professionals—but the outlay represented a huge hit for him. Maybe he thought it was funny. Maybe he was just being unfiltered. Whatever the motive had been, the comment didn't go over well.

What the hell? He's just so damn rude, she thought. How could she have such good gaydar and such horrendous heterosexual radar?

The evening wrapped up with John seated in an armchair in the living room of Pat's apartment. John pulled out a bag of tobacco and a pipe, pressed a pinch into the pipe's briar bowl, and lit it. He kept telling stories and chatting. Pat supplied brief interjections for a while, but the week had been long, and the evening had gone stale. She fell asleep.

John woke her to say goodbye and left. As he drove off into the night, he cranked down his window and let humid air buffet about the ancient Volvo. Here and there, loose clusters of fireflies flickered in the darkness over the fields of corn and soybeans. He figured he wouldn't see Pat again.

* * *

At the kitchen table, as we page through John's course pack, I stumble onto a poem by Rebecca Stone that he's included. It describes a breast-cancer diagnosis. "But out of dusty memory and myth/The Amazons came striding/Perhaps to welcome me/To their proud tribe," it reads in part.

"Why the Amazon poem?" I ask him.

"So 'typical-atypical,' 'political-apolitical'—the 'a' prefix means 'not' or 'without,' Okay?" John says. "'Amazon' means 'without breast.' To be sure, that's folk etymology—lore. The Amazons were these tall women, and they didn't like men, right? They defended their island against invaders. This is, of course, Greek mythology."

"OK," I say.

"And they would cut off their right breasts, so they could, absent their right breasts, better pull their bowstrings back or fling their spears or wield their swords," he said. "What Rebecca Stone is saying is that she just had a mastectomy. And to me, the poem was a good way to help students remember that 'a' means 'not' or 'without,' and that you can expand your vocabulary if you know this 'a' in front of some words negates. But I love the poem, especially that one line: 'But out of dusty memory and myth, the Amazons came striding.'"

"Yeah, it is great stuff," I say. "And on the topic, I wanted to talk about a different kind of Amazon. You talk about 'scratching your itch.' But not everybody can do that. They need jobs in places like Amazon warehouses. How do you reconcile that?"

"As a society, if everybody scratched their itch, there would be a lot of hungry people," John allows. "Second of all, you would not be able to shop." He thinks about it for a moment. "Look at me, though. I could never have afforded, never in my wildest dreams, to go to Europe. What I did was, I found a job that would allow me to go to Europe and get paid for it. So I think, you know, if people have the will, and if they have a definite dream . . ." he searches for what he's trying to say. "Most people don't, it's sad to say, have dreams," he continues. "The students I teach at the University of Michigan, chances are they're going to be able to get a job and make a lot of money. Then the question becomes whether they should."

"How so?"

"The six words to be happy in life—six words to avoid years and years of psychotherapy: scratch your itch—not your parents' itch, not society's itch—and, of course, *quid pro quo*," John says with the conviction of the religious man he isn't. "So many kids—as an example, I've had about six of them in the last forty-two years who wanted to be forest rangers. But their parents wanted them to be doctors or lawyers. So they ended up being doctors or lawyers."

"Did it work out? Were they happy?"

"No idea," John says. "Maybe. Maybe not. I mean, you started out as a consultant. Were you happy?"

I will never forget John's disappointment when I told him about that first job, nor his saying, when I insisted that I'd keep writing, that I'd never have time. "Scratch your itch" gnawed at me. I was 30 before I finally did. "I met Carol. I did some traveling. But no," I admit.

"Right," he says. "The problem is, you were raised—most of the kids who go to Michigan were wealthy. You were wealthy."

111

"We were upper middle-class, yeah," I say.

"Which is wealthy. It's especially hard for girls because they're used to having a car at their ready disposal and four or five pairs of shoes, going to summer camp—stuff I never got used to. I never had any money, and I was brought up dirt poor. But I can easily distinguish between my needs and my wants. I may want a Mercedes, but I need a ten-year-old Honda Civic. I want to go to Chop House in Ann Arbor; I need to stay home and cook."

The gift of poverty. His dying father was, in a way, right. John takes a long look at the Amazon poem and continues.

"You know, my sister always talked down to me because her husband was an insurance man who owned his own agency and made a lot of money," John says. "What the fuck? I didn't care. That wasn't my itch to scratch."

"Totally. Scratch your itch, man," I say.

"Scratch your itch and *quid pro quo*—that's all you need to know in life," John says.

* * *

At the Corner Vise the day after the dinner at Chi Chi's, Pat expected John to stop in and say "Hi" as had been his habit. He didn't. Nor did he the following day or the day after that. She stopped expecting him, and, with time, he left her thoughts, too. Then one day the door jingled as a beautiful young woman with long, dark hair walked into the shop.

"My dad said you'd know how to frame this, but he wants it done really cheap," she told Pat.

Pat, who took pride in doing quality work for fair prices, was a bit taken aback. "How cheap?" she asked.

"He said about $10," the young woman said. "And he needs it this afternoon."

Ten bucks for a rush job. Unbelievable. "What's your dad's name?" Pat asked.

"John Rubadeau," Becky answered. She explained that her dad hadn't dropped it off himself because he'd been busy selling insurance.

Pat shook her head in mild disgust but managed a smile as Becky handed her the wedding invitation John wanted framed for the big event the next day. "Okay, but tell him he owes me one," Pat said, forgetting to get the girl's name before she left.

Becky was 18 now and headed off to the College of Saint Mary in Omaha, Nebraska, in a couple of months. As she drove back to Lebanon, she realized that she'd recognized someone else in the woman behind the counter—someone from a long time ago.

Back at her dad's apartment, she found him at the kitchen table which was crowded with yellow legal pads crammed with his cursive scrawl. "Dad, I think you should go out with her again," she said.

John leaned back in his chair. "Go out with whom?" he asked.

"The picture-frame lady. Pat," she said.

"Really?" John said. "What makes you think so?"

"Well, you like her, right? And she seems so nice, and she's really pretty," Becky said. "You know, she looks like mom."

"Like Nancy?" John said. "I don't see it at all."

Becky shook her head. "No, she looks like *Barbara*."

Barbara.

That's right, Becky had been old enough to remember her. And while he hadn't considered the resemblance, there was something to the impression.

"Huh," John said. For a long moment he seemed to be looking right through Becky. His focus returned again to the legal pad at hand. "Well, thanks for dropping it off," he said. "What time are you going to pick it up?"

"Oh, I'm not picking it up," Becky said, dropping the keys on the table with a clank. "*You're* picking it up."

Pat dug into the Corner Vise scrap bin and pulled out some simple molding that would make for a good frame for a wedding invitation and did a job she was pleased with. She affixed a sticker with the store's logo on the back and gift wrapped it knowing John would be pleased with yet another free service. When it was time for the shop to close, John had yet to appear. She stuck around reconciling the day's receipts for a few minutes longer—still no John. She put the framed-and-gift-wrapped rush job in her bag, locked up, and headed home. The phone rang. She knew it was John, so she let it ring. And ring. Let the man sweat, she figured. She finally picked up.

"Pat, thank goodness I caught you," John said. "Can you come back downtown and give me my picture? You did finish it, didn't you? I'm desperate."

No, she couldn't come back downtown, she said. She'd had a long day, she'd stayed late, she'd done him a huge favor, and he hadn't even bothered to pick it up.

He begged: "Please, please . . . Please?"

This was becoming well worth the discount frame job.

"Pleeeease?"

Pat let him sweat in silence for a long moment. "OK, you can come by my apartment," she said finally. "I brought it home with me."

He hung up without saying goodbye.

When John arrived a few minutes later, he told her he'd pay her on Monday—he had missed the bank, too.

He did show up on Monday, and, for the first time, Pat found him rather attractive. Maybe it wasn't so crazy, either: one of her employees had mentioned the same thing to Pat. He asked her to lunch again.

"My daughter thought you were really nice," John explained. "She said I should give you another chance."

"Really. Another chance," Pat set a frame down on the counter. "Another chance at what?"

"To go out with the handsomest man in the whole wide world," John said, referring to himself with both index fingers.

Pat laughed. "Sure. But only if you treat."

This time it went well. On the drive back, the red Volvo passed a field of daisies. Over the hum of the engine and the whooshing of the open windows, John said, "*Carpe diem; carpe rosam.*"

"What?" Pat said.

"Oh, that's Latin for 'Seize the day before it's spent; gather the roses before they wilt.' It means 'Live life to the fullest.'"

He dropped Pat back at her frame shop where she caught up with orders. Before long, John stood in the entryway with a big bouquet of daisies he had gathered from the field. "For you," he said.

That evening, John picked Pat up again. Pat's daughters were with their father, so she was free. John wanted to introduce her to his friends. The first stop was at a gas station in Lebanon. The Volvo's tank was pushing empty, but the real point was for Pat to meet a friend of John's. "You'll love the guy that owns this place," he said as they pulled up to a pump.

The man approached the car with a big smile and a bigger bulge in his crotch. "I'm sooooo excited to meet you," he said. "John's told me sooooo much about you." He turned in profile with his pelvis jutted forward. Then he reached into his pants and removed an oil can.

John drove a few blocks to the home of his friends Jack and Alice Porter. Jack was the local family doctor, a throwback who made house calls, delivered babies, and cared for families whether they could pay him or not. Jack dabbled in calligraphy and cared for his English garden as if his plants were his patients. Pat shook hands with this wisp of a man who had longish dark hair that resisted taming, a scraggly beard, and thick glasses. The smoke from the pipe he held in his opposite hand smelled of something acrider than the Borkum Riff John preferred. Jack's wife Alice soon came downstairs; she was equally slender with gray hair that fell to her waist and the raspy voice of a longtime smoker. It was a Thursday evening, and John and the Porters had a standing date to hang out, drink wine and nibble on cheese, and talk about books.

Jack walked them back to a kitchen straight out of an old farmhouse, a kitchen with copper pots and pans hanging from the ceiling, jars of spices stacked here and there, and wallpaper featuring floral-and-herb drawings. Rather than talk about books, they got to know Pat and vice versa, and then it was time for slugs.

Any self-respecting Midwestern gardener wages a continual war with these snails who couldn't be bothered to grow proper shells, and Jack was no exception. He had set out traps of beer and cornmeal, akin to putting out filet mignon traps for a dog infestation. He reached into his armamentarium and pulled out latex gloves that Alice, John, and Pat snapped on. On the way out the door to the backyard, Jack grabbed a pair of wooden tongs and a bucket that Pat would later learn was partially filled with saltwater. Pat observed as Jack plucked three drunken slugs from the first trap and popped them into the saltwater. She could swear she heard them sizzle as they sank. John did the slug-plucking at the second trap and again at the third; Pat declined Jack's slug-hunting invitation.

After slug hunting, they returned inside and had the sort of grand time people enjoy when they meet someone new and interesting. When it was time to go, Pat and John drove back to John's apartment. It was empty because Becky, Nick, and Pace were at Nancy's that week.

Upon entry, Pat was confronted with walls heavily adorned with sheets of paper. Many were yellow which, upon closer inspection, Pat recognized as legal pulp that had been densely filled with penciled cursive writing. Also hung liberally were white sheets of paper beautified by John's son Pace's kindergarten artwork. The coverage was extensive to the point that Pat wondered if John's financial difficulties hadn't been brought about by bulk paper purchases. There was a single reading chair in the corner, a small desk, a chair pushed against a wall, and a TV on the floor. In the adjoining kitchen, she noted a table with chrome-plated legs and a clutch of mismatched chairs. Before John excused himself to use the bathroom, he suggested that Pat sit in the reading chair—but slowly, or it would tip backwards. Pat thanked him and chose one of the kitchen chairs.

John emerged and asked Pat if she might like a strawberry daiquiri, which, for a light social drinker, he blended with remarkable skill and, for a teetotaler, drank with marked enthusiasm. Soon neither Pat nor John was in any condition to drive Pat back to Zionsville, so they decided she would stay the night.

Becky had a room of her own; the boys slept in the second bedroom with John. That space was unadorned save for two mattresses, a double and a twin, both lacking bedsteads. The room would have looked right at home in an opium den. Whether these mattresses were normally pushed together Pat didn't ask. The fact that the double was a couple of inches thicker than the twin led her to strongly suspect otherwise. They started on separate tiers; they ended up at the same altitude.

Deep in the night, Pat stirred. John was gone. She wrapped herself in a sheet and followed the light. She squinted at a clock: 4 a.m. At the living room's threshold, she stopped. There John sat at the little desk, hunched over another pad of legal paper, working on his novel.

9

Two at Purdue

Nay, 'tis universally so, *Vitam regit fortuna, non sapientia.*[*]
— Robert Burton
(The Anatomy of Melancholy, 5th Ed., 1638*)*

T he Porters' garden had withered, and the slugs had slithered off to wherever it is that slugs overwinter when Jack and Alice hosted Pat and John's wedding at their home among a small group of family and friends. The Porters supplied the wine and cheese; John and Pat, the hors d'oeuvres. An old army buddy of John's had partaken enough of the wine by the time he officiated that he named the soon-to-be Patrice Rubadeau "Patrish" and declared them man and wife in the state of Illinois rather than Indiana which technically had legal jurisdiction.

It was January 1983. John and Pat had already moved in together and combined families in a two-bedroom apartment on the second floor of a house in Lebanon. Pat's daughters Heather and Lexi shared one room; John's sons Nick and Pace shared another (Nick was full-time with John now; Pace split time with John's ex-wife Nancy, though she often dropped him off before breakfast and picked him up after dinner on her weeks—call it payback for John's past absenteeism). John's daughter Becky was off at college. John and Pat slept in the living room, couch-surfing in their own abode.

Most couch surfers don't stay in the living room for five years, but so it would be for the Rubadeaus. It was what they could afford, and

---

[*] Chance governs our lives, not wisdom.

they were so busy that they couldn't be bothered to look elsewhere. John was teaching at Purdue, selling insurance, and, during school breaks, chipping away at his magnum opus. Pat continued to run the frame shop as before but added to her entrepreneurial, management, framecrafting, and family obligations a heavy academic load at Purdue. She intended to finish the degree she had broken off at Miami of Ohio years before.

She majored in Russian. Rather than work slowly toward the degree as most people with full-time jobs and families do, Pat shouldered eighteen credits per term. John studied along with her, reading Dostoevsky (whom he hated) and Tolstoy (whom he loved) to inform his edits of her papers for content as well as grammar. Pat jammed her classes into Mondays, Wednesdays, and Fridays and slept the hour's drive to and from West Lafayette as John piloted the aging, but smoothly running, red Volvo. Tuesdays, Thursdays, and both weekend days she spent at the Corner Vise Frame Shop, running her eyes across readings when she could and then doing most of her classwork late into the night.

She had help at the shop. Heather, barely a teenager, did the books. Lexi, in elementary school, cleaned the bathroom and took care of random tasks. Nick worked on frames, as did John, who also helped manage the place and happily chatted with customers out front when Pat was tied up working on something in the back.

John and Pat treated each other's kids like their own. Heather and Lexi thus got to experience John's parenting style, even if Becky and Nick still bore the brunt of it. Fellow parents who observed it characterized that style as one entirely uninformed by a role model.

John was strict, demanding, and obsessed with the kids' educations and personal and physical development. He was a strict college teacher, too. But in the classroom, his strictness was leavened by two factors: he considered students as potential future friends, and so his sharp fraternal instincts came into play; and students were only required to deal with him for a couple of hours a week in class and during occasional office hours during the confines of a single semester.

His own kids were captive over the long-term. With them, it was, as his old friend Barbara Bone from his Red Cross days in Germany put it, "his way or no way."

As with most other aspects of John's life, there are a lot of good stories. This man who swore liberally and repeatedly admonished "Don't be fuckups" would abide nothing of the sort from his kids. "If Nick or I ever said 'it sucks,' we'd get backhanded," Becky recalled, though the backhanding was figurative. He was known to return Father's Day cards with red-pen corrections.

When Nick was in the eighth grade, a teacher offered extra credit for learning the preamble of the Declaration of Independence. John asked the teacher what Nick would earn if he learned the entire Declaration by heart. An "A" for the semester, the teacher replied, assuming he had been presented with an outlandish theoretical construct. But indeed, John saw to it that Nick memorized the entire 1,320-word body of this nation's founding document. Nick then had the pleasure of reciting it verbatim in front of his class plus all the middle school's teachers.

On family road trips, John generally forbade sleeping the car.

"But dad, there's nothing to see," Nick might protest.

"Goddammit, look alive! You're not going to sleep your life away!" said the driver, who could power through 12-hour shifts with only the occasional, desperate bathroom break from his pleading offspring to stop him.

Before Pat came into the picture, John had, deliberately and periodically, triggered one of the apartment's smoke alarms in the depths of night. He held a cup of icy water that he had stored in the refrigerator. Nick recalled that, if he didn't wake up and move fast enough, his dad threw the water in his face.

"Goddammit, you have to be prepared!" John barked. "Everyplace you rest your head for the night could be a tinderbox! Be alert!"

His old friend Ron Pace summarized: "John sees danger around every corner."

As Nick entered high school, John focused on making a man out of him. For a boy who had inherited his biological mother's quiet nature, this was, at times, tough. He had Nick do grip exercises "because—that was one of his things—every time you shake someone's hand, try to fucking break it because it's a sign of strength," as Nick recalled. John's insistence on his kids developing physical strength and courage extended to the high diving board at the local pool. He went up the ladder behind Becky. She begged to be allowed to climb back down. He made sure she descended via a single, long step into the water. Once she had finally done it, John worked his way back down the ladder.

John occasionally called his shy older son "Peter Pout" and "Wally Wimp," nicknames that upset Nick but, he recognized with the passage of years, helped him develop a thick skin that would come in handy later in life. John, the son of an alcoholic, expounded on the dangers of drinking and drugs, both of which Nick avoided in high school entirely. Sex was another educational necessity. At one point, John swung through the family-planning center in West Lafayette, grabbed a big handful of condoms from a bowl, and brought them back to Lebanon where Nick and a friend, both about 16 and both in absolutely no position to employ such devices, were hanging out. "All right, you little fuckers," John said, tossing condoms at the boys like candy from a parade float. "Be careful. Safe sex."

John's intensity as a parent did have its upsides. When Becky was 14, he pestered his old German friend Bernd Munderloh to help organize a summer homestay in Hamburg for her. John somehow scraped together enough money for her flight. When Nick showed interest in tennis, John managed to pay for a tennis camp in Kentucky that lasted much of a summer. (John also enlisted his friend Rick Mount, the Indiana basketball legend, to serve as Nick's tennis coach.)

Of course, things could get weird, too. Becky met a guy named Stu her junior year in high school. Stu stopped by the house to pick her up for a date. He rang the doorbell; Becky answered with a nervous look on her face. Stu noted his date's father just inside the front door. The man was doing sit-ups on a bed pillow, which was itself odd. Stranger still, he wore nothing but black socks. Becky quickly joined Stu outside.

"I'm never going into your house again," Stu told her.

Later, Becky explained that "he just likes shock and awe. Instead of having the gun on the chair, my dad took a different route. He's not a sexual being at all or a pervert."

Stu and Becky stayed together through high school. A big part of the reason John sent her to college in Nebraska was to make sure she completed her education and avoided the long interruptions her biological mother and Pat's early marriages had inflicted on their educations. Age 18 also represented a watershed year to John. It was the year Becky went to college without him paying for it, and she was on her own. As Pat put it, "You're out. He's raised you."

Becky stayed with Stu and ultimately married him.

* * *

John is going back home to Ann Arbor tomorrow. We're wrapping up many hours of recorded interviewing about grammar, teaching, and his life.

"This is it," I say. "You're going to miss this microphone in your face all the time, aren't you."

"I think I'll take it home with me," John says. "I'm going to take it home with me or shove it up your ass."

"Maybe take it home with you," I say.

He gets up and then kneels to pet Oscar, the family puggle. Oscar licks him on the nose in reciprocation.

"He licked me on the nose—right after he licked his penis. Good dog," John says. "By the way, do you know why a dog licks his penis?"

"No," I say. "Why?"

"Because he can."

John returns to the kitchen table and its various books and papers and the microphone he may or may not shove up my ass. "My mind is wandering. It's settled on something important," he says. "I'd like you to read two poems. They're called *carpe diem* poems. One is by Andrew Marvell, 'To his Coy Mistress.' And the other one is 'To the Virgins, to Make Much of Time,' by Robert Herrick. This is for your own benefit because they talk about living life, not thinking about life. It's like *Zorba the Greek*. Have you read *Zorba the Greek*?"

"No."

"My favorite book of the twentieth century—except for mine. Nikos Kazantzakis," John says.

I search on my laptop and find 'To His Coy Mistress' at poetryfoundation.org. Our faces crowd the screen. He scrolls down to a poem written in 1681. "Read this," he says. I read:

> But at my back I always hear
> Time's wingèd chariot hurrying near;
> And yonder all before us lie
> Deserts of vast eternity.
> Thy beauty shall no more be found;
> Nor, in thy marble vault, shall sound
> My echoing song; then worms shall try
> That long-preserved virginity,
> And your quaint honour turn to dust,
> And into ashes all my lust;
> The grave's a fine and private place,
> But none, I think, do there embrace.

"It's all about dying and about the end of living. It's all about seizing the day while you're still young and passionate enough to enjoy young life absent the impediments of advancing age that always come. Although he's telling the world that you should lose your virginity while still randy and robust, it's not necessarily about sex. See, that's the whole point. It's *carpe diem, carpe rosam*: seize the day before you're old; gather the roses before you and they wilt. You know? I just love this poem. But that's just for you," John says.

I open another browser tab for Herrick's 1648 poem, which is much shorter. "Read that first part," John says.

> Gather ye rose-buds while ye may,
> Old Time is still a-flying;
> And this same flower that smiles today
> Tomorrow will be dying.

"And we've done that, by the way," John says. "We've seized the day. We've done things while we were young," John says.

"Yeah, we have," I say.

"You're probably too young," John says—something I don't often hear as a soon-to-be 50-year-old—"but it's a wonderful source to begin the reflection on what you've done in your life. I never made any money, but goddamn I had a lot of fun." He stands and moves back to his chair by the microphone. "But I wouldn't be happy if I hadn't had the tragedy, too, to compare it against."

"Do you think?" I ask.

"I know," John says. "I know."

* * *

Meanwhile, at Purdue, John taught introductory English and composition classes during the school year. Wearing slacks and button-down shirts and even a sport coat whose elbow patches Pat periodically replaced, John looked the part of college instructor when, in fall 1983, Chris Meyer walked into his required freshman English class. The clean-shaven Professor Rubadeau surveyed the group and said, "Not one of you is getting an A."

Meyer needed an A. Purdue was a good school, and he knew that when he had applied without having visited campus from his parents' home in Westchester, New York. It hadn't been his first choice, but his first choice—and second choice, and third choice—hadn't panned out. Upon arrival in West Lafayette, he quickly concluded that he wanted out of the Midwest and back to the East Coast. He needed As to do that.

"John was like, 'You don't know shit about the English language,'" Meyer recalled.

Brutal edits to early papers backed up John's opening line. He would teach them and point out mistakes, but it was ultimately up to them to get up to speed, John told them. He mentioned the writing lab.

Some quietly accepted their doom. Meyer started spending time in the writing lab, donning headphones and listening to cassette tapes on such topics as comma and semicolon usage. A big part of it was that he wanted to escape West Lafayette. But John had tapped into something deeper—a competitive instinct Meyer knew from his time as a high-school athlete but had never felt in the classroom.

"I think I just wanted to say 'Fuck you' to him because I didn't like the challenge of him saying I wasn't going to get an A," Meyer told me.

John, as ever, slung F-bombs in the classroom and said such things as, "You know what I'm doing? I'm writing a book about scatology"— even if the book he was actually writing was a Juvenalian assault on the Catholic Church from a semiautobiographical perspective separated by two layers of fictitious alter-ego authors—"You know what that is? It's the study of shit."

Meyer recognized what later generations of East Coast students of John would instinctively sense if not explicitly articulate: this sarcastic, frank, cantankerous Midwesterner was, in essence, a New Yorker without the accent. Despite John's demands on them and all the red ink, the class was fun. Meyer started stopping by John's office hours, and John showed interest in this lonely 18-year-old far from home. He recognized that Meyer was putting in the time and effort and that his work was paying off. When grades came in, Meyer's was an A. Meyer later transferred to, and graduated from, Brandeis University, earned a law degree as well as a master's degree in environmental law at Vermont, wrote screenplays, ran a chain of funeral homes, and is now a tech entrepreneur. Thirty-six years later, he described what made John's class a turning point in the course of his life. John had, wittingly or not, been the first to channel Meyer's innate motivation and competitiveness—traits he had left on the baseball and football fields of Westchester—into the academic realms that would now shape his future.

Meyer was back East by the fall semester of 1984 when Matt McKillip walked into John's freshman-English classroom. John's teaching approach had remained consistent; his appearance, though, had changed. He still wore the slacks, button-downs, and the sport coat, but now he sported a beard that continued to grow throughout the semester.

Facial hair had been an on-and-off-again thing for John over the years: there was a lot of red in it he wasn't quite sure he liked. But he was allergic to many aftershave products, and Pat found herself breaking out in a rash from the Clubman Osage Rub he had settled on. Pat suggested he just grow a beard. By now, he was in his mid-40s and, while the sideburns came in dark, the gray dominated the nest of whiskers that left John's neck to the imagination of all who would consider him frontally. From that day forward, it would be shaved just once more—two decades later, for a skin-cancer check. By then, Pat had grown so used to the beard that she found herself staring at her clean-shaven husband as if he were a stranger.

The first day of the semester, John was indeed a stranger to McKillip and his classmates, but he soon broke the ice with what had already become pedagogic mainstays: the paramount importance of *quid pro quo* and scratching one's itch to success in life, the idea of making the private public in one's writing, and the use of the word "fuck" and its derivatives as noun, verb, adjective, or expletive. McKillip was, like Meyer, another fish out of water despite McKillip having grown up an hour's drive east in Kokomo.

McKillip had chosen to major in computer science despite not having programmed much and found himself out of his depth among those who had programmed much. It was one of those majors where, at the introductory lecture, the professor says, "Look to your right. Now look to your left. One of you won't make it through the semester." John, being eminently approachable, was an outlier among McKillip's professors, all of whom maintained a certain distance from their students. "It was kind of we-against-they," McKillip said. "A chasm between us that wasn't to be crossed. John broke that down. He had some unorthodox methods and made it fun.

"We felt free to open up and talk. You've always got some students who just are not comfortable participating and talking and engaging in whatever the discussion is. He was always good at getting those students to really participate and engage."

John sensed that McKillip was a bright kid who was temporarily out of his depth. He told McKillip as much and said that, if he applied himself, he would do well at whatever he studied at Purdue. "He lit a fire under me," McKillip said.

McKillip indeed caught up with his more technically trained peers and did well. An internship at Procter & Gamble led to an offer for a full-time position after he graduated. At a multinational company where managers and executives were expected to pitch small projects on up to billion-dollar initiatives in a single page or less, John's lessons on how to write and communicate effectively paid dividends, McKillip says.

"P&G is infamous for the one-page memo. The idea is that if you can't express it in one page, basically it's not worth expressing,"

McKillip said. "I felt like I hit the ground running because John taught me how to do that."

Pat was working on her degree in Russian all the while. In 1987, she graduated magna cum laude. John, as well as her Purdue professors, encouraged her to consider graduate school. Always supportive and in awe of Pat's intelligence, he wanted her to aim high, proposing Harvard and Berkeley. She wasn't tied to Lebanon or Zionsville, but she did want to stay in the Midwest. In the meantime, she had a small business to consider: given her desire to pursue a PhD, the Corner Vise Frame Shop was now a mooring from which she had to release herself. While applying to grad schools, she sold the shop with the understanding that she would work with the new owner for a few months to get the woman up to speed on the finer points of a guillotine chopper and all the rest.

Among the places Pat applied to was the Department of Slavic Languages and Literatures at the University of Michigan. Neither she nor John had any connection to Ann Arbor, but it was a good program. On the application, there was a box to be checked if the applicant needed no financial support. Seeing as most check boxes involve the affirmation of a fact or statement phrased in the positive, and as Pat definitely needed financial support, Pat checked it.

She was accepted—great news. Less great was her realization that her acceptance had been predicated upon her mistaken declaration that she was rolling in dough despite having slept in the living room of a two-bedroom apartment while working and going to school seven days a week for the better part of five years. It took little in the way of calculation to see that she would run out of money after her first semester.

The Slavic department chair was unavailable at the time when Pat visited campus after she'd sold the business and committed to relocating. Omry Ronen, a Slavic-literature star, showed her around the Modern Languages Building instead. He was courteous at first, but then said this: "We really don't want you here, but you indicated that you don't need financial support."

There was no turning back now. In July 1987, Pat, John, Heather, and Lexi moved to a married-student-housing unit on the university's

North Campus. Pace stayed in Lebanon with Nancy for the time being; Nick had started at Purdue the year before; and Becky was off at college also. For the first time, John experienced a relocation without having instigated the familial uprooting and replanting.

Pat applied for a part-time job at a University of Michigan library to lessen her future loan burden. John looked for work, and did what any good insurance man would do: he worked his contacts. One of them had taught him years before when John was a Wisconsin undergraduate and was now a full professor of geology at Indiana University. This old friend may not have seemed like a terribly hot lead, but the geology professor had a good friend in the University of Michigan's Geology Department who, in turn, knew someone in the University of Michigan's English Department. William Holinger was a lecturer, but he was also a close friend of the department chair. John and Holinger hit it off, and that led to an interview with Lillian Back, a lecturer who led the department's undergraduate writing program. Back offered John a job as a lecturer.

"I would be thrilled, but I have to go home to discuss this offer with my wife," John told them. Back hadn't experienced such a response, she said later. "No male would have ever said that. There was something very special about him."

Pat was enthusiastic, and she had very good news of her own to share with him. Months back, she had applied for a prestigious Jacob K. Javits fellowship which would bring a four-year full-ride PhD scholarship plus an additional $10,000 a year for food and housing. She hadn't been all that hopeful and had forgotten about it as the months had passed. But that very same day, she learned she had landed the Javits. Later that afternoon, the library offered her the part-time job. She turned it down, so she could focus on her studies.

On a single day in July 1987, some combination of preparation and luck had turned a precarious leap to a new city and a new life into concrete opportunities for them both. Now it was a question of what they would do with them.

10

The Human Condition

Whether you think you can or you can't, you're probably right.
— Attributed to Henry Ford and others

John taught introductory classes in the University of Michigan Department of English: English 125 and its follow up English 225. Lillian Back had created English 225, a course devoted to writing persuasively to support a point of view. Typically, a lecturer such as John would have taught three classes of twenty students each. But Back recognized his enthusiasm and respected his teaching skill and experience and instead had him instruct two classes and spend the extra time mentoring graduate-student teaching assistants.

Jean Rosella took both of those classes during John's first couple of semesters at his new university. She was a married mother of two young daughters and had gone back to school after working as a nurse for years—a 35-year-old woman among 18- and 19-year-olds. Such nontraditional students had been common at Lincoln Memorial University. At Michigan, they were a rarity. In big lecture classes, Rosella could sit up front and be anonymous among the dozens or hundreds of students in cavernous lecture halls. In John's class, there was nowhere to hide. At home after that first day, when her daughters were out of earshot, Rosella told her husband about this English professor who used the word "fuck" as though it were the word "the."

John's classes had no fixed seating arrangement, but, after a few classes, he seated Rosella among three freshman girls to quell their chit-chatting. John often let the subsequent chatter go until Rosella chimed in with a word or two at which point he scolded her jokingly for talking in class.

Rosella had been in enough classrooms to recognize that John's was different. He managed, within the span of a few class periods, to create a seminar strangely free of the typical undercurrent of tension from unspoken social, cultural, or religious differences. That, in turn, rendered unnecessary the need to talk around those differences: the linguistic yoga of what would later come to be known as political correctness—a budding movement by the late 1980s—never found a mat in John's class. Lillian Back later described it like this:

> John knew he had to break with traditional ways of thinking about prejudices. How could he create classrooms that functioned with Muslims, with Jews, with African Americans, with Asians, with Hispanics, and with gays talking to each other with respect? How could he help these people understand they had so much to learn from each other—in fact develop a loving of the different cultural approaches? And therein lies the eccentricities of this teacher: he began by breaking the mold of quick, nonthinking responses. It was easier for him because he really had so few inbred prejudices: he had honestly developed a love for Jews, for Chinese, for Muslims, for gays, and for all those "others." Consequently, breaking the mold meant words like "fuck" could become tolerated. The mold was broken. Many of the responses that were "built in" for polite (but often nonanalytical) society no longer had a stronghold on the analytical part of these students' minds. Instead, what these students took away from his classes through the years was a strength to look at ideas in their own unprejudiced ways. Ideas that would norm-ally not be tolerated, ideas that were "outrageous," led these students on an unknown path.

In other words, John's own lack of bias—be it racial, religious, socioeconomic, gender based, age based, or otherwise, be it inborn or somehow acquired over all those difficult years in Madison and beyond—had paved the way to a unique teaching style. Here was a man who had habitually developed lasting friendships with cleaning people and company presidents, doctors, and dog groomers. He wasn't colorblind (or religion- or class-blind, either)—he, like everyone else, could not help but see differences in skin color, religion, gender, sexual orientation, and all the rest. But unlike most of us, John openly noted all these differences, and, in so doing, he made it clear that they were but minor permutations in the embroidered patterns of humanity. He had used foul language as a habit since the moment he had learned it, so why not swear for the greater good? And to be clear, he didn't like everybody. He routinely formed low opinions of people even if he were more generous in his assessments than most of us might have been. But he made a point of basing his distaste on behavior—not on who he or she was.

How much of all this John was doing consciously he himself couldn't say. But it worked.

"That's how it's supposed to be, right? I think college is the place where you're supposed to ask these questions. To have these arguments." Rosella said. "Young people should be able to express their differences—whether religious or political or otherwise. That just gives us a better understanding of our world."

John brought a copy of the student-run newspaper *The Michigan Daily* into class one day and asked, "Did everyone read this article on STDs?" Rosella, the nurse, recognized an especially important topic for the cohort surrounding her—a topic more typically discussed in health clinics with doors closed than in an English class. One of the chatty girls raised her hand and asked if she could ask Nurse Jean a question. Sure, John said.

"Can you get vaginal warts from sitting on a toilet seat?"

Rosella smiled uncomfortably as young faces shone on her like so many spotlights.

"Oh, Jill, can we please talk about this after class?" she said finally.

My mother looks down at her
half-empty plate and begins to
shake her head slowly. I cannot
tell if she is shaking in disbelief
or disapproval, either of which may
be expected at a time such as this.
I look around nervously to see if
anyone is listening, but our
waitress is busy greeting a family
that has just walked through the
door, and the elderly couple is
sitting too far away to hear my
confession. After a minute, she
finally looks up at me and takes a
deep breath. I prepare for the
worst.

"So, you're saying you're gay?"
she asks in the most deadpan tone
that I have ever heard from her.

The conversation becomes so much
more awkward for me at this point,
for I am not "gay." I have feelings
and desires for both men and women.
Ever since age fourteen, I have
always known that something isn't
"normal" about me because I have
feelings for both sexes.

One can probably imagine how
astoundingly difficult this feeling
is to tell someone about
(especially one's Mexican-Catholic
mother) because it raises so many
questions:

"So, which one do you like
better?"

"Does this mean that you can
love two people at the same time?"

"So, you're a swinger?"

I sometimes think gays and
lesbians have an easier time coming
out than I do because their sexual-
ities (to me, at least) are so

131

```
black and white — I, on the other
hand, am a shade of gray.
```

— From a student essay

Eric Rogoff had come to Michigan from suburban Pittsburgh. He knew from the start that he wanted to study business—a two-year program starting in one's junior year. He had visited the English Department and inquired about a class that would help him write better.

"I was not interested in writing literature; I was not interested in writing poetry. I wanted to be more persuasive," Rogoff said. "They suggested Rubadeau."

In January 1992, Rogoff joined nineteen others in John's English 225 class. He encountered a teaching approach that would take the separation of many years for Rogoff to articulate: "He was just different than everyone else on campus because—in my words today—he was himself and he truly was able to be himself in a really free way. Swearing, wearing what he wanted to wear, teaching what he wanted to teach, communicating what he wanted to communicate without all those constraints—the cages we all live in day in, day out."

Rogoff absorbed John's lessons on writing and communicating in ninety-minute intervals twice a week. The class sat in a big circle with John's chair oft-abandoned as he leapt to the chalkboard or paced about or held forth on topics of fluctuating relevance to the theme at hand. He told jokes; he gave people nicknames; he kept it light. Rogoff heard, too, as John expounded on the catchphrases that, like any good marketer, he repeated many times through the course of a given semester: *quid pro quo*; scratch your itch; make the private public; *carpe diem, carpe rosam*. And, of course, "Opinions are like assholes: everyone's got one, and most of 'em stink."

In addition to writing essays and sharing them with the class, students were expected to critique the essays of their fellow students. John expected several pages of analysis and criticism, and he insisted that it be constructive and polite. Learning how to couch negative comments in a positive way—one that assisted, rather than angered or alienated, the writer—was itself a communication skill essential in business and other realms of professional life, John believed.

"Frame your negative comments in a positive fashion so you don't piss off your audience," he urged students.

For his part, John marked up essays heavily with underlining and marginalia reminiscent of his legal-pad novel drafts. Students handed in their critiques; he read and included them in grading. John's course-pack Grammar Review dominated class time during the first couple of weeks; after that, the focus was on essay workshopping. The technical aspects of writing remained front-and-center, albeit sneakily so. The essays being workshopped served as stocked ponds for errors to be fished out for John's explanations and remediations; they also provided fertile ground for lessons in composition and rhetoric: how to organize ideas, how to transition between them, and how to back up arguments with concrete examples rather than abstractions.

The bulk of the writing load for his classes went into the critiques, and they were the main driver for learning. Some of it was simple psychology: cleaning up one's own mess was a drag, but pointing out someone else's mistakes had a certain "Where's Waldo" pleasure to it—not to mention serving up a dose of good old *schadenfreude*. But, Rogoff and others soon learned, recognizing problems with grammar, spelling, and structure in a fellow student's draft was also a surprisingly good way to improve one's own writing. Such blemishes are scarcer or completely absent in professional writing that's polished to a high gloss.

Rogoff was accepted into the business school and with that was done with the College of Literature, Science, and the Arts. After graduating, he a got a job at a New York investment bank—just the sort of position that he had envisioned and worked so hard for. When he was occasionally back in Ann Arbor to recruit for his firm, he stopped by to see John and Pat.

They had stayed in touch for twenty years when Rogoff's phone rang. He was in the throes of a divorce and had flown to Jackson Hole, Wyoming, to get away and clear his head over a long Fourth of July weekend. John assumed his former student was in New York. "What are you doing?" he asked.

"I'm getting divorced," Rogoff told him, and explained where he was.

"If I could afford the flight, I'd come out there right now, and we'd have a real heart-to-heart" John said.

"I can afford the flight if you want to come out here right now," Rogoff said.

They spent the better part of three days together. They toured the Tetons; they hiked; Rogoff talked; John listened. John told him his own stories, too: about Barbara's suicide, about the divorce with Nancy, and about his and Pat's partnership. John became, in those couple of days, "the father I wish my father was," Rogoff said. Rogoff loved his dad, but the man had led by example: how to make money, how to provide for a family. As was the case with so many fathers raising sons, he did not probe feelings and emotions.

"John could share with me his own experiences with divorce and what it means and what it doesn't mean," Rogoff said. "Here was an older, more experienced individual who had been through similar situations, a man who could provide real perspective over the course of time on what can bring happiness to a relationship."

It was only with the passage of years that John's mantras really resonated. "Following your passions, making the private public, *quid pro quo*—they were wedged in my mind somewhere," Rogoff said. "When other life events forced me to learn some things that I didn't learn at age 19, his words came back to me."

> The sound of voices jolts me back into consciousness. Harsh fluorescent lighting floods into my eyes, forcing me to promptly re-shut my lids. *Darkness—darkness is better*, I decide.
> But the voices do not agree; they are trying to get me to open my eyes again. The voices have hands, and their hands are squeezing my shoulders. "Mmmeh-uhh," I say, which is drunk for: "kindly stop squeezing my shoulders

because you're making me nauseated
as fuck, and I am not going to open
my eyes because my head will
explode on account of the bright
lights."

"Beck, open your eyes," the
voices plead, persistent. *Wait, how
do they know my name? Who are they?
Where am I?* I am curious enough to
open my eyes halfway. Through
quivering slits, I see that the
voices belong to two blobs that
slowly evolve into my aunt and a
doctor, a sight that confuses me
because they definitely were not at
the bar with me last night (although "your aunt and a doctor walk
into a bar" could be the uninspired
opening of a mediocre joke). As my
eyes gradually adjust, and the
world momentarily stops feeling as
if I am a dreidel on the first
night of Hanukkah, I become aware
that I am sitting pantsless in a
wheelchair, wearing nothing but a
papery gown. *Shit.*

— From a student essay

In April 1991, Pat was 39, wrapping up the coursework for her
Michigan PhD in Slavic linguistics, and moving ahead on her dissertation. The year before, she and John had moved the family into a one-
story house they bought in the wooded Northside neighborhood
tucked in between Pontiac Trail and the Huron River. Pace had joined
them a couple of years earlier. Beyond the demands of Pat's classes and
dissertation, she ferried Pace—a budding trumpet player—to music
practice and basketball games, and she also drove him, Lexi, and
Heather to swim meets and the girls' other activities. The term "soccer
mom" had yet to be coined, but it was as formidable a part of her
portfolio as the Old Church Slavonic of her studies.

That month, Pat had emergency surgery at the University of Michigan Hospital for severe endometriosis. The procedure went fine, but, even after she had recovered, the shortness of breath that she had begun to notice before the surgery increased. Months of doctor visits and X-rays, CT scans, MRIs, and a bronchoscopy brought a diagnosis in early November. It came in the form of a single, sesquipedalian word: lymphangioleiomyomatosis (LAM).

LAM struck fewer than one in a million people, nearly all of them women in their prime childbearing years. Via mechanisms that remained—and remain—poorly understood, LAM triggers a mass, unruly proliferation of bastardized smooth-muscle cells that renders the lungs increasingly dysfunctional. There was no cure, and the prognosis was much clearer in terms of its endpoint—a form of suffocation called "respiratory failure"—than the path or pace of its progression, which typically took longer than eight years but which varied widely. Lung transplantation was an option but only for cases far more advanced than hers.

John had yet again been dealt a reason to live his philosophy of living in the present—not in the past; not in the future. This worked well in some ways and less well in others. As the shock of the diagnosis wore off, the estrogen-cutting drugs Pat was on (estrogen remains a suspect in the progression of LAM) contributed to a fifty-pound weight gain. John, while fine with all sorts of body shapes in the world at large, was less forgiving of it within the walls of his home. He was also busy both as a teacher as well as socially—a lecturer whose growing fame was leading to favorite-professor dinners at sorority houses and all sorts of other invitations. Their relationship suffered. Years later, Pat admitted that "we had some really tough times, but we worked through them."

```
    The hardest part of getting
catcalled is the lack of choice.
Sexual harassment isn't something
you can actively avoid unless you
become a hermit crab and never
leave your bubble. It's not even
what they say that gets to you but
```

how they look at you. It's feeling
their eyes on your ass as you walk
by and not being able to do anything about it except internally
scream. It's a constant struggle of
asking yourself conflicting questions: *Do I stick up for myself by
giving them the finger or telling
them to fuck off and put myself in
danger by angering them? Do I just
keep walking, take the harassment,
and suck it up? Is it my responsibility to tell them what they're
doing is wrong? How do women who
live in big cities do this every
day? Are they mentally stronger
than me? Do so many of them wear
headphones to drown out the noise
of their daily harassers? How much
can one woman take?*

— From a student essay

Evan Hansen and Susannah Nichols took John's class in the fall
semester of 2001. Hansen was from New Baltimore on the shores of
Lake St. Clair northeast of Detroit; Nichols was from the older
Baltimore on Maryland's Atlantic coast. They were both senior
English majors, and they were dating. The first day of class, John said,
"Everyone here is gonna be friends, but nobody should start dating
because it's gonna fuck up the class bonding so important to writing
honestly to one another."

So they kept it secret, even if everyone but John had figured it out
by the time they came clean midsemester.

Nearly everyone in the class was a senior. Years earlier, the English
Department had moved John to upper-level writing courses—English
325 and 425. These classes were identical and generally paralleled his
lower-level classes. Administrators made the change because students
outside the English Department—those studying engineering or
premed or business or other fields—had gotten wind of this bearded

wonder but couldn't enroll because his classes didn't satisfy their programs' upper-level language requirements. A smattering of athletes typically rounded out the mix. Bonnie Campbell, an English Department administrator, said John routinely had more students on his waitlists than were in his classes—often twice as many.

John found that older students who had lived away from home for three or four years and who were forging their way into adulthood had amassed more "grist for the mill of their creative minds"—another Rubadeau favorite—than had been the case with the teenage freshmen and sophomores he had been teaching. These older students were more likely to have had their hearts broken by girlfriends or boyfriends, or to have come out as gay, or to have been betrayed by someone they trusted, or to have recognized that maybe the binge drinking was less voluntary than they had otherwise convinced themselves, or to have experienced enough separation from their upbringings to question their received beliefs, or to have wondered more seriously about who they were and where they were going. The essays became much more personal; often, they were confessional.

"Making the private public" proved to be a beneficent cycle: the more private stories students made public, the more bonded the class became. Also contributing was "the experience of being vulnerable and having it pay off. It's utter fulfillment with an unofficial minor in grammar," as Hansen put it. John encouraged his students to get together outside of class, and end-of-semester potlucks became fixtures.

There were three main reasons why confessional essays made for such good fodder in an English class. First, they were interesting, diverse, and surprisingly universal, so one ended up with a course about the "human condition," as John called it.

"It's as much about the people as the content being taught," Nichols said.

Second, writing from personal experience provides a shortcut to developing one's "voice." Voice differs from writer to writer like fingerprints differ from hand to hand. Voice in writing enhances readability, authority, and novelty. Voice is the difference between a wire report on a football game and a sports columnist's take on a bitter rivalry. Developing voice is a high-level writing skill. "I would say I was a good writer before I came into his class," Hansen said. "But the idea of really using my voice and cherishing it, in a way, was not something that had ever really occurred to me."

Third, the goal of John's class was to improve his students' writing, so he wanted them focusing on that skill—as opposed to devoting time and effort to gathering information about the characters of *Othello* or the failures of the Treaty of Versailles or the role of currency hedging in corporate finance or whatever else their other classes were force-feeding them. If students wrote what they knew, they could focus on the craft. That also made it more interesting for John: despite having taught essentially the same course for decades, a new batch of students with unique perspectives and experiences provided fresh material, class after class, year after year, further fueling John's enthusiasm and joy in teaching.

"Students learn more about grammar than they ever could by diagramming sentences or memorizing rulebooks. They improve their rhetorical skills, and they build a genuine confidence in communicating their ideas," Nichols said.

Nichols spoke as a student as well as a teacher of English at a highly regarded private high school in metro Detroit. At the Roeper School, she adapted John's approach to a junior-senior expository writing course. She put loose boundaries around how much private to make public at this small school where everyone knew everyone. She didn't censor, but she took a look at essays before the writers handed copies out to the class, so she could be prepared for heavy topics. Some kids wrote about coming out or being in recovery for eating disorders; others wrote about their cats. "It runs the gamut—but we talk about how you don't have to write about the most devastating thing you've ever experienced for it to be a good essay or for people to be interested in what you have to say," Nichols said.

John's teaching approach worked—and continues to work—for her, too, she said.

        This myth that college football
     players get laid simply because

they play football is basically a
complete lie. Yes, there are those
superstars who bang as many chicks
as Tiger Woods while he was
married; however, those lucky
gentlemen are few and far between.
I, the subpar fullback who is
better known for his mangy, wet
doglike hair, rather than exemplary
play, am not so lucky. As a matter
of fact, I am practically the
opposite of the stereotype. No, I
am the fucking complete opposite (I
am aware this is an absolute
statement).
        I thoroughly believe that
playing college football has made
me worse at talking to girls. I am
constantly surrounded by testos-
terone-filled meatheads who
struggle to formulate coherent
sentences. That kind of environment
can only breed morons who can't
communicate with the opposite sex.

— From a student essay

After graduating, Evan Hansen took a job in marketing and communications with the university. John occasionally stopped by the office to see him. More than once, he brought what Hansen described as "his giant-ass polar bear of a dog" which would then aimlessly browse neighboring cubicles and surprise their occupants as John chatted with his former student. They were friends now, with John addressing Hansen as "Asshole" or "Dicklick" and Hansen returning the favor with "Dumbfuck."

"Hey, use my honorific," John said.

"Okay," Hansen said. "*Doctor* Dumbfuck."

"Better," John said.

Hansen and Nichols had stayed together. In early 2004, they decided to get married. While they had friends in the new and old

Baltimores, they were closest to those whom they had met at Michigan. They booked an outdoor wedding at the Dearborn Inn in its namesake Detroit suburb and considered their options for an officiant. Both had been raised Catholic but now weren't religious at all, so a priest wasn't their first choice. Hansen recalled how John had told him how his stepdaughter Lexi was going to have him do the honors at her wedding but then, to his disappointment, had backed out at the last minute.

He and Nichols asked their favorite professor if he'd be willing to lead the ceremony, and he agreed. The couple visited John at home and helped him apply for credentials on the Universal Life Church website. With a click of a Get Ordained Instantly button, the atheist became a man of god without the hassle of divinity school much less a vow of celibacy.

The ceremony took place in late July. It had rained the night before, providing for Floridian humidity as the midday temperature climbed into the mid-nineties. The 150 or so guests perspired through the mere act of existence. Hansen and Nichols had written their own vows; John had composed the lead-in. He welcomed everyone and said a few words, and then announced it was the birthday of Hansen's father who hadn't wanted the occasion to be recognized. John led a mass chorus of "Happy Birthday" before getting down to business. It went like this:

> When Evan first asked me to officiate at his wedding, my initial thought was what to say, how to come up with something especially appropriate on this especially meaningful day when we gather as a family of well-wishers to celebrate this union of two separate individuals into one distinct family unit. One of my mantras is from Mark Twain. I quote, "The difference between the right word and the almost right word is the difference between lightning and the lightning bug." I wanted to come up with just the RIGHT word, but no words were forthcoming.
>
> Tongue-tied and, therefore, at a loss for words, I did what any lover of literature would do when called

upon to come up with just the right words for a particular occasion. I rushed to my bookshelf, grabbed my dog-eared 125th Anniversary Edition of *Bartlett's Familiar Quotations*, and flipped through the pages of its index until I came to the word "marriage." Under "marriage," much to my initial delight, I found eighty-six entries—a veritable goldmine where I could scratch and dig about and mine a gem of a saying. Surely, I thought, amongst these eighty-six observations reflecting the collected wit and wisdom of the ages' sages, I should find words that would establish a fitting tone to reflect the happiness that all of us gathered here today feel about Susannah and Evan's marriage.

Truth be told, truth is, oftentimes, stranger than fiction: What follows is the God's honest truth. Since I had eighty-six quotations to choose from, I decided to go in numerical order. The first quotation listed in Bartlett's index was from the Greek dramatist Menander (342–292 BCE).

I quote, "Marriage, if one will face the truth, is an evil, but a necessary evil."

Somehow I sensed that these words did not set the happy tone I was striving to reach.

The second listing was from Cervantes' *Don Quixote*, one of my favorite novels. I quote, "Marriage is a noose." With two down and eighty-four to go and no favorable words about the joy of marriage, I considered advising Susannah and Evan to continue living together in a state of blissful sin and avoid marriage as if it be the plague—as it certainly seemed to be from Menander and Cervantes' perspectives.

Distraught now but not dissuaded, I decided to abandon an ordered search and just pick citations at random. I closed my eyes and let my pen fall where it might on the page of the index I had turned to. My pen fell on these words from John Haywood, whose book *Proverbs*, first printed in 1546, is the earliest collection of English colloquial sayings. I quote, "Marriage is destiny—and hanging likewise."

Now growing dejected and beginning to doubt the wisdom of my decision to marry my own wife, I made one more attempt to find something pleasant to say about wedded bliss. Closing my eyes and letting my pen fall where it might on the page, I let it drop. It fell upon a quote from Robert Louis Stevenson. Again, I quote, "Marriage is like . . . a field of battle and not a bed of roses."

Thoroughly disheartened, I called those individuals who would be giving readings at the ceremony and begged them to find something propitious and appropriate to say that would express happiness about this joyous occasion.

Family and friends then read John Donne's "The Good-morrow," Tennyson's "Marriage Morning," and Kahlil Gibran's "On Marriage." John pronounced his former students who hadn't fucked up the class man and wife. Hansen and Nichols kissed, and they left the gazebo to the string quartet's rendition of the Michigan fight song, "The Victors."

You're still wearing the same jeans and nice striped sweater that you wore to your classes, all of which were long and dreary. There's nothing you'd rather do than change into sweatpants, plop on the couch, and play *Call of Duty*.

But your roommate is out of town. You knew he would be gone, and you told her this. That is why she's coming over tonight.

Whenever you match with someone on Tinder (for John the Luddite:

143

it's a popular dating application),
it's always one of two outcomes.
The conversation fizzles out, or it
ends a couple of days later with a
night of drinks, fooling around,
and desolation.
Tonight, it will be the latter.
Whenever you meet someone through
Tinder, it always is.
Your phone emits a small and
empty ding. Your fingers abruptly
stop mid melody in response to the
sharp peep, lingering with antici-
pation. That's your cue.
You check your place one last
time before you head down. The bed
is tidy, the booze is copious, and
the mirror confirms that you are
presentable for the night.
Time to begin the show — the
same show you've done over and over
again.
You see your audience in the
lobby. She stands out with her
ginger hair, kissed by fire.

— From a student essay

It took those in charge of the University of Michigan graduation ceremonies little time to recognize that John, when outfitted in a black robe, hood, and cap rather than faded jeans and flannel, looked more the part of senior professor than just about anyone in Ann Arbor with actual tenure—a genuine Dumbledore doppelgänger. Starting in 1989, he served as lead marshal of the left flank of dignitaries proceeding onstage for winter, spring, and graduate commencements. The spring commencement, by far the largest, was held in the Big House football stadium. In return for leading a line of people in lockstep with a similar line on the right flank, John was rewarded with handshakes and photographs with sixty-six commencement speakers over more than two decades: Kofi Annan, George H.W. Bush, Hillary Clinton, Larry Page, and Sandra Day O'Connor among them. His run ended in 2010 when what John described as a "huge donor" wanted to be onstage with Barack Obama and bumped John. University officials offered a tent-marshal role as consolation—with a 6 a.m. start time.

John's response (direct quote): "Fuck you."

Volunteering for commencement ceremonies fed straight into what became a spring tradition. Starting right after the Big House festivities, John toured Ann Arbor to visit the graduation parties of the seniors who had taken his class. Pat had done the logistics in advance, figuring out a proper path and typing up street addresses in geographical order. For several years, she joined him on the adventure and snapped countless photos until her slowly advancing lung disease made the six or so hours of chasing after her husband too grueling. John's close friend and German lecturer Kalli Federhofer then accompanied him. In the early 2000s, Evan Hansen took over.

Hansen's work started in the days before the event: with an online map, he charted a course. Geography was a key consideration, but so was food.

"He'd want to know which ones would have either Jerusalem Garden or Zingerman's" —John's favorite restaurants— "and I'd always plan the route around them," Hansen said. They started off on foot, then Hansen drove them to the parties on the outskirts of town.

In his classes, John assigned a student to keep track of the topic at hand to keep John's digressions from straying so far into the wilderness that they would never make it back. Hansen played this role on graduation day—one vital in keeping them on schedule. Before the selfie era, he also served as designated photographer, using John's camera—first film, later digital—to capture hundreds of photos each year of the still-robed-and-hooded lecturer with students, family members, and friends. If kids under the age of about 14 were around, John pulled out the old separating-thumb trick. Often, because students had written about their families, he would know something about the people he was meeting: "Oh, you're the grandmother who did such and such!" as Hansen recalled. John adeptly confused mothers with older sisters. "He was always buttering up mom," Hansen said. "She might be 85, and he'd still try and pull that joke out."

145

John introduced Hansen in various ways, but his standby was "This is my retarded son Evan. You'll have to speak slowly if you want him to follow." Hansen found that, while most chuckled and talked to him at a normal pace, others bent down a bit and spoke slowly. "Sometimes it got a little weird," Hansen said.

By the time they wrapped up, the two had visited forty-five to fifty-five graduation parties over six or seven hours. (One graduation day, they visited seventy-two houses.) John clearly enjoyed these days among the students he loved. But it was a lot. Hansen once asked him why he did it.

"It's the fulcrum on which our relationship tips from student-teacher to a lifelong friendship," John told him.

A trendy topic focuses on "the talk" that parents of adolescent Black boys will eventually need to have. In addition to sharing safe-sex tips, parents will be expected to teach their sons how to project a nonthreatening presence. We'll be expected to tell them, once they reach adolescence, to always keep both hands visible if apprehended by an officer. To calmly request a call to the shift manager if the situation oddly escalates and becomes heated. To never forget that to some, their blackness will always signify a threat and to avoid situations where they are alone with these types of people.

I refuse, perhaps prematurely, to have this conversation with my sons; and not because I'm naive enough to think that they don't need to know these things. While their adolescence feels far away and the haze of their childhood restricts my vision to problems no worse than bedtime battles and

never-ending ear infections, I
refuse. Today, I firmly believe
that warnings like these create
boys who internalize the lies told
about them and put too much effort
into preparing our boys for the
threats they are the least likely
to face.

— From a student essay

Even after the digital-photography revolution, many of the photographs Evan Hansen took of John ended up being printed. Their destination: John's office on the third floor of Angell Hall.

The first photo of John and his students was snapped his first year at Michigan: Lillian Matsumoto asked to take a picture of her class, and she gave John a copy of it. He pinned it to a cork bulletin board, and, over the next couple of semesters, similar photos joined it, crowding the bulletin board and radiating onto a nearby wall. As John moved offices more than once in his early years on campus, resettling the photos became a burden. Pat came up with the idea of gluing the growing hordes of faces to two-foot by three-foot foam-core boards and mounting the boards to the wall with those tiny clear-plastic screw-in mirror clips. Office moves became a matter of removing the feather-light boards and hanging them in the next space. By the time Hansen took the graduation-party baton, John had been in a third-floor Angell Hall office for years. Its walls, ceiling, and windows were covered with photos, and, with each new class, new photos continued to stack up.

John was at a loss as to how to continue the practice. The office had a high ceiling, and a student came up with the idea of filling that lofty vacuum with photo mobiles. These mobiles would be made by cutting one foam-core board in half vertically and gluing its halves down the center of a fresh board. Pat, the former framer, ran with the idea. The result, observed from the top or bottom, looked like a "+" sign. Year after year, mobile after mobile filled the higher reaches of John's office. Entering his workspace was to walk into a dizzying three-dimensional collage, an explosion of the students he loved and, his own children noted, doted on to a degree rarely seen in the Rubadeau household. Even when alone, he was surrounded by his students, and that's the way he liked it.

For a very long time, just one photo of students was framed. It was of Marc Zeplin and Lee Trepeck. Both had been in John's class in the late 1980s. Both had been to dinner at John and Pat's several times.

Zeplin asked John if he would write recommendation letters to what became Zeplin's first employer and, later, to the Michigan MBA program. John was happy to. Zeplin graduated, returned home to New York, and soon found success as a trader with Cantor Fitzgerald. Together with their two boys, ages 3 and 10 months, he and his wife Debra moved into a big, new house in Westchester. They had lived there just a couple of months as of September 11, 2001, when Zeplin went to work on the 104th floor of the World Trade Center's North Tower. He made a trade at 8:20 a.m. Twenty-six minutes later, American Airlines Flight 11 struck a few floors below.

John wrote a letter to Zeplin's parents. It read, in part,

> Over the years, we lost touch, but I always had an especially fond place in my heart for him. Not that any of my babbling in any way assuages your pain, but I want you to know something: on my office walls, I have over 4,000 pictures of students whom I have taught over the last fifteen years. However, on the windowsill behind my desk sits a sole framed picture, the only framed picture in my office. That picture was given to me—just before they graduated—by Marc and his buddy Lee Trepeck. So even though I haven't spoken to Marc in over ten years, I have seen him every day, first thing, when I walk into my office and sit down at my desk.
>
> I truly wish that I could somehow find the appropriate words that might ease somewhat your pain and suffering. Sadly, there are no such words. All I can do is write to you and tell you how much I liked

Marc and what a wonderful young man I thought he was.

A thousand people attended the memorial service. Len Zeplin, Marc's father, read Marc's Bar Mitzvah speech. Then his mother Leona spoke about her son. Len closed with one more reading: John's letter.

My mother, I know, I have always known, never had a dream that looked anything like me.

My Mother's Dream is lighter by three shades and twenty-five pounds and wears skirts that fall below her knees.

My Mother's Dream accepts the flimsy black-cotton bras that she buys in seedy backrooms of alleyway clothing stores in her native India and would never darken the doors of a Victoria's Secret. My Mother's Dream loves math and medicine. She spends weekends with her hands in the dark, rich earth as she tends to heirloom tomatoes and unpronounceable squashes.

My Mother's Dream would play Scrabble with her every night and go to church every Sunday. She would be a National Merit Scholar and a Bharatanatyam dancer. And my Mother's Dream would never allow my father to use the phrase "your mother's daughter" as the worst insult in his arsenal. She would never allow it to split open her unfurling, now torn, already too-complicated love.

I am not my mother's dream. But I am my mother's daughter.

— From a student essay

149

The class list read "Vincent Pagano," but he went by Vince. He had been a business student, realized he hated it, and decided he wanted to be a doctor. That required year-round classwork to make up for having learned the basics of accounting rather than those of anatomy. As a senior in 2007, Pagano had more than enough credits for priority boarding to John's class. He aimed to improve his writing for personal statements on his med-school applications. John entered the room, his long strides imparting excessive speed, his hair color having caught up with that of his beard. Roughly in the middle of roll call, he read the name "Vincent Pagano," and as Vince raised his hand, John asked, "Can I call you 'Vinny?'"

Nobody had ever called him "Vinny," but Pagano figured what the hell. Over the next few months, the class unfolded as it always did. "There were some incredibly heartbreaking stories. Some people took things that were completely embarrassing and made them funny," Pagano said. "One girl had cancer. You would have never known."

The semester ended in late April. Pagano, having crafted a personal statement, asked John if he would review it. John said, "Of course," and invited him over to the house for dinner.

Pagano, who liked to cook, ended up doing so. He, Pat, and John got to talking. Pagano, from Shelby Township north of Detroit, was the son of Sicilian immigrants and the first in his family to go to college. His father and a brother were alcoholics. John and he had more in common than they knew.

Pagano made a habit of making meals at the Rubadeaus. It was he who came up with the idea of doing foam-core mobiles for John's overpopulation of student photos. Working at a lab in Ann Arbor while studying for the MCAT and applying to medical schools—twenty-one of them, all told—he and John went for long walks and talked about their "shared, painful experiences," as Pagano put it, but also whatever else was on their minds.

John and Pat helped him hone his personal statement as well as narrative answers in the secondary applications many medical schools require. Pagano had carried a 3.8 GPA at Michigan and scored in the 98th percentile on the MCAT—a strong candidate. And yet rejection after rejection came in until every single one of his applications had been denied. Perplexed, he called the admissions office of a school he had considered a backup option. "You're never going to come here anyway," he was told.

"It was the most terrifying moment of my life," Pagano said.

John had by then taught enough doctors-to-be to staff a hospital. Pagano, in John's mind, was solid physician material and a good guy. He walked over to the Michigan Medical School's admissions office, sat down with an assistant director, told him that Pagano was as sharp as any of the many students he'd referred to the school, and repeated his belief that "Vinny" was MD material.

Pagano was offered a spot. At the ceremony marking the beginning of medical school, John was there to put the white coat on Pagano. Meanwhile, Pagano had met a girl in the Ann Arbor lab. Alyse, a year younger than Pagano, had finished up her nursing degree. With Pagano renting a room and the couple not wanting to sign a year-long lease (Pagano would probably end up elsewhere for his medical residency in a few months), Alyse was poised to return to her parents' place in Portland, Oregon. John and Pat offered her the guest room in their basement. She stayed for four months.

"This could have been the moment in our lives—the stress, the distance—that ended our relationship. And here come John and Pat to the rescue," Pagano said.

John was there again four years later to hand Pagano his medical-school diploma. Pagano continued with a three-year anesthesiology residency at Michigan and was chosen chief resident in his third year—the team captain, so to speak, among 120 young MDs. Alyse and he squeezed their wedding into the brief gap between the end of Pagano's residency and the start of his cardiac anesthesiology fellowship. John officiated at the ceremony—"the irreverent reverend," he called this persona—as he had, by then, at more than 40 student weddings as far away as Germany and South Africa. When Pagano's fellowship wrapped up in 2017, he launched his cardiac anesthesiology career at Kalamazoo Hospital. "Vinny" had, indeed, been MD material.

"Ok, I'm done."

I cannot think of more romantic words he could have uttered to consummate the loss of my virginity. I am seventeen years old and just had sex in a tiny room beneath my basement stairs.

This eight-by-six, glorified closet is adorned with NSYNC posters, Beanie Babies, and a sexy picture of me from 9th grade when I had a gleaming mouth-full of braces, eyebrows that were comparable to a Muppet's, and bangs that looked as though a blind man with a severe tremor had cut them.

As I awkwardly stumble around in the dark, grasping aimlessly for my clothes, I am trying to process what happened. *You just had sex in front of your fucking stuffed animals. Do you have no shame? What if* Toy Story *is true?! Great. You just perverted your whole childhood, you dirty, dirty whore.*

My internal ramblings are suddenly interrupted when I catch a glimpse of white glowing beneath me. My bleach-white athletic socks, contrasting against the pitch-black backdrop, are screaming at me as if to say, "Look what you've done! You had your fucking socks on the whole time!" With my head hanging low, staring at my stupid fucking socks through tear-filled eyes, I realize how truly meaningless and superficial my deflowering was.

– From a student essay

Elise Yu took John's class in the winter semester of her junior year in 2009. She had been 19th on the waitlist but showed up anyway. None of the first eighteen on the waitlist did; nor did one of the twenty who had gotten enrolled. There's probably a life lesson in that.

By this point, John was as famous on campus as an English professor could be. He had won his Golden Apple award four years prior, and the glowing reviews on RateMyProfessors.com stoked his legend further. His reputation had preceded him to the point that Yu found herself surprised that the creature who loped into the fourth-floor classroom in Angell Hall was indeed a mere human being. The profanity, the energy, and the clothing that wouldn't have looked out of place on someone whose worldly belongings would fit in a shopping cart were all there as advertised. "It was like, here he is, in the flesh, kind of this crazy person," she recalled.

One of the first essays the class considered was by a young woman who wrote about her love of chocolate. Others followed with often deeply personal recollections. Yu wrote about the idea of being proud to be an Asian American and how she came to grips with what that meant—in particular, her own deep-seated desire to be her "best, genuine self" without feeling a need to "whitewash" herself to fit into a Caucasian-dominant society. The girl who had written about chocolate remarked, "Man, I feel like such an asshole. You wrote about all this personal stuff, and I wrote about fucking chocolate."

John told the chocolate lover that what she had written was perfectly fine: "You wrote about how chocolate makes you feel and the guilt you often associate with it."

Yu, the daughter of immigrants, had come from a Korean-American community in the Detroit suburb of Troy. They were members of the region's largest Korean-American church. Her peers and her friends tended to be a lot like her: high-achieving, socially conservative, polite Asian Americans. She gravitated socially toward the same kind of people at Michigan. John's class was different, having all sorts of people and all sorts of majors. One of the guys was old enough to have a daughter in high school. Through their essays and their interactions in and, later, outside of class, she really got to know them all. "I think, maybe for me, it was my first sort of step out of the world that I'd created for myself," Yu said.

Yu went into law, a Caucasian-dominant field. John wrote her a glowing law-school recommendation letter because he believed in her intelligence and work ethic. She worked as a legal assistant for a year at an Ann Arbor firm and then started at the University of Michigan Law School. She was, by this point, working as what John referred to as his "amanuensis," a term which describes not a medical procedure but, rather, a typist. John somehow never learned how to type, so, for years and years, he paid a series of former students to type for him. Yu typed countless emails that appeared to be from John's fingertips; she also helped prepare and upload recommendation letters.

John had, by the early 2010s, written many hundreds of recommendation letters for his students and former students. At the bottom of his own resumé, he explained under the heading ADDITIONAL PUBLICATIONS OF A SORT: "While the lion's share of the faculty publishes novels, articles, reviews, *et cetera ad infinitum,* I 'publish' letters of recommendation. Since 1987, I have written well over 1,500 letters supporting my students' desires to attend medical school, or law school, or graduate school, or to find employment as teachers or investment bankers or social workers or—you name the profession, and I can, with great assurance, tell you that I have written on someone's behalf to support that individual's desire to pursue that particular career path. I have made the penning of such letters a cottage industry—one that I greatly enjoy."

There was some cookie-cutter language that would apply to any student who performed well enough in his class to inquire about the possibility of a recommendation letter; he dictated the rest to Yu. The stronger he felt about the student, the more he dictated. In addition to his time, he was spending ten bucks an hour on Yu's help, a small sum that added up given the volume of correspondence he was taking on.

The bearded septuagenarian's words—and more generally his approach to life—started rubbing off on her. She found herself swearing exponentially more. She continued to have a filter, but she also recognized the value in selectively chucking that filter and just calling something that was fucking stupid "fucking stupid."

"I don't think I was going to be like crazy old John terrorizing Ann Arbor like he does," Yu said. "But I think there's something really useful and good about not giving a fuck about what anybody else says."

After law school, John connected her with Eric Chisholm, a former student and Chicago attorney. Yu joined his firm. She and her boyfriend Carl, who was working in the Detroit area, survived the long-distance relationship, and, when it was time for them both to move back to Ann Arbor after a couple of years, John connected Yu with yet another former student, Jon Jurva, whose law firm she joined. Carl proposed; Elise accepted. They wanted John to do the wedding ceremony. Her father, who knew John from dinners together and was fond of him, resisted. What if he swore during the ceremony? John could say whatever he liked at the reception, but an actual man of religion should lead the ceremony.

"He's done all these weddings, and he's never sworn during a ceremony," Yu pressed. "Maybe he can do a reading or something?"

"No, do not let this man speak at our church. John cannot speak at our church because he's going to say something like 'shit.'"

John and Pat attended the wedding and were as proud as Yu's parents. And John didn't say shit.

It was because of Houston that I came to appreciate the suggestively leering emoji. Once, he sent me an unprecedented "I'm so fucking horny" while I was at work. Though I was not a sexting aficionado, I was pretty sure that responding with "It's 9:32 a.m. on a Tuesday. Calm down." would not have been well received. Fortunately, Apple had engineered me an effective exit strategy. With one character, a little yellow face with a subtle glance and a knowing smirk provided me with a silver bullet to dissipate the awkwardness caused by his unreciprocated sexual escalation.

155

Conversations with Chicago were quite the opposite. Disregarding any virtual foreplay, he plunged right into the deep end. I would tell him of my summer fitness goals and how I was blending salad leaves into my breakfast smoothies. He would tell me "veggies make your pussy taste good." I would send a good-morning selfie of me smiling in my carpool on the way to work. He would return my greeting with a soft-core porn meme depicting positions he wanted to do with me.

Whether it was my greater measure of physical attraction to Chicago, his unapologetic in-your-face personality, or some other factor entirely, I was considerably less taken aback by his continued messages than Houston's sole deviation from "normal." Though none of Chicago's and my exchanges sexually excited me, I appreciated his bold, aggressive nature. Opening one of his messages was like seeing a raunchy reality TV character slap a co-star. I would think *that's appalling!* while simultaneously reveling in the entertainment that is outlandish behavior.

– From a student essay

Tim Cavnar's first memories of John were hazy, but they had to do with "a lumberjack-looking guy with this huge dog stomping through the backyard" to talk to his parents. The Cavnars lived around the corner from the Rubadeaus, and John was, from the time Cavnar was old enough to remember, the Northside neighborhood's designated urban trapper.

It had started with a backyard skunk. Skunks must be trapped in cages they can't see out of. Otherwise, they'll spray you. John had learned this lesson the hard way. His trapping targets quickly expanded to include raccoons, groundhogs, and opossums. Pat tolerated this avocation despite opossums being, as she put it, "good for the yard in that they eat grubs that ruin the grass."

Unlike the skunks that John had executed gangland-style back in his days as a dogcatcher in Madison, he now transported his captors to what became known as the Rubadeau Nature Preserve, an undisclosed location a fifteen-minute drive from home and presumably crammed with generations of suburban-wildlife émigrés.

Summers were high season for urban trapping: John might capture three to four dozen animals during the warmer months. One summer alone, he trapped forty-eight raccoons. He expanded his collection of traps to include several different sizes and expanded his targets to squirrels and chipmunks. These rodents—all told more than a hundred of them over the years—were relocated to what he called the Kellogg Eye Center Chipmunk Hotel. He appropriated the bathroom scale to weigh his various captives and recorded the biggest specimens on a whiteboard he hung in the garage. Not all were on his most-wanted list.

Twice he found a blue jay waiting patiently for release. Another time there was a fox, "the coolest thing he ever caught," in Pat's estimation. This was also released posthaste, for foxes were beneficial to nature and gardens. The same with the neighbor's cat which had been attracted to the Thanksgiving-turkey carcass John had used as bait. The cat, as thoroughly sated as it was steeped in turkey grease, darted away. Sometime later, the neighbor, a Michigan professor, remarked that his cat had recently come home covered in some slimy toxic material.

"How very strange," John said.

Cavnar went on to attend the University of Michigan. He lived at home. His parents suggested he take John's class. But, as Cavnar recognized, "At that point in his career, it was basically impossible to get in because he was so famous." The bearded phenom had little influence on the registration process—despite, in Cavnar's estimation, wanting "to get his hands on me in part because my parents are strongly devout Catholics."

"You know how John likes to push people's buttons," Cavnar said.

By the start of the spring 2012 semester, Cavnar had already digested Richard Dawkins and was calling himself an atheist. John spotted him in an Angell Hall hallway and told him to come to his class—someone might drop after John explained how much work he expected.

Someone dropped. As the class progressed, John recognized Cavnar as an exceptional writer and sharp editor of his classmates' submissions. After the class had wrapped up, John asked his neighbor and now former student if he would be interested in being his amanuensis.

"Your what?" Cavnar asked.

This would be for a project, John explained. He wanted to finally finish a book he had been working on since 1977, his magnum opus. Various typists—in Constanța, in Lebanon, and in Ann Arbor—had digitized the handwriting from all those legal pads. John had spent the bulk of his summers rewriting and adding to it for years now. He had edited the big book himself a dozen times. Pat had read and edited an earlier draft and wasn't up for a rerun. It was time for another set of eyes. Those eyes would be paid ten bucks an hour. Would Cavnar be interested?

John had alluded to his literary life's work in class, repeating, as he habitually did, that he expected it to make him posthumously famous. Cavnar felt helping out on it would be a "huge honor to have him trust me with something really, really important to him." They had a deadline: John had written Cavnar a recommendation letter for a prestigious Princeton in Asia program in China; Cavnar would depart for it eleven months later in August 2013.

Cavnar had no idea what he was getting himself into. The book's contents included such diverse topics as critiques of the Catholic Church, rundowns of 1940s-era radio shows, analyses of 1970s-era breakfast cereals, assessments of famous court cases, the takeover of popular culture by the lowest common denominator, a thorough plumbing of masturbatory impulses, a torrent of literary references, and off-color jokes ("What do you call a gay, male dinosaur? A Megasoreass."). There were footnotes on footnotes on footnotes.

Adding to the challenge was that, in the persona of the persona of the author, John had made hundreds upon hundreds of "mistakes"— very few of them easy to spot—for his fictitious editor Clyde MacHound Sr. to correct in the footnotes. One example which, in the story, is part of a first-person reflection by the fictitious author of his thoughts as a guilt-ridden young teenager: "In ghastly musings and horrific nightmares, I reflected on the condition of my sin-defiled soul, and the prospect of the Stygian netherworld it would occupy unnerved me. I imagined my soul, bloated and decaying, breaking away from its millstone mooring at the bottom of the Styx."

The sentence is marked with footnote number 1,050. The footnote reads: "This entire metaphor is simply indefensible. Would any thirteen- or fourteen-year-old child have been that conversant in Greek mythology to imagine such a scene? (Editor's note)."

The editor's note is in turn marked with a small crucifix that references a footnote-to-the-footnote that begins with "I was, Professor MacAsswipe. And if I were, then there is no reason why my protagonist could not, at a similar age, also have acquired the same knowledge base . . . . (Fitzpatrick note)"—Fitzpatrick being John's fiction-writing alter ego whose fictional persona, Joseph Kelly, is the asylum-dwelling, novel-within-a-novel-writing protagonist *A Sense of Shame* revolves around.

Got that?

Pat told Cavnar: "This fucking book. I can't believe you're reading it."

John's magnum opus had been a sore point for more than a decade. Summers were sacrificed when Pat could still travel without having to lug oxygen concentrators around for sleeping—LAM would, they both knew, eventually demand that and more. Even when physically present, John was mentally elsewhere.

"When he's writing, he's writing. There's nothing else," Pat said. "You can't have a conversation. It's twenty-four hours a day. You can say, 'What do you want for dinner? Hamburger or chicken?' 'Burger' he'll say. That's about it. I'll be talking away, and I look at him, and he's glazed over. And it's always about the book."

The printed manuscript resembled a whitewashed cinder block. Cavnar took sections home, edited them, and returned with markups. He soon recognized a contemporary analog: "It's like a cracked-out *Infinite Jest* about Catholicism," he said, referring to the David Foster Wallace novel. "It demands so much from you to follow it and take it on his terms."

He had lots of suggestions for John, ideas which John typically ignored. Cavnar then invented what he called the Penis Rating Scale "based on how much of a dick he was being. One dick to five dicks. It gave him a lot of pleasure to just be viciously mocked," Cavnar said. "That's an interesting part of his psyche. On some level, he wants it to be effortless, beautiful prose, stunning everybody, great literature. He's incredibly ambitious. And on another level, he's an editor and critic and that voice comes out in Clyde MacHound: 'this is garbage; no one wants to read this shit.'"

They had arguments that would, as Cavnar put it, "descend into both of us being really pissed off with each other." A serious tiff about a footnote at one point led John to fire his young neighbor during an editing session: "Timmy, you have no idea what I'm trying to do here—get out! Just get out!"

A few hours later, John called to apologize and hire him back, "probably because he realized that he was fucked without me. There was no way somebody else was going to figure out this novel," Cavnar surmised.

They got it done. Cavnar flew off to China where he realized he loved to teach. He would come home three years later and enroll in a master's program in applied linguistics at John's alma mater in Madison, Wisconsin, to be followed by a PhD in second-language acquisition. "I get a lot of satisfaction and enjoyment out of the mentoring aspects of teaching and just getting to know my students," Cavnar said. "John's outlook as a teacher and mentor—someone who's extraordinarily supportive and funny—has played a huge role in my career trajectory and what I want to be as an instructor."

In early 2014, Bhavin Shah, a former student, footed the bill of more than $11,000 to have 250 copies of *A Sense of Shame* published. John sold them for $69.00, a nod to the risqué material therein. He vowed that it would be the last book he ever wrote. Posthumous fame, John was sure, would be his reward.

> In a way, I am my own seed, a
> small speck of life capable of
> becoming more. I was once suicidal.
>   It took a while to admit that
> fantasizing my own funeral wasn't
> exactly healthy, that picturing the
> eulogy my mother might give wasn't
> making me feel any more loved, that
> imagining the tears that might fall
> from the eyes of all those who knew
> me didn't make my relationships any
> more authentic, but I got there. I
> had lost myself down the spiraling
> drain of all the things I had
> wanted and didn't seem to get:
> things I believed I wasn't worthy
> enough to receive. All I wanted was
> someone to notice. I was nothing
> more than a wrecked car on the side
> of the highway, desperately waiting
> for someone to light up a flare.
>   But no one pulled to the shoul-
> der; that other car never came.

– From a student essay

Nina Bailey was a semester from graduation in 2007 when her son Ezra was born. She had started at Michigan with her twin sister Shianta; she wouldn't finish with her. Instead, Bailey moved to a house near Seven Mile Road and Mound Road on Detroit's east side, not far from the enclave of Harper Woods where she had grown up. She found a job with the U.S. Census Bureau's regional office in Detroit. As Ezra entered first grade in 2012, a second son, Eli, arrived. She and the boys' father broke up right around then. Bailey liked her job, and her bosses liked her enough to keep her on as a field supervisor working from home when the Detroit office closed. But she couldn't stop thinking about finishing up her English degree.

It wouldn't be easy. While the boys' father remained a part of their lives, Bailey was a single mom now. She would have to keep working and run the household on her own. Ann Arbor was an hour's drive away. She enrolled anyway.

In January 2014, seven years and two kids after she had left the University of Michigan, Bailey returned to get that degree. She landed in John's class by chance. In the graybeard strode, larger than life, spelunking through the etymology of the word "fuck," telling everybody they'd be working hard and it would be worth it.

Bailey was the only Black person in the class, the only mother, the oldest by years. Her parents, civil servants who worked with welfare recipients, had frugally raised four kids. Bailey again sat among the children of doctors and lawyers and Lord knows whom else—the elite, the privileged. She felt she had nothing in common with any of them.

Being a self-described introvert didn't help. Her first three-and-a-half years at Michigan had been strictly business: no parties, no football games, no social anything: she and Shianta had taken the Greyhound bus home most weekends. Now, with the boys ages 7 and 2 and living fifty miles away in Detroit, the main difference was that she was commuting four times a week rather than one. Her schedule: up at 6 a.m., get the kids ready and off to school and daycare, drive the hour to Ann Arbor, go to class, do Census Bureau work in the gaps between classes, drive the hour back home, pick the kids up, cook, do Census Bureau work, put the kids to bed, hammer through schoolwork until she fell asleep in the wee hours, repeat.

In John's class, she absorbed his grammar lessons, but, more importantly, she learned that making the private public and writing what you know—sharing one's unique experiences, perspectives, and voice—can bring greater readability, appeal, and impact. She had never considered doing such a thing much less felt the freedom to attempt it. Bailey also read and listened to the stories of her classmates: the struggles with substance abuse, with relationships, with coming to terms with where they had come from and where they were headed.

"It was interesting in a sense to learn how humans struggle, and you just don't see it," Bailey said. "We deeply got to know each other through these essays. When we had the conversations around the table, I could see myself as being more like them."

Bailey opened up, too, writing about the dilemma of raising her boys to believe that they possessed the same essential dignity as anyone else while knowing that the color of their skin put them in a different category in the eyes of far too many. The class potluck was the first college house party she had ever gone to. "It was like having everything that happens to everybody else in four years of college happen in one semester," she said. "Professor John," as Bailey calls the man, influenced her profoundly. "I can talk about my life and be able to do that without hesitation because he didn't teach with hesitation. I'm an overthinker about everything. It's okay to talk about yourself in the world and be yourself in the world."

When the semester ended, John introduced Bailey to Dan Varner. Varner had been a student of John's more than twenty years before and, like Bailey, had been the only Black student in the class. Back then, Varner had been impressed by the time and energy John spent on student papers—"I swear there was more ink from what he had written on it than there was from what I had typed for him"—and by his frankness and directness in "calling bullshit when he thought something was bullshit." John's deep interest in a paper Varner had written about a day in the life of a student of color sealed what would become a long friendship.

John had been happy to write Varner a law-school recommendation letter but had warned him that he'd hate the practice of law. A law degree was about money, John knew. Varner had confided in John that he really wanted to be an English teacher in Detroit.

John had told him: "Being a lawyer is not going to make you happy. Being a teacher will. Everybody thinks money will make you happy, but, in the end, it won't." Then he added: "I'm not gonna be the one who has to live with the results of the decisions you make. If you want to believe in God, believe in God; if you want to go into the army and kill people, go into the army and kill people; if you want to go be a lawyer, go be a lawyer. Scratch your itch—not my itch, not your parents' itch, not society's itch."

Varner got a full ride to Michigan's law school. He graduated, served as a clerk for NFL Hall of Famer and Minnesota Supreme Court Justice Alan Page, and joined a boutique firm in Detroit.

He lasted a couple of years. In 1996, he and a friend launched Think Detroit, a sports program for urban youth. The program grew and ultimately merged with the Detroit Police Athletic League; Varner took on leadership roles in other nonprofits. By the time John reached out to Varner about a student named Nina Bailey, he was the executive director of Excellent Schools Detroit. Varner had learned that, if John recommended someone, "This person's worth talking to. Period. No question. He has taught and mentored and coached so many people, I know he's a great judge of character and talent."

John had picked up on Bailey's passion for kids and, more generally, her passion for improving Detroit, where about half of all children lived in poverty. The three of them had lunch in Ann Arbor; sometime later, Bailey joined Varner's organization as a receptionist, a position that led her to another nonprofit and then to Greenlight Fund Detroit. There she looked for stories in data to understand where and how nonprofit investments were paying off. She was passionate about the work, she said, which wasn't something she had been expecting from a job.

"I wasn't thinking about my dreams and what I wanted. I was being a mother with kids. Now I'm on a path doing work closer and closer to what I want to do," Bailey said. John's class, she added, "changed the entire course of my life. I'm on a path people go to college for because of his course. His course was the college experience for me."

```
Down. Up. Down. Up.
You study the skin as you bob.
The dark, tan, rippling muscula-
ture. You wonder how many push-ups,
sit-ups, crunches, curls it takes
to get skin like this.
```

And you hate it — this horribly
beautiful skin.
   You hate the way it looks, the
way it feels, the way it smells.
You hate the way it twitches as
your tongue flicks across the
surface.
   You are repulsed, disgusted.
Down. Up.
   But the taste —
   The taste is what you hate the
most. You don't hate it; you de-
spise it. You loathe it because it
lingers. The smell, the sight, the
feeling — those fade. They are
swallowed up by inky night and
washed away by icy showers.
   But the taste —
   The taste stays with you. The
taste of a man lingers long after
the man disappears. It clings to
your tongue, your cheeks, the back
of your throat. You will try to
wash it away with moonlight and
Merlot.
   It won't.

— From a student essay

   The student essay the above excerpt came from won a writing
award. It also set in motion the series of events that led to John's firing.

11

No Joke

As flies are to wanton boys, are we to the gods. They kill us for their sport.

— Shakespeare

John described the work from which that final excerpt came as "One of the best essays I've received in forty-one years at the college level, the last thirty-one at Michigan. While the subject matter is perhaps a tad risqué, the writing is absolutely gorgeous—full of wonderful details to show excellent parallelism, superior and very mature diction, subtle use of leitmotiv, et cetera."

John wrote that in his nomination for a Granader Family prize for excellence in upper-level writing. The judges agreed with him. At the awards ceremony in April 2017, nominating professors and lecturers introduced the winners—two each representing sciences, social sciences, and humanities in the College of Literature, Science, and the Arts. John walked to the podium and surveyed the audience. There were about a hundred people assembled. He recognized a few faculty colleagues, but the crowd was mostly students, parents, and siblings of the six honorees. Some were just kids.

Five essays had already been recognized, the nominating professors and lecturers talking mostly about the content of the works—challenges facing refugees rejoining the medical field after resettlement, gender differences in students' ability to identify sexual assault, food insecurity among college students. These serious topics were discussed at length, and folks in attendance had been listening for well

over an hour already. John said, "Ladies and gentlemen, I thank you
so much for this award. Being as old as I am, I had no idea I was still
eligible for such an honor. But I accept it graciously, and I appreciate
being nominated for it. Thank you."

With that, he walked back to his seat and sat down. There was an
awkward silence of the sort that makes ten seconds feel like ten
minutes. Then John yelled, "Wake up, people! It's a joke!"

Amid murmurs and scattered chuckles, he walked back to the
podium and asked the actual nominee, a junior named Claire from his
English 425 course the previous semester, to join him at the podium.

He could have talked about the essay at that point, or, perhaps read
from this powerfully sad story about lack of self-esteem and a longing
for true love. But John couldn't have accessed those deeper themes
without exposing a thick overburden of sex. An excerpt couldn't have
avoided something like this: "In minutes, you hear it—the sad,
choking-turtle sound. He is there. A breath, and liquid squirts into
your mouth. All at once, then barely at all."

No way.

He improvised. It went more or less as follows.

"Many people don't know that Claire and I have been friends since
before she was born. I had actually dated her mother at one time. She
married somebody else; I married somebody else. But I feel like I'm
Claire's father. I mean, I did drive Claire's mother to the hospital when
Claire was born. I brought her to her christening where she got
indoctrinated into the Roman Catholic Church. I organized her first
birthday party—everybody loved that. She was so cute. And I could
see then that she was going to be the beauty she is today. And when
she went to kindergarten, I took her there, picked her up every day,
and took her home. We've just become such fast friends over the years.
And then, when she was in fifth grade, she was starting music lessons,
and I bought her a trumpet to help her along, so she didn't have to rent
one through the school. And in seventh grade, I remember, because
her mother was busy and her dad was working, we went to the store,
and we bought her first training bra. We've been so close."

While Claire's smile and subtle head shaking should have tipped
off those paying attention, John's delivery was convincing enough that

it wasn't totally clear that he was kidding. John continued, "I'm pleased to give her this check for $2,000—minus my 10% finder's fee—as this is one of the best papers I've read in forty-one years of teaching at the college level."

They sat back down, the event ended, and soon so did the semester.

A couple of weeks later, John was called in to meet with David Porter, the English Department chair. John walked up the stairs, said "Hello Huffy!"—his standard greeting for the receptionist named Huff, who had told John years earlier that he could nickname her thusly. Then, a few steps later, he asked an administrative assistant, "Wanna hug?" which she declined as she had for nearly twenty years. John answered "OK—you lose!" as he always did. John entered the chair's office and sat down. Porter explained that his colleagues had been unhappy about the Granader-prize improvisation.

"Well, it was fuckin' hilarious," John said.

"Yeah, well, your colleagues didn't think so," Porter said.

"My colleagues have no sense of humor. They're so straight and so uptight." John then explained what had happened. Would reading a passage about fellatio have been better? He couldn't believe he was being taken to task for it.

Porter, a soft-spoken specialist in the Chinese influence on England in the centuries leading up to about 1800, was in a tough spot. For the better part of two decades, the English Department chair's office had been occupied by a faculty member who had, typically out of a generosity of spirit, agreed to deal with the sorts of political headaches and administrative minutia that English faculty tend to run from. In exchange, the department chair got a lighter class load and the use of a weighty title for a few years. That meant that the department chair was at once the boss and a temporary caretaker who, generally, would have preferred to be working on his or her next publication. It was at moments such as these that the title's cost was most dearly paid.

Three of John's colleagues had complained about the incident, Porter explained. They had found John's behavior inappropriate and disrespectful.

"I think they're full of shit," John said.

Porter considered his response, then asked, "OK . . . but what are we going to do about it?"

He wouldn't get an answer. John stood, handed him a business card—that of an attorney, a former student named Eric Scheible—and told Porter he had to go to the airport to pick up Pat and then would undergo a partial knee replacement early the next morning. Then John stood and said, "I really like you as a person. But I told you: you're gonna make a lot of enemies when you become department chair. Remember that? And I don't want to be an enemy because I like you. But I can't talk about this right now."

And with that, John walked out.

Why, one might wonder, had John not offered at least a half apology? Or an understanding tone? Or an "I wasn't trying to offend you"? Or an "I'm sorry if my approach bothered them—that wasn't my intention"? Or an "I'll do better next time"? Any of these might have gone a long way on that May afternoon.

But then, why had John coated his office with thousands of student pictures? Why had he written probably 3,000 recommendation letters over his decades of teaching? Why had he taken to underlining the entirety of every student essay he read to ensure that he maintained focus? Because John was John, and John thought these were all good ideas—just as he thought handing the person who signs off on the English Department's hiring and firing decisions his pro bono lawyer's business card and abruptly walking out on the meeting was a good idea. It would prove to be not a good idea.

This wasn't the first time that complaints from colleagues had crossed an English Department chair's desk. An open office door seemed to John to be an invitation to walk in and chat. Sometimes it was; sometimes it wasn't. He called his friends in the department "assholes" or "fuckers" within collateral-damage earshot. A job candidate for a professorship had once been brought by John's office to check out all the photos. The visitor asked, "Do you have a martini bar in here, too?"

John responded, "No, it's a titty bar."

English faculty are not known for their happy-go-lucky ways—they are, by and large, bookworms: serious, analytically inclined people who are pursuing tenure or justifying it with serious publications. A lecturer who the day before winter break appeared with jangling bells, dreidels, and a strand of blinking Christmas lights nested in his beard (or for whom Pat had, before every Halloween, dyed his beard orange and added Velcroed-in jack-o-lantern eyes, nose, and mouth) was welcomed by many colleagues as a dose of levity.

However, others viewed him as an annoyance, a clown, or worse. That's all to say that the near-universal acclaim John enjoyed among his students did not extend to his colleagues. Perhaps his enormous popularity triggered resentment among less-beloved colleagues.

That said, Lincoln Faller, who chaired the English Department from 1999 to 2002, said he fielded no complaints about John, one of 140 lecturers and faculty at the time. Faller said John was "just considered a very popular teacher and very eccentric." Faller, who retired in 2013, recalled John's beard blinking away before the holidays and John asking him for hugs, which Faller was fine with giving.

"John always seemed to me to be on the edge, but he had such a large and enthusiastic student following," Faller said.

Curious as to whether subsequent English Department chairs had fielded complaints about John, I emailed Sidone Smith (chair from 2003 to 2009) and Michael Schoenfeldt (2010 to 2015). Smith responded, writing, "I'm not inclined to talk with you on the subject. It's been a long time and I have no notes to help my memory." Schoenfeld didn't respond at all. Porter, who took over as chair in 2015, declined to comment.

Also, a few months before, in January 2017, John had had a rare clash with a student. It centered around a "personal pronoun."

The English language has two sets of pronouns for people: he/him/his and she/her/hers. These work for most of us. But for a subset of us, these pronouns don't quite fit. A February 2017 *American Journal of Public Health* article estimates that about four in 10,000 people are transgender; the National Center for Transgender Equality, in turn, estimates that about two-thirds of these identify as either male or female. The rest, known as "genderqueer" or "nonbinary transgender," identify as neither exclusively male nor female. On the Ann Arbor campus of about 29,000 students, perhaps forty would fall into this last group.

In 2016, the University of Michigan formed a Pronoun Committee. It involved eleven professors, administrators, and lawyers from the Ann Arbor, Flint, and Dearborn campuses. For a year, they hashed out how to address the pronoun question. The result was that students could establish a "designated pronoun" through a new Gender Identity tab in their campus personal-information profile. The pronoun, if so designated, then landed in a new column on class rosters. This change went into effect in the middle of the fall 2016 semester.

The story announcing the Pronoun Committee's work in the *The University Record*—the university's newsletter for faculty, staff, and retirees—included a comment section. Among the twenty-four commenters, three were supportive: "So proud of my alma mater and employer! Much love and excitement for another step in the direction toward inclusiveness," wrote one. Most were less charitable.

"My pronoun is Mr. UM Sucks."

"My preferred pronoun is "Grand Sensei Mixmaster."

"My pronoun is Lord-Commander-of-the-Clit."

"How ridiculous this University is to bend to this baloney. I would refuse to call anyone 'Ze.' ["Ze" being a common gender-neutral pronoun.] How stupid."

John had missed all this. But in January of the following semester—winter 2017—a person in his class with a typically female name told him her personal pronoun would be "ve." So instead of "I'll go if she goes," it would be, "I'll go if ve goes." Others in the class chimed in and told John of the new pronoun policy. John checked the class roster and, indeed, there it was in a new "pronoun" column next to the student's name, student ID, major, and year in school: "ve."

John was a political liberal but a linguistic archconservative. He had, for example, long railed against the use of "they"—a plural pronoun—as a substitute for the cumbersome "he or she" or "s/he." Sentences like "Everyone [singular] can do as they [plural] please" drove him fairly nuts. More than two years earlier, a student had anonymously commented in John's post-semester evaluation, "The best course I've taken at this university. Everyone should take a course like this one during their time here. John will run into problems if he rejects the singular 'they' like he does, however, if a transgender person were to take this class."

And here ve was. John recognized a pedagogical opportunity. Off he went, explaining how gender representations in language needn't be taken literally: "Everyone agreed to the proposal to a man" and "Man can't live on bread alone" refer to all humanity regardless of gender; how it's not just English: the French word for "prostate" is the feminine *la prostate*, and the German word for "bra" is the masculine *der Büstenhalter*, examples he followed with a translation of the German joke that every woman needs a man because it's *der Büstenhalter*. Besides, in a setting such as his classroom, people soon enough use given names rather than pronouns, personal or otherwise. He was on a roll now, holding forth with examples and tangents for a solid twenty minutes. He wrapped up with his introduction of audience and purpose as keys to successful writing. In this case, the primary audience was John (and classmates were the secondary audience), and he expected them to adhere to his norms—just as, when these overwhelmingly privileged students graduated and left the liberal bastion of Ann Arbor with all its safe spaces and trigger warnings, they would have to adhere to the norms of employers in the real world.

"Are we clear?" John asked, finally.

"We're clear, but I insist on being a 've,'" ve said.

"But we talked about this for the last twenty minutes!" John said.

Ve looked at John with what he interpreted as a sneer. "This is nonnegotiable," ve said.

While passengers in his car are more likely to see it than his students, John has a temper.

"Why don't you nonnegotiate your ass out of my class," he suggested.

Out of his class ve and two friends walked.

The incident had been noted by March 31, 2017, when Porter sent John a letter to tell him the department's executive committee had voted to approve another five-year contract—John's seventh. The letter, though, was more scolding than congratulatory. It noted that the committee had been "deeply concerned regarding issues raised by a number of student comments in your course evaluations. In particular, the [committee] was concerned by allegations that language used in your classroom was felt to be racist, sexist, mocking, and dismissive, and contributed to an ongoing classroom climate that students find deeply uncomfortable." Porter then threatened disciplinary sanctions.

The committee's actual language rings rather differently: "In the years under review, our committee also found a few student comments that raised concern . . . . While such comments are numerically few compared to the overwhelmingly positive comments that constitute the majority, our committee encourages Dr. Rubadeau to attend to both the matter of favoritism (real or perceived) and to the fact that some of his comments are being taken as racist or sexist by his students."

Curious about these student comments, I dug into a five-inch-thick stack of student evaluation forms spanning John's Michigan career. He has often repeated that his numerical rankings related to "Overall, this was an excellent course" and "Overall, the instructor was an excellent teacher" were higher than any other teacher's over his thirty-one years of teaching in Ann Arbor. While neither I nor the Office of the Registrar can easily confirm this, John's prolonged, stratospheric appraisals would be tough to beat.

In ten semesters over the five years spanning 2012 to 2016, John taught 586 students, of whom 497 left anonymous comments in addition to numerical rankings. The comments were indeed "overwhelmingly positive." There were occasional criticisms: questionable time management (despite, as mentioned, John tasking a student to keep him on track, it was sometimes impossible to reel him in from what he called "tangents of discovery"); nebulous grading; too much of a focus on grammar at the expense of time critiquing essays; and perceived favoritism toward star students, repeat students, and athletes.

Just four students wrote comments related to the concerns Porter had emphasized in the renewal letter. The first one described having felt uncomfortable when John remarked about students' appearance or clothing. The second recalled John wondering whether a girl in a story the class had referred to were "well endowed." The third wrote, "While John at times can be inadvertently offensive or not politically correct, I know he is a good person with the best intentions." The fourth wrote his or hers after the fall 2013 semester three-and-a-half years earlier, and it ranked among the longest of any John had ever received. It went:

> *John is undeniably passionate and makes every single class period thoroughly engaging."* Later, the student continued, *"I was often offput and even offended by some of John's views regarding race and gender. I have no problem discussing these issues and am not squeamish, but the discussions did not make me (or other students with whom I spoke) feel safe. I have no problem with John expressing his own views about some things, but when he's using words like "bitch," "nigger," and "raghead" in class, it makes me uncomfortable. When I expressed my disagreement with John rather than engaging in discussion, he would often turn instead to mocking me or encouraging other students to voice their agreement with him. One girl who constantly voiced her opposition to John's sexist views was regularly dismissed as "feisty." I felt John spoke down to her. I think he really does love his students and means well, but when it comes to speaking in a way that makes students feel actively targeted and harassed, that's just not acceptable . . . . John needs to understand he makes students feel uncomfortable.*

I asked John about the various points raised. He never used the word "raghead," he said. "Nigger" he used in class now and again in the context of the word having particular force when quoting (and thereby more clearly defining) the sort of small-minded racist who would employ it—or as a means of explaining the concept of reclaimed language in which some African Americans use it as an endearing term among themselves. The word also came up when, to show the power of parallelism, mindful repetition, and the use of detail, the class reviewed Martin Luther King's "Letter from the Birmingham Jail."

John didn't shy from pointing out that the feminist movement reclaimed the word "cunt," either. "Bitch?" Of course, though not in relation to a student in the room—he only called people "bitches" behind their backs.

There's a difference between pointing out sexist and racist language—which John did routinely—and being a sexist or racist. Was John mocking or kidding around? Was this student a discriminating analyst or a nitpicking snowflake? One would need more perspective, ideally gathered years earlier, to sort that out. The committee itself had recognized that: "While we do not have the context in which such comments were made (were they made directly, or were they in reference to a quotation from a work under discussion?), we do think it important for Dr. Rubadeau to be alert to the ways in which students process such language."

Rather than reflect the tone of those who had actually evaluated John, Porter had used the vague "a number of" to enumerate the comments of fewer than 0.7% of John's students over the past five years. Then, to support an argument of chronic classroom misbehavior, the department chair built his case almost exclusively on the criticisms of a single student commenter from eight semesters ago.

It's worth noting that the "other students" with whom the commenter had apparently spoken had rather different takes on the experience, based on the fourteen of the twenty in the class who also left comments. They read like the vast majority of them had since 1987: "This course was taught extremely well"; "John is an incredible teacher"; "This course was interesting every day, even when we were talking about boring grammatical shit"; "We learned about much more than just English. Thank you!"; "Literally the BEST class I have taken at this university"; "John's got a reputation for being the best English professor ever for a reason"; "THE BEST"; "This course is the best English course I have ever taken"; "This was the best course I have

taken throughout my entire career at the University of Michigan";
"Excellent. I've learned the most in the class over any other through
the quality of instruction"; "John is amazing. I learned so much not
only about the English language but also about life—how to approach
each day and to live positively"; "John is a marvelous and engaging
instructor"; "Very awesome instruction in this course. John is great."

What's clear is that, by the time John cut short the training-bra
discussion and walked out of Porter's office in May 2017, he already
had a target on his back. Whether because Porter was bending to
pressure from a small group of joint English-and-Women's-Studies
faculty appointments that one source described as "some very strong,
aggressive women who really found a lot of fault with John's devil-
may-care attitude," personal animosity, or something else, Porter set
the wheels in motion to get John out. The chair would choose the
wrong vehicle.

12

Fired

Oh God, if there be a God, save my soul, if I have a soul.
— Joseph Ernest Renan

On July 13, 2017, John was back in another meeting with the English Department chair David Porter. This time Pamela Heatlie, the Title IX coordinator for the University of Michigan's Office of Institutional Equity, was also present. The OIE's self-described role was to "support diversity, inclusiveness, equal access, equitable treatment, cultural understanding, and the prevention of discrimination and harassment" at the university.

The meeting's topic: personal pronouns.

John brought along Eric Scheible, a former student who was now a partner with a suburban Detroit law firm whose name consisted of six names with fourteen syllables. Twenty-seven years before, Scheible had taken John's class as a college sophomore. He had come away with a B grade—"I'm still pissed at him about that," he told me—and a nickname unsuitable for mixed company.

Scheible the law partner was clean-shaven from crown to chin, quick to laugh, and direct in the way of the litigator he was. Scheible the student had sported a full head of hair and had still been feeling out the situation when, during the vocabulary-enrichment portion of the class, Rubadeau had asked a fellow student named Rob Dwortz to look up the word "shithead" in the *The American Heritage College Dictionary* to illustrate the difference between vulgar slang and offensive slang.

John had previously bequeathed Dwortz with the nickname "fuckin' Dwortz." That name had stuck to the point that, by the time Scheible told me this story over lunch at a Bloomfield Township restaurant, "even our mutual friends call him 'fuckin' Dwortz. 'They're going to see 'fuckin' Dwortz this weekend.'"

Scheible's and Dwortz's acquaintance had been limited to a few weeks of Rubadeau class sessions as Dwortz paged to the definition. Dwortz then ignored "*n. Vulgar Slang.* A highly contemptible or objectionable person" and instead pretended to read: "Shithead. Noun. Definition: Eric Scheible."

"People are falling out of their chairs laughing," Scheible recalled. "Rubadeau thinks it's the funniest thing ever. And from that day forward, I was 'Shithead Scheible.'"

John had written him recommendation letters for law school and a clerkship, and they had stayed in touch. John had asked him to sit in on the meeting with Porter; Scheible had driven the hour to Ann Arbor. When he got there, he told John, "We're here to listen. We don't know anything except they called a meeting, and you made a stink that you wanted your lawyer there. So let's go listen."

The meeting was Heatlie's. She declined to comment, but it went more or less as follows. She spent first few minutes praising John's stellar student reviews, his Golden Apple award, and other such accolades. John, unsure of where the meeting was headed, leaned over and whispered in Scheible's ear, "Shithead, what's she buttering me up for? Is she gonna fuck me or fire me?"

Scheible kicked him under the table.

When the meeting's true purpose emerged, and John took up the topic of "ve," Heatlie didn't quite hear him at first. She asked, "Did you say 'ze'?"—"ze" being a more common nonbinary transgender personal-pronoun alternative.

"No, it was 've,'" John said, "as in 'vulva' or 'vagina.'"

Scheible kicked him under the table again.

Why not "'ve' as in 'Victors valiant'"? But this was John, and this was John's way of showing what he thought of the meeting.

Heatlie—unperturbed, as Scheible recalled—then explained to John more or less the following. This millennial generation was unlike any other since the baby-boomer generation that was here in the 1960s. They were transforming the campus in every sense of the word: in terms of sexuality, in terms of technology, in terms of openness. John would need to adapt or be left behind. She told him she understood his resistance from the standpoints of grammar and applicability in the real world. But the university had a personal-pronoun policy, and it was part of John's job to respect it.

John wasn't apologetic, but he said he understood the policy and would, henceforth, honor it. Scheible felt that the meeting had gone well.

The first day of the fall 2017 semester, John announced to his classes that pronoun selection was up to the individual student, not up to him. One asked John to call him "nabob of naughtiness," to which he briefly complied before mastering the student's name.

By then, the OIE was quietly investigating the senior lecturer. OIE investigator David Baum told John about it in a December 13, 2017, email that read, in part, "Several members of the University have come to our office with concerns that you may have engaged in behavior that potentially violates the University's Sexual Harassment Policy (see spg.umich.edu/policy/201.89-0) and its Discrimination and Harassment policy (see spg.umich.edu/policy/201.89-1)." Baum requested two meetings, the first on January 8, 2018.

Scheible drove back to Ann Arbor on a cold day to join John in a hot little room in the university's Administration Building on State Street. There, Baum and Alexandra Matish, a human-resources associate director who was helping Baum with the investigation, awaited them. Baum and Matish walked through allegations of a half dozen women. Scheible listened as they described one witness relating how John had pointed out a miniscule garland of "cocks" on a Christmas sweater depicting copulating deer; the witness also explained how John had, over many years, asked for hugs that she had always declined. Another witness had taken offense at John popping into her shared office space and asking, "Are you the Turkish girl?" despite her not being Turkish; another noted John saying, after a handshake upon first meeting, something to the effect of "I love a woman with a strong grip." Another, an Indian woman, took issue with John's confusing her with another Indian woman. Another noted John swearing in a hallway. Another viewed with suspicion John's offering her dog biscuits for her dog, offerings which had been accepted for well over a decade without apparent concern.

Scheible couldn't quite believe it. "Under Michigan law, this wasn't anything I'd spend more than two seconds on," he told me. None of it was teacher-student. None of it was threatening or pervasive. None of these people were reporting to John, so there was no exploitation of power. They were coworkers—some not even English Department people—in an environment where coworkers rarely interacted. Their jobs were to work with students and do their research and publishing.

"This is the kind of stuff we're talking about? When he's got the highest scores in all the student-evaluation rankings, the Golden Apple, and everything else?" Scheible told me. "So I started thinking, 'They're looking to broom him.'"

Scheible asked for a written copy of the accusations; Baum and Matish refused, saying there would be a written report later. As Scheible and John walked back out into the January cold, Scheible said, "There's more coming. I think it's bullshit, you think it's bullshit, but they're watching you. Take that for what it's worth."

Meanwhile, events even further beyond John's control were working against him. On October 5, 2017, *The New York Times* published an investigative piece by Jodi Kantor and Megan Twohey, "Harvey Weinstein Paid Off Sexual Harassment Accusers for Decades." Five days later, *The New Yorker* posted to its website Ronan Farrow's investigation into Weinstein. On October 15, a friend of a friend of actress Alyssa Milano had tweeted that "If all the women who have been sexually harassed or assaulted wrote 'Me too' as status, we might give people a sense of the magnitude of the problem." Milano then retweeted that email with the comment, "If you've been sexually harassed or assaulted write 'me too' as a reply to this tweet."

Fifty-three thousand people left comments by the next evening, and the hashtag "#MeToo was tweeted nearly a million times within forty-eight hours. While the use of the term "me too" dated to a 2007 campaign by gender-equity advocate Tarana Burke, it caught fire just as John was being investigated. By late December—when *Time* magazine featured "The Silence Breakers" including Milano, Burke, and several others as their Person of the Year—hundreds of people, overwhelmingly men, had been outed as sexual harassers or worse. Allegations had emerged from all over the map: the diverse realms of entertainment, media, science, industry, gastronomy, finance, government, politics—even libraries and children's publishing had their real or purported sexual harassers. Some reports were new; some were decades old; some made sense: the U.S. Equal Employment Opportunity Commission estimated that three-quarters of sexual-harassment cases went unreported.

Another development loomed over University of Michigan leadership. Larry Nassar, a Michigan State University and USA Gymnastics team doctor, was on trial for dozens of counts of sexual assault over decades. On January 24, 2018, Nassar was sentenced to forty to 175 years. The day after that, MSU President Lou Anna Simon resigned. Fears of a massive financial hit would prove well founded: MSU later agreed to a $500 million settlement for hundreds of Nassar's victims. The University of Michigan had no intention of enabling the next Nassar.

On March 8, 2018, John again aborted a meeting with Porter—this time Dominick Fanelli, a university labor-relations representative and lawyer, was to sit in. John was solo but intended to record the conversation. When Fanelli didn't give permission (though under Michigan law, John could have secretly recorded it anyway), John said, "Fuck you!" to Porter and Fanelli and walked out.

"When people are really doing something wrong, and you know inherently that it's wrong or evil, it's such a marvelous feeling to let loose with a 'Fuck you!' It's like the petcock releasing all of the steam," John explained to me later. "It's release—complete release. And you can't do it very often because, you know, you'll get fired from every job. There has to be a reason for it, and it has to be an ethical reason, and you have to have a moral spine and backbone."

That sense of release would be short-lived. A week later, Porter sent John an email with many bullet points regarding behavior that he expected to be changed, including seven prescriptions as narrow as "before addressing colleagues in their offices, you will need to knock and request permission to enter; absent a prior acquaintance, you will also need to introduce yourself." The missive also instructed John to "address all faculty and staff colleagues in the department by their given names" and "avoid engaging in unsolicited physical contact with others and asking others to engage in physical contact with you." More broadly, Porter said John needed to "observe high standards of professional decorum in all interactions with faculty, staff and students." Porter mentioned no consequences should John fail to observe all this. Though John objected to them all, thinking them downright silly, he made a point of addressing them top to bottom.

On April 23, 2018, a few days after *The New York Times* team and Farrow shared the Pulitzer Prize for Public Service Journalism, John was back meeting with Porter and Fanelli. Scheible wasn't with John this time. Instead, he was joined by Kirsten Herold, the vice president of the Lecturers' Employee Organization representing 1,600 lecturers across the university's three campuses, and her colleague Moe Fitzsimons. John hadn't thought much about the lecturers' union besides occasionally grousing about the 1.33% of his gross pay that went for dues. Employment-related disputes had to go through the union.

Herold had known John for years. Her husband Niels, now a tenured Shakespeare scholar at Oakland University, had been a visiting assistant professor at Michigan in the late 1980s and early 1990s and had become friends with John. Herold herself had landed in Ann Arbor in 1986. Born in Aarhus, Denmark, she had graduated from high school and stretched a gap year into three, working as an *au pair* in the United States and Berlin. She met a guy from Maine and moved there. She attended and graduated from Colby College where, having worked part-time in the administrative offices, she learned, "What everybody cares about is office space. That was a small place; The University of Michigan is a very vast place. But some things aren't that different."

She told me all this over lunch in Ann Arbor. We ate outside on an afternoon in July. Herold struck me as a person who looked a decade younger than her sixty years, was pleasantly direct, and seemed mildly entertained by whatever chapter of the endless story of human folly one might be discussing at a given moment.

Herold earned an English PhD and became an English Department lecturer in 1992. In the early 2000s, she happened upon the movement to establish a lecturers' union. The English Department in particular seemed to take umbrage at the idea. "People said, 'You're not a real union.' We said, 'We're not coal miners. But we're underpaid; we have no health insurance in the summer, no raises, no job security.'" She paused and continued, "They really just wanted to keep doing what they were doing—which was whatever they pleased."

For a few years after the union formed in 2004, her end-of-the-semester reviews always included some issue with her teaching, an issue which she would address only for something else to come up next time around. At one point, a supervisor reprimanded her for making a racist statement. Her transgression: she had explained to students that the goal of college-level writing is to enable the expression of complexity and nuance because, as she had put it, "The world's pressing issues are rarely simple matters of black and white."

In 2010, her contract was not renewed—a de facto firing. *The Michigan Daily* noted that her dismissal coincided with a new union-bargaining round which she was involved in; the timing looked a lot like retribution. The publicity led to a short-term gig in the university's Career Center after which Herold landed a lecturer contract with the School of Public Health, where she still teaches: the union job was, and is, part-time. She had seen enough over the years, though, to recognize that John was in trouble. The #MeToo movement clearly was working against him, too.

Sexual harassment was a real problem, Herold recognized, and a place such as the University of Michigan provided fertile ground for it. Professors there were often high-powered—the sorts from whom a recommendation letter could make a career or a dubious assessment could ruin one. "There's lots of potential there—the combination of powerful, entitled men and young people, some of whom are very lost. Sometimes they're lost; sometimes they want sexual adventure" she said. "Power plus older men and young women—it's not always that way, but it often is—it's not a good combination."

Some cases were clear-cut, but many weren't, and she had been seeing a lot more of the latter. John's fit among those, and, given her personal experience with the bearded lecturer, she was skeptical that he belonged under investigation.

Before that April 23 meeting, Herold told John that his extraordinary success as a teacher, his long tenure, and his lofty appraisals by thousands of students meant nothing now. The English Department and the university were in the driver's seat.

John showed up late, stormed in angry, called Fanelli an asshole, and in general showed his disdain for the proceedings. He had a nasty black eye from losing his balance (vertigo—a new development) and bonking his head on a bedpost.

"My God, John, what happened to you?" Porter asked.

"Same thing that happened to the last guy who insulted me," John said. "If you think this looks bad, you should see what this guy looked like. He could barely walk away."

John settled down, and they reviewed the draft document containing both the allegations and John's responses. Porter also levied new accusations of John asking for unrequited hugs and using nicknames. These had to do with the same administrative assistants he greeted on the way into Porter's office nearly a year earlier: he asked for the hug from the admin who ritually refused, and he said "Hello Huffy," as always, to the woman named Huff. These new transgressions had, in fact, been reported earlier that very day. Porter also discussed an incident related from a graduate student regarding "highly sexualized comments regarding pornography."

John had apparently, a week before, waited in a hallway to ask a close friend and department staffer a question as the graduate student, a young guy, went on and on about art with the staffer. John, not known for his patience on his mellowest days and bored with what he considered a dilettantish summary, finally butted in and said, "Excuse me, but, you know this is all very interesting, but I myself, I just prefer to turn on porno flicks and look at pussy."

This despite John having, as he told me with what I assume was at least some exaggeration, "never looked at porno flicks in my life."

The OIE report—which is, along with other documents referenced for these paragraphs, available on the website accompanying this book—was sent out on April 30, 2018. Its eighteen pages contained more detail about the accusations John had now heard about in two meetings.

Witness 1, an associate professor in the department since 2003, indeed brought up the ugly Christmas sweater featuring copulating deer that John had worn a single time five years earlier in December 2013. (John had long since given it away—to a female student who loved it.) He had, she said, asked her to "look at the cocks" and exclaimed "They have cocks!" They have cocks!" She then described his requests for hugs in 2013 and 2014 when stopping by her office. By 2015, she had asked him to stop asking her for hugs, which he did before apparently forgetting by September 8, 2016, on which exact date Witness 1 recalled John having asked her for several hugs, describing her as "so huggable" and giving her "an appraising inspection from head to toe." She then stopped by to talk to a colleague, identified as Witness 7, during which conversation she said John brushed her back with his hand. Witness 7 did not corroborate this, and John denied it—as well as having anything remotely approaching a physical interest sufficient to spur an "appraising inspection." He also noted that both he and Witness 1 were wearing jackets at the time. Using the legalese "respondent" for John, the report continues that his behavior

> "makes [her] extremely uncomfortable" and that she feels his behavior that day "was lewd and, because of previous conversations [she had] had with [Respondent], aggressive." She added "because he was fully aware of my feelings against requests for hugs, he was intentionally demeaning me; the fact that he considered his request with obvious ogling, pursuit, and actual touching, suggests that he knowingly sought to harass me."

Witnesses 2 and Witness 3 were graduate students, one pursuing a PhD in History; the other, in Comparative Literature. They were officemates. Witness 2 recalled that, on September 12, 2017, "an older white man with a white beard whom she did not know standing in her office." John, who asked "Are you the Turkish girl?" The report continues "Witness 2 was bothered by the fact that Respondent assumed she was from a foreign country because her skin is brown and also because he referred to her as a 'girl.'" There's more, but that's the essence. She reported the interaction to her supervisor—who ran the English Department Writing Program and also happened to supervise Witnesses 3.

Witness 3, who is in fact Turkish and whom John had confused for Witness 2, described John walking into her office during office hours on September 7, 2017, and asking where she was from. He offered to introduce her to a colleague whose wife was Turkish. (A friend of John's, knowing his familiarity with being a cultural outsider from his years in Europe, had suggested that he reach out, John told me later.) John and Witness 3 chatted a bit and then John left. A few days later, on September 12, Witness 3 and a classmate were standing in an Angell Hall hallway trying to find a classroom, she told investigators. John happened to walk by, stopped, asked what they were looking for, and pointed them in the right direction. Then she overheard him say to a male professor down the hall, in a joking tone, something to the effect of "Where the fuck do you think you're going?" or "What the fuck do you think you're doing?"

Witness 4 was a lecturer who had been with the university since 2012 and had been, according to the OIE report, "appalled" by John's "training bra" comment at the writing-award ceremony. She took issue with John introducing himself, shaking her hand, and saying "I love a woman with a strong grip." John told her he was looking for her officemate, a close friend of his, to tell him that John was nominating him for "Department Asshole." (John told me later that his exact words were "the very prestigious Department Asshole Award.") She perceived John to be looking down her shirt. She described accompanying John to his office at his request to check out the floor-to-ceiling photo gallery, which she described to investigators as "very weird." She then recounted to investigators a joke John had apparently told a male colleague—Witness 4 had heard this secondhand—that involved John saying "fucking sheep." (The joke's punchline is, in fact, "tupping sheep," a Shakespearean term.)

"Witness 4 described her interactions with Respondent as 'uncomfortable,'" the report says.

Witness 5, an assistant professor of English since 2014 and an Indian woman of color, viewed as "aggressive" John's calling her "Aliyah," which was not her name but that of another assistant professor and Indian woman of color in the department whose name was, in fact, "Aliyah."

Witness 6, a full professor of English who had been with the department since 1999, took issue with John having offered her dog biscuits, as had been the case on and off for the past fifteen years or so. This had started during an Ann Arbor power outage during which she had brought her kids and dog to work. What Witness 6 first saw as an act of friendship between two dog lovers "slowly began to become tedious, as he would hand her a biscuit at inopportune times, such as when she was on her way to teach." Perhaps seven years back, she had asked John to stop (John disputed this), but John kept offering dog biscuits on roughly a monthly basis. Four or five years earlier, John had even thrown a dog biscuit toward her in a hallway. Another time, the plastic bin attached to the wall outside her office was halfway filled with about thirty dog biscuits. The report continues,

> "Since this past fall, about the time the #MeToo movement started, she says she has stopped looking at him or acknowledging his presence wherever possible . . . . She says that Respondent's persistent behavior feels to her like a "weird, sexist power trip." She adds that "[a]s a former Director of Undergraduate Studies, as a tenured professor, and as a woman, I seem to irritate or provoke him. Handing off this biscuit to me as if I am his own pet, in need of his reward, bizarrely expresses, and placates, his own issues with women, and perhaps with women in authority."

Baum and Matish's report concluded that "the preponderance of evidence" established that John's behavior was, despite the general vacuousness of that preponderance and John's point-by-point spoken and, later, written rebuttals, "sufficiently persistent and pervasive as to have created a sexually harassing hostile environment." This is, as we'll see, a gross misinterpretation of the state and federal laws and subsequent courtroom interpretations from which the University of Michigan's sexual-harassment policy was derived—and to which that policy must adhere.

The investigators themselves seem to have recognized the limits of their case. "Action should be taken to ensure that Respondent does not repeat similar behaviors, so that those with whom Respondent interacts can enjoy a nondiscriminatory, respectful, inclusive and welcoming environment," they concluded.

Porter had something else in mind. On June 27, he cited the report as well as John's "porno" interaction, having called Huff "Huffy," having asked the admin for a hug on the eve of the April OIE meeting as evidence of "your continued inappropriate and unprofessional behavior within the Department."

"In order to protect our staff from your continued harassment, inappropriate sexual behavior, and derogatory forms of address, the Department has chosen to move forward with a Notice of Intent to Terminate Appointment," Porter wrote.

After thirty-one years of exceptional service, and in the darkness of the academic summer, John was being fired.

13

Retired

The graveyards are full of indispensable men.
                    — attributed variously

Eric Scheible had spent a gorgeous day with the families of old friends kayaking in the upper reaches of Michigan's Lower Peninsula. It was the Fourth of July weekend, and Harbor Springs bustled with vacationers. This was neither the time nor the place he had envisioned pacing a parking lot in a heated conversation with a University of Michigan lawyer on his cell phone, but there he was.

"You've got to do better than this," he told the attorney. "You're carving a guy out who's been there for thirty years? And you're not offering him any money? And I can tell you right now: this thing's going to blow up."

"We're not afraid of any media pushback," the attorney told him. "We think we made the right decision."

Scheible was not wont to yell when it came to work. He made an exception now—in part because he was mad; in part because, as he told me later, "I wanted them to know what they were doing was flat-out wrong."

"Right now, you're not even giving John anything to think about," Scheible hollered. "You put fifty on the table, now he's got a decision to make, and I have to start making recommendations. Right now, my recommendation is, 'Don't do it.'"

Porter intended to fire John during the Fourth of July holiday week. The department chair and university officials held a perfunctory meeting with John and representatives from the lecturers' union on Monday, July 2, to rehash the accusations and dismiss John's defenses. The official termination would fall on Friday, July 6. Scheible pushed back, and the process stretched out another month, with John's new termination date set for August 3, 2018. This timing still worked from the university's perspective: just as long as the process was over before the summer break—which had started before that April 23 meeting and would continue into August—ended and students came back to complicate matters.

Students attempted to complicate matters either way. John's typist Parker Procida launched an online petition that quickly gathered 680 signatures. She also sent out a note to John's former students explaining the firing and suggesting they write University of Michigan President Mark Schlissel to ask him to reconsider. Over the next few weeks, students sent Schlissel 129 letters, many of them cc:ing Andrew Martin, the College of Literature, Science, and the Arts Dean; Porter; and others. All the students received boilerplate responses from university spokesman Rick Fitzgerald. These were so similar that the University of Michigan Chief Freedom of Information Officer Patricia Sellinger kindly suggested that I save the money and she save the staff time it would take to amass and review them. And so it went like this:

Dear President Schlissel:

. . . Forgive me, but I can't put this any differently: John gave a shit about me. Not about my grade, not about my future career, not about his reputation. He just cared about me. And every single other student he has ever had. How many classes did I take in those four years? How many professors did I encounter? How many office hours did I attend? Countless. But John is the only professor who left a profound and lasting impact on me, and who made me feel seen.

John once docked me an entire letter grade on an essay for forgetting to paperclip the papers as instructed. It left me near tears, but it was a bold lesson that I've shared in every job interview since: "I won't miss a detail." John's class connected me to classmates I never would have pursued relationships with, that are now friendships I maintain to this day in Manhattan.

All that said, the thing I like best about John is that I really didn't like him all that much. I didn't like that he was dismissive of my or any religious beliefs. I didn't like that for someone so intelligent, he swore often and could be quite crass. I even didn't really like how cluttered and chaotic his office was. But that is the most important lesson of John's teachings: you will encounter people all over this earth that you may not like or agree with, or who do things differently than you, or who perform the same job as you but in a way you may not understand. Even so, you absolutely must respect those people. You must gather with them, listen to them, support them, and learn from them . . . .

To which Fitzgerald answered:

Thank you for your email message to University of Michigan President Mark Schlissel. He has asked me to respond.

It is university policy not to discuss personnel matters. Our approach is designed to respect the privacy of our employees.

We can tell you that the university takes the termination of any employee very seriously and in each case these matters are carefully considered.

Dear President Schlissel:

. . . By this time, I'm sure you've received numerous emails from former students on behalf of Dr. John Rubadeau. I took John's Advanced Essay Writing class my last semester of college while I was also in my last trimester of pregnancy. It was a very difficult time for me emotionally, physically, and psychologically as I was about to be a college graduated single mom off to take on the world. I got weird looks from people while walking around on campus with my big belly, felt more than a little excluded by my friends, and overall needed some support and sensitivity.

John is not a sensitive guy, by any means, but this big, over-the-top, goofy guy said something to me that I will never ever forget. It was the

191

end of the semester, and I was going to give birth any day. He said to me again, "Congratulations! I'm just so excited for you." Rather than do my usual smile and nod, I replied, "How can you possibly be excited for me? I'm about to be a single mom. Everyone says congratulations, but what they mean is thank-god-it's-not-me." He looked at me astonished and said, "You made the decision to have this baby and give it a wonderful home. It was a good choice. You're a good woman, you'll be a good mom, and to hell with what anyone else thinks. Own it."

So I have. I have lived my life by those words. I made a decision, I knew it was the right one, and I owned it . . . .

Thank you for your email message to University of Michigan President Mark Schlissel. He has asked me to respond . . . .

Dear President Schlissel:

I was appalled to hear about your decision to dismiss Dr. John Rubadeau, one of the most talented and beloved professors to have ever taught at the University.

Dr. Rubadeau has changed the lives of countless students, including mine. Years ago, I arrived in the United States as a teen-aged refugee from a war-torn country. I spoke little English but dreamed of attending a top law school, an aspiration most people considered unrealistic. Today, I am one of the leading regulatory lawyers in the U.S. and the world. Dr. Rubadeau taught me to write with impact and humor and instilled in me the confidence to pursue the impossible.

But Dr. Rubadeau is not just an extraordinary teacher; he is indeed one of the kindest people I know. Dr. Rubadeau has sacrificed a lifetime of his personal, "off-the-clock" time and dedicated it to his students. He has taught young people not just to write properly, but to write sensibly, eradicate sexist language, and use the power of words and grammar to promote justice and fair treatment. It is then perhaps not surprising that Dr. Rubadeau has been a champion for women and minorities long before social media and the Me Too movement. It is most shocking and hypocritical that a professor who dedicates his career to using the English language to promote diversity and affect change is dismissed by a leading university for the mere use of "colorful language" or teaching methods that other professors may dislike . . . .

Thank you for your email message to University of Michigan President Mark Schlissel. He has asked me to respond . . . .

Dear President Schlissel:
. . . John facilitated an open forum for his students to express the things they could not share with others in their lives and taught us about not only English grammar and writing brilliant essays, but also about how to live our lives after college by going after things that set our souls on fire. John created a safe space for us that grew rare, profound friendships between classmates. I wrote my essay on the sexual harassment I experienced in my life which was met only with respect, gratitude, and open arms. John applauded my essay, shared it with the rest of his students that school year, and claimed it to be an important subject we could all learn from. He helped me become a much better writer, a more confident writer, and a better advocate for social change with my writing . . . .

Thank you for your email message to University of Michigan President Mark Schlissel. He has asked me to respond . . . .

Good evening:
I am contacting you as a former student of the brilliant John Rubadeau. I was lucky enough to have him for English 125 and he was, by far, the best professor I have had to date. As a freshman who felt a bit lost at a huge university, John helped me to feel like an important member of the UM community. He transformed my writing and instilled in me a love of education that I try to pass on to my students as a middle-school educator. I attempt to emulate his way of connecting individually with each of his students. Because of John's unique style of teaching, I was inspired to become an educator and attempt to make a difference in the lives of my students as he did for me and countless others. When my sister recently visited John on campus, he immediately

asked about me and my best college girlfriend by name—this after not having seen or spoken to me since I graduated in 1994. His style of teaching may be slightly unorthodox, but that is precisely what connects him to his students and inspires them to push themselves to do better and be better. Firing John is a disservice to the current and future students of the University. I hope that you will reconsider your decision.

Thank you for your email message to University of Michigan President Mark Schlissel. He has asked me to respond . . . .

Dear President Schlissel:

Undoubtedly, John is a treasure forged from blinding gold. His classes weave the rarest thread of intellectual curiosity, ineffable bravery, and unbridled honesty into his students. These lessons, these values, these experiences are all immeasurable in worth . . . . My own life would not be the same without this man. John has given me the courage, confidence, and wisdom to achieve endeavors meaningful to myself. His time, essence, and impact mean more to me than I am capable of putting into words. I shan't forget him or his classes for the rest of my days . . . . John is something we each so rarely see in our lives. I beg you not to deprive us of John, and I implore you not to deprive John of us.

Thank you for your email message to University of Michigan President Mark Schlissel. He has asked me to respond . . . .

Dear President Schlissel:

I majored in computer science, but the best class I took at Michigan was John's English 325 class "Essay Writing." I learned a lot about grammar and communication, of course, but it was the best class because of the incredible community John built within his classroom. It taught empathy and about the human condition. John's class was an amazing space where students felt comfortable and volunteered to bring forward and talk about being an immigrant, discovering that he or she is LGBTQ, having an abortion, just being lost. I wrote about a pain that

194

I held deep about my father dying from cancer; it was deeply cathartic . . . . We want more educators like John at the University, they're rare. If these allegations are true, then sure, fire him and stone him in a public square; the John Rubadeau I know would approve.

Thank you for your email message to University of Michigan President Mark Schlissel. He has asked me to respond . . . .

Dear President Schlissel:
. . . John is better than the allegations. Even if the allegations can be characterized as his faults, he is better than his faults. Are you not better than your faults, President Schlissel? Are we not all better than our faults? This betterment is what binds us as a university, as a body. We are all better than our faults, and if we cannot look at one another and see the good beyond the fault, then there can be no room for grace to improve us as a University and, in the crucible that we are currently facing in America, as a nation . . . .

Thank you for your email message to University of Michigan President Mark Schlissel. He has asked me to respond . . . .

Hello President Schlissel:
. . . In John's classes, I, of course, learned things like comma placement, whether or not adverbs take hyphens, and that using "like" as anything other than a simile was complete idiocy.
More than that, though, I was taught the importance of listening to myself. That what we learned in the classroom was to equip us in meaningful ways, but that the most meaningful takeaway was learning how to live. I pursued a graduate degree and a big move out to Denver from Ann Arbor three years after graduation for several reasons, but one of those reasons was John's voice in my head saying, "scratch your itch." When someone challenges you to live meaningfully and deliberately, to take ownership of your life, you listen up. And I am so glad I did . . . .

Thank you for your email message to University of Michigan President Mark Schlissel. He has asked me to respond . . . .

Dear President Schlissel:

As I'm sure you know, John was recently fired from UM, essentially for not being sufficiently politically correct. Some of John's behavior can certainly be interpreted as vulgar, crass, or inappropriate—of that he's guilty as charged. And, obviously, being aware of and attuned to others is a key aspect that allows all of us to interact in society. However, excessive political correctness can also lead to an atmosphere that stifles thought and freedom. In today's environment of political correctness, you may find that terminating John is the correct answer; however, it is the wrong answer for your current and future students . . . .

I know that my letter will not change events and that John's termination is final. After all you've already chosen to terminate one of the most popular professors on campus. And in doing so, you've chosen to ignore the dozens or hundreds of current and former students and colleagues who have already written to you in support of John. So what more could my letter say? Nevertheless, I felt compelled to write to you and share my perspective, and in doing so try to right a wrong. And taking action on a strong belief is yet another lesson instilled in me by my years of friendship with John.

Thank you for your email message to University of Michigan President Mark Schlissel. He has asked me to respond. . . .

And so on. One hundred twenty-eight of them. It wasn't 129 letters in support because a student from that winter 2017 class out of which "ve" had nonnegotiably walked took the opportunity to applaud the firing. He or she cited the ethical dilemma he or she had faced in not walking out in solidarity, then wondered if John's intentional mangling of foreign-sounding student names (a running joke that those with such names didn't seem to mind) and his habit of giving beard rubs (John's playful brushing of his beard in the face of a victim he knew reasonably well) themselves amounted to terminable offenses.

Fitzgerald was only the messenger. He later told me in an email that his public-affairs team often assisted with responses—but only after the president's office had reviewed the emails in question. "The president is keenly aware of the messages received in his office. Neither I nor my team act as any sort of firewall for any messages sent to the president's office," he wrote.

Nor would one plausibly expect the president of a major public university to spend undue time on the apparent plight of a lowly English lecturer—though it would have been nice, and one might have hoped, perhaps, for a request that some tiny fraction of his many minions take a closer look at the case. The same could be said of Andrew Martin, then dean of the college the English Department belongs to and now chancellor of Washington University in St. Louis.

The point of excerpting from the thick stack of support for John is, rather, to share a sample of their beauty, eloquence, and diversity. What makes these letters all the more striking is that the vast majority of these writers had no inkling of the accusations against John. They simply couldn't fathom that he was a sexual harasser.

And he wasn't. The accusations remained secret because the lecturers'-union contract, valid until his firing, indeed stipulated confidentiality, and Scheible and others had advised John to keep quiet as they and the university went back and forth on a potential settlement that would give John something to think about. One thing was clear in John's case: Fitzgerald's bit about "Our approach is designed to respect the privacy of our employees" is hogwash. The university's approach served to protect the university itself.

* * *

John's firing landed on the front page of *The Michigan Daily*'s weekly summer print edition on August 3, 2018. The file photo above the headline, "Award-winning lecturer fired amid misconduct allegations," shows John in his office reading from "A Handbook to Literature," sixth edition, with zillions of student photos blurry in the background. The print story is truncated with reference to the online edition. That continuation quotes Kirsten Herold, the Lecturers' Union representative.

"Herold said she has represented several LEO members in collective bargaining with the University, several of which she thought were rightfully terminated," the story reads. "She does not believe, however, Rubadeau was given a fair chance."

"You would think the evidence would be significant but you would be wrong," Herold told the reporter. "He is not being found guilty of sexual harassment. It's a series of much smaller things that they used to make this decision. There are no allegations of sexual harassment. He's not been found guilty of things normally used to fire people."

Herold wrote a ten-page grievance and sent it to College of Literature, Science, and the Arts human resources officials on September 9. Given her own history having been de facto fired by the English Department, she thought hard about her own motivations before embarking on it, she told me.

"I don't think I fought for John because I wanted to stick it to English," she said. "I think it was because this institutional overreach has gone too far."

In the grievance, Herold offered up background on John's teaching career, reviewed the timeline from his five-year contract renewal that was to extend into 2022 on through the process that led to his firing, and then savaged the proceedings for violating several aspects of the union's contract with the university. Was the employee adequately warned of the consequences of his conduct? No. And given that the entire firing process happened during the summer, John had no real opportunity to address the concerns raised in the Office of Institutional Equity report. Was the employer's rule or order reasonably related to efficient and safe operations? Reasonable people may disagree, but that's certainly a stretch. Did management investigate before administering discipline? Yes. But only via a highly biased, tiny sample. Was the investigation fair and objective? No. Did the investigation produce substantial evidence or proof? "Emphatically no." And here Herold expounded on the accusations of the witnesses. It went more or less like this:

Regarding Witness 1 (hugs), Herold pointed out that hugs weren't inherently sexual ("Our culture is becoming increasingly huggy; even President Obama hugged Joe Biden all the time!"), that John only asked for hugs from people he knew well (hence no hug requests for Witnesses 1-5), that he had asked men as well as women for hugs and received them from both, that he never insisted on hugs when rebuffed, that hugs sometimes turned into running jokes, and that John was "hardly the only faculty member at the University to engage in occasional hugging of colleagues and students."

Regarding Witness 4's belief that John looked down her shirt, Herold restated John's vehement denial and noted that the man stood at least six-foot-four and looked down at basically everyone who wasn't on the Michigan basketball team. His office door had been open when John introduced his room-sized photo gallery to this witness whose reaction was as if he had been proudly showing off a human-skin lampshade collection. The accusations of Witnesses 2 (non-Turkish girl), 3 (actual Turkish girl), and 5 (non-Aliyah) being apparently too ridiculous to bother wasting the ink to address (Herold can't discuss the details of John's case, so I couldn't confirm or deny this), she then talked a bit about power.

Witness 1 and Witness 6 were tenured professors, Herold pointed out. Tenured professors have enormously more status and power in the University of Michigan Department of English and everywhere else in academia than do lecturers—even lecturers as long-employed and beloved as John was. With the exceptions of the thousands of students who had never mentioned John being a sexual harasser, John had had no power or supervisory responsibility over anyone. In fact, Witness 1 was technically one of John's supervisors. A disparity in power exercised by the harasser over the harassed—an essential element in valid sexual-harassment cases—was utterly absent here.

What Herold does not point out is that Witnesses 2, 3, and 4 all reported to the head of the department's Undergraduate Writing Program who reported to Witness 1 who reported to Porter. The possibility that their testimony emerged through collusion or organizational pressure goes unmentioned in the OIE report despite the close relationships among a majority of the accusers.

Herold slammed the dismissal on two other points: (1) "Were the rules, orders, and penalties applied evenhandedly and without discrimination?" and (2) "Was the penalty reasonably related to the seriousness of the offense and the past record?"

No and no.

She then wrote that the university had violated the just-cause protections of both the collective-bargaining agreement and the university's own Standard Practice Guide of policies and procedures; Herold then asked that John be reinstated with back pay for time missed.

"Firing a man who has dedicated 31 years of his life to this University, based on these kinds of allegations, is not only a contract violation; it is morally wrong," Herold concluded.

Herold's grievance stops short of considering the legal backdrop against which sexual harassment cases are to be measured. We'll take a look at that in a moment. First, a few words on sexual harassment.

Sexual harassment didn't get its name until 1975, when the term was coined in reference to a Cornell University administrative assistant named Carmita Wood's suffering under Boyce McDaniel, a prominent nuclear physicist. How did such an obvious evil become so deeply enmeshed in the social fabric of the workplace as to somehow go nameless for hundreds—thousands—of years? The biggest reason was that, in what were so often paternalistic, sexist environments, the blowback a woman endured from calling out a harasser was worse than just quietly toughing it out. Plus the perp wouldn't pay much of a price—if any—anyway. So on and on it went.

The big legal breakthrough with respect to sexual harassment didn't name the term, either. Title VII of the landmark Civil Rights Act of 1964 prohibited certain forms of discrimination in the workplace, including discrimination based on sex. But it would take twenty-two years for the U.S. Supreme Court, in *Meritor Savings Bank v. Vinson*, to definitively hold that sexual harassment violated Title VII. *Meritor*, which revolved around a bank manager and a junior employee, defined sexual harassment as unwelcome conduct of a sexual nature that was "sufficiently severe or pervasive to alter the conditions of [the victim's] employment and create an abusive working environment."

According to a unanimous Supreme Court decision, sexual harassment was unlawful and joined various other types of workplace discrimination. The floodgates opened for decades of lower-court decisions to flesh out exactly what "sufficiently severe or pervasive," "abusive," and other broadly stated terms meant. They're summarized nicely in an April 2018 Congressional Research Service (CRS) report, "Sexual Harassment and Title VII: Selected Legal Issues," a sort of Fodor's for a journey into despicable male (though also, very occasionally, female) behavior.

It's worth noting that Congress's interest in a deeper understanding of the courts' interpretation of sexual harassment cases was not merely academic. By the time that CRS report came out, the #MeToo movement had spurred allegations that had led to the resignations of Senator Al Franken (D-Minn.) and U.S. Representatives John Conyers (D-Mich.), Blake Farenthold (R-Texas), and Trent Franks (R-Ariz.).

The courts, the CRS report's authors write, consider a few factors in determining whether sexual harassment has, in fact, occurred. Among them: was the conduct unwelcome? Did the accuser consider the harassment as creating an abusive work environment? Would a "reasonable person" also *objectively* (emphasis theirs) view the work environment as abusive?

That last one is tricky. What's an environment a "reasonable person" would find "abusive"? A 1993 Supreme Court decision, *Harris v. Forklift Systems, Inc.*, elaborated. In the unanimous opinion, Justice Sandra Day O'Connor wrote, "This is not, and by its nature cannot be, a mathematically precise test.... But we can say that whether an environment is 'hostile' or 'abusive' can be determined only by looking at all the circumstances. These may include the frequency of the discriminatory conduct; its severity; whether it is physically threatening or humiliating, or a mere offensive utterance; and whether it unreasonably interferes with an employee's work performance."

In the 1997 case *Faragher v. City of Boca Raton,* the high court reaffirmed that "conduct must be extreme to amount to a change in the terms and conditions of employment" and that such a standard was needed to avoid Title VII becoming a "general civility code."

"A recurring point in these opinions is that 'simple teasing,' offhand comments, and isolated incidents (unless extremely serious) will not amount to discriminatory changes in the 'terms and conditions of employment,'" the court wrote.

The 2018 CRS report offers many examples of conduct that lower courts concluded had failed to meet the high court's standard. Among them: the supervisor looking the accuser up and down and making a sniffing motion as he focused on her groin, constantly following her, and him telling her he was "getting fired up." The boss intentionally touching the employee's breasts using papers he was holding and saying she was voted as having the "sleekest ass" in the office. The supervisor propositioning the employee multiple times for sex and telling her he would deny her vacation request unless she had sex with him. The harasser placing his chest against her breasts "for 30 seconds," then following her, forcing his way through the door ahead of her, and placing his hand on her stomach and rubbing his pelvic region across her hips and buttocks.

I note these not to nod in agreement with these various federal-court decisions—much less insinuate that this kind of behavior belongs anywhere on planet Earth—but to show just how high the legal bar really is. (Or, at least until recently, how high it has been. The courts are, thankfully, less forgiving now, a labor attorney told me, particularly in cases involving supervisors' misbehavior toward subordinates.) And like them or not, the University of Michigan must play by federal laws (and state laws—in Michigan's case, the Elliott-Larsen Civil Rights Act of 1976) when firing someone on sexual-harassment grounds. Beyond the union-contract violations Herold had noted, John's firing depended on the testimony of accusers who fell miles short of any objective "reasonable person" standard, and for behavior that no court would recognize as sexual harassment.

John's firing was, in sum, illegal.

* * *

As the leaves turned and the Big House filled with maize- and blue-clad fans on football Saturdays, someone, somewhere in the University's administrative hierarchy must have grasped this fact. The university became a bit more serious about giving John "something to think about," as Scheible had put it. Neither Scheible and Herold nor the university's representatives were interested in taking it to arbitration as the union contract required—although John adamantly wanted to do so, for he was certain that he had done nothing wrong.

"When you get into arbitration, at least half of it you're not going to like," Scheible explained.

After negotiations that ran well into the winter, John, Scheible, and the university arrived at a settlement. John would be retroactively retired and given a $100,000 settlement, little more than a year's salary. He was forbidden, under a nondisclosure agreement, from discussing the case publicly.

John was heartbroken.

"I'd give them back the $100,000 in a second. I so miss my students and the classroom. Ask any of my students—they'll tell you, to a man, that I told them that I wanted to teach until I was at least 100," he said.

He would not get his job back, and he would not be able to clear his name.

His name needed clearing. Google "John Rubadeau University of Michigan." High in the search results you'll find not only the aforementioned *Michigan Daily* front-pager from August 3, 2018, but also a follow-up from August 9. That story, "Claimant comes forward in misconduct case against John Rubadeau, LEO files grievance against 'U'" starts on page three of the print edition and again refers to the student newspaper's website. The piece devotes more than 800 words at the top half of the story—the length of a typical op-ed column—to a single, anonymous source describing John as "creepy," "strange," "making me uncomfortable," and "inappropriate."

John couldn't comment, and the writer elected to post the piece before the time window she had given Ralph Williams, a popular English professor and longtime friend and colleague of John's, closed.

Williams's words never made the story: "I can speak of my sense of his presence in the Department. He has been an active, supportive colleague, dedicated to the well-being of our students, interested in the ideas and careers of his colleagues, solicitous of our personal and professional well-being. He has frequently recommended students to my courses—students of lively intellect, questioning, thoughtful. In manner he has been colorful, pricking pretense, a figure the students have described to me as one of humor and plain fun. His courses in writing they have felt have made them much better, clearer writers. He has always, to my knowledge, tried to act on principle."

My emails to the reporter and to *The Michigan Daily* editors asking about their decision-making went unanswered. I omit the writer's name here because we need good journalists, and she may become one. But this was a story that an experienced editor would have put on ice pending better reporting or spiked outright. Despite falling far short of the *Daily's* usual standards, this tripe will now be out there until the sun boils the oceans.

Only because John was angry enough to bring me a stack of documents on his visit to Denver in late 2018—after his firing and before the settlement with the university was signed in January 2019—did I have the material necessary to write the above. Even then, I wasn't sure about whether I should.

So why did I write the above? Legitimate sexual harassment remains a serious problem at the University of Michigan and elsewhere, as the recent case of disgraced former Provost Martin Philbert illustrates. With hundreds of the famous #MeToo men to choose from—some of them undoubtedly innocent by legal standards—why chase down one involving an obscure (outside of Ann Arbor) lecturer who was well past standard retirement age anyway? As the story morphed from a dirty grammar book to a biography and an inside look at how a malevolent and/or misguided cabal looking to bring down an idiosyncratic odd-duck professor with sexual-harassment allegations amid the 2017-2018 manic phase of the #MeToo movement, I had questions for myself, too. The big one: would my long friendship with, and admiration for, John open me up to accusations of biased reporting?

The answer was, of course, yes. But show me an environmental reporter who is pro-coal. I'm pro-John. There it is. But I'm a reporter, too, and facts are facts. I was prepared to be anti-John, too, if the facts led me that way. I wrote this account because I thought John's life and firing would make for a good story—not because I was looking for a good grade three decades after graduating.

But I'm not anti-University of Michigan, either—and nor, you should know, is John himself. The institution I've been taking to task was, after all, smart enough to hire and hang onto John Rubadeau for more than three decades. Through two decisions the university made in 1987—the wise one to hire John and the questionable one to accept me, just another upper-middle-class white kid from Dearborn—I was gifted the opportunity to meet John in the first place. So yeah, I was ambivalent about going after a $10 billion-a-year behemoth that had provided me with four memorable years, a great education, and a soccer team and a fraternity to play and drink and grow with. What tipped the balance was not some burning desire to avenge John (though that was one motivator), but, rather, my hope that the University of Michigan and other institutions can learn from an injustice done to one old man and be better for it.

What lessons might they learn?

Sexual-harassment guidelines and their interpretations should align more closely with established legal precedent. There's an old saying in business that you don't want to do anything you wouldn't want to see on the front page of the *The Wall Street Journal*. The University of Michigan should avoid doing anything it doesn't want to see argued before the 6th Circuit Court of Appeals.

Freedom-of-speech as well as academic-freedom considerations should be taken into account. As an instructor working for a publicly funded university, John enjoyed First Amendment (freedom of speech) protections that a corporate employee would not—not to mention the added safety of the broadly understood tenets of academic freedom. The University of Michigan stomped all over both of these in the process that led to John's firing.

Academic department chairs need a better understanding of what sexual harassment is and isn't. While Porter had earned a Stanford

PhD and had authored *The Chinese Taste in Eighteenth-Century England*, something few experts in labor law could pull off, he had no obvious management experience before taking on the department chairmanship—essentially a business unit with about 200 employees and a $17 million annual budget. While this is standard operating procedure in liberal-arts academe, situations like John's demand specialized legal and HR expertise. Despite the abundance of such expertise on campus (among the University of Michigan Law School, The Ross School of Business, and the institution's vast administrative functions), Porter apparently failed to tap into—or, if he did, heed—any of it for a second opinion. Whether that heedlessness was intentional, inadvertent, or a precipitate of incompetence remains an open question—I can't tell you because Porter wouldn't talk to me.

To be fair, a department chair doesn't fire a lecturer as prominent as John in a vacuum: associate deans, human-resource specialists, and, ultimately, the college's Dean Andrew Martin had their say. Their inability or unwillingness to recognize the deep flaws in the case made against John also calls into question their motives and, perhaps, competence.

Whoever's to blame, he or she or ve cost the university a hundred grand and a legendary teacher.

The university's own sexual-harassment guidelines contributed to the overreach. While the school's definition of sexual harassment largely follows federal guidelines borne of legal precedent, it also strays into the hypothetical. After explaining that sexual harassment most often happens when one person has authority over another—power disparity being, as mentioned, a basic prerequisite for sexual harassment—or those of equal status of rank, the policy continues, "It is also possible for a person who is not in a position of power or authority over another to sexually harass that person, such as a professor being sexually harassed by a student or a supervisor being sexually harassed by a supervisee."

Maybe mail clerks have sexually harassed provosts, but it's overwhelmingly the other way around. "It is possible" opens the door too wide for suspect accusations. How about something like, "While harassment typically involves supervisor-employee—or, less frequently, peer-to-peer—relationships, in rare cases other manifestations occur and will be considered on an individual basis"?

Nondisclosure agreements (NDAs) should be banished from sexual-harassment settlement agreements. Now, this is controversial: lawyers representing harassment victims will tell you that confidentiality agreements help avoid painful trials and lead to bigger financial settlements. But the fact is, these NDAs overwhelmingly benefit institutions, not individuals, and they further the interests of the powerful over those of the powerless. NDAs let institutions cover up abuses such as John's firing and provide cover for bad actors who will have less motivation to change their ways.

John, a lone individual lacking a public-affairs department, is now permanently silenced with respect to the proceedings. Forbidding NDAs in settlement agreements would benefit victims of legitimate harassment, too: for example, because of NDAs, former Fox News hosts Gretchen Carlson and Megyn Kelly still can't discuss the abuses of Roger Ailes and others at that entertainment and propaganda organization. By suppressing the truths of sexual harassment, NDAs enable its perpetuation as organizations simply pay off victims in exchange for silence, thereby protecting profit-driven predators who then harass again and again. Doing away with NDAs would have helped John and will help others unfairly accused. Had John been able to share the allegations and mount a public defense—even after the settlement agreement—would the University of Michigan allowed this mess to have gone forward?

Ending NDAs in this context is not a new or radical idea. Enacted in January 2019, California's law (Senate Bill 820) already bans NDAs from settlement agreements. It also allows alleged victims to maintain confidentiality if they wish to. It's an example more states—Michigan included—should follow.

Finally, #MeToo advocates should be wary of overreach. This is a sensitive topic, I know from my own dinner table. When I suggested as much to my daughter Lily, who's 16 now, she considered me as she might something our dog left behind in the yard. She then said, "That's very Boomer of you," her generation's shorthand for "closed-minded, doddering loser." I noted that I was technically Gen-X but that we do have our own problems. Then I put it like this.

#MeToo is good. But it can be taken too far. The wheel is good; 40,000 people a year perish in car accidents in this country alone. Fire is good; people die in them. Water is good; people drown. Good things have dark extremes. That's why we have seatbelts, fire extinguishers, and flotation devices. Right now, it's not clear that the equivalent—call it due process—exists for the #MeToo movement. It's not clear that hardcore #MeToo advocates agree that due process needs to exist.

It needs to exist. The term "witch hunt" has perhaps been debased by Donald Trump's abuse of the term to describe legitimate investigations into his own perpetual misconduct. But as John's case demonstrates, witch hunts do happen. In John's case, the University of Michigan's system of due process failed. But at least the university had such a system. That's important, because—as the victims of the Salem Witch Trials, of the Spanish Inquisition, and of the countless pogroms and lynchings would surely have attested—self-perceived righteousness is very different from fairness and justice. Rather than #BelieveWomen, it should be: Listen to women. Take their accusations seriously. Then listen to men, doing the same. Consider the context, the organizational rules, and the legal basis upon which those rules rest. Do the analysis. Let the facts of the case see the light of day—probably with the alleged victims maintaining anonymity if they want it that way. That's hard to fit into a hashtag. Most nuanced solutions capable of covering the grays—and not just the black and white—are.

I'm not the only one saying it.

From *Time* magazine's 2017 Person of the Year story: "While everyone wants to smoke out the serial predators and rapists, there is a risk that the net may be cast too far. What happens when someone who makes a sexist joke winds up lumped into the same bucket as a boss who gropes an employee? Neither should be encouraged, but nor should they be equated."

From Daphne Merkin, a critic and novelist, in a January 2018 *New York Times* op-ed: "The fact that such unwelcome advances persist, and often in the office, is, yes, evidence of sexism and the abusive power of the patriarchy. But I don't believe that scattershot, life-destroying denunciations are the way to upend it. In our current climate, to be accused is to be convicted. Due process is nowhere to be found."

From Debra Katz, the lawyer who represented Christine Blasey Ford during the Brett Kavanaugh Supreme Court nomination process, in Jane Mayer's *New Yorker* feature on Al Franken: "All offensive behavior should be addressed, but not all offensive behavior warrants the most severe sanction," Katz told Mayer. "To treat all allegations the same is not only inappropriate. It feeds into a backlash narrative that men are vulnerable to even frivolous allegations by women."

From historian Jill Lepore, as told to *The New York Times:* "I find a lot of the rhetoric of the #MeToo movement incredibly troubling, which is not to undermine that sexual violence, sexual assault and sexual harassment are terrible and we fail to prosecute them effectively. But the evidentiary claim of the #MeToo — that there's an asymmetry in the law, that we've always just believed men, and therefore should just believe women — there's a thousand ways I disagree with that."

And finally, in the wake of Tara Reade's accusations against Joe Biden in the runup to the 2020 election, from Harvard Law School professor Jeannie Suk Gersen, also in *The New Yorker:* "What is emerging unmistakably from this Biden episode is a later-draft, more refined #MeToo, in which 'Believe women' stands for the imperative to listen respectfully and investigate thoughtfully. It is not about a right to be believed, much less automatically vindicated, but essentially a right to be heard and to have one's claims examined with care."

This "later draft" #MeToo came too late for John, who should have been allowed to keep teaching. Yes, he was an old man. But his reviews had remained lofty and his students were as bedazzled, entertained, and motivated as ever. Besides, who decides how old is too old? (The 1964 Civil Rights Act also covers age discrimination.)

He wanted to teach; he loved to teach; he lived to teach. He would teach no more.

Among those whom John would not teach was Ryan Zeplin, whose dad Marc perished in the World Trade Center collapse. The University of Michigan had told the family back in 2001 that, should

Marc's boys Ryan and Ethan choose to attend Michigan, they would be offered scholarships. The university had kept its word. Ryan, a Michigan undergraduate business student, had intended to take John's class in fall 2018, exactly three decades after his father had taken it. He and 480 others over the next four years wouldn't get the chance.

John's firing came about through a poisonous brew of stubbornness, incompetence, misplaced zealotry, hypersensitivity, blinkered perspective, bad faith, personal friction, professional jealousy, and shoddy investigative work—all of which led to over-reaction and injustice. The University of Michigan, or at least John's corner of it, failed itself. A place famous (and to some, infamous) for its liberalism—read open-minded, compassionate, inclusive, unprejudiced, and unbiased—now seemed to legislate and enforce that liberalism such that it has become strangely conservative: demanding of conformity and oppressive to voices that didn't obey their increasingly nitpicky norms.

But why should we be surprised? We have seen this in politics where the loudest voices pull our parties to the fringes and ultimately impose their abnormal norms. These are generally people least connected to practical concerns, the most simple-minded (regardless of intelligence or education level), and the most embracing of the black and white and the black-versus-white.

All that said, John was far from blameless. He failed to recognize that the gregarious-to-outlandish behavior that had worked decades ago had run its course. He was unwilling to change his ways. He refused to admit fault—which is, at times, the most advantageous course. He failed to recognize Porter not as an implacable enemy out to get him, but as the person best positioned to put the brakes on a misguided investigation based on dubious accusations. They had, indeed, been friends—Porter had invited John and Pat to his Chinese New Year parties for years. Maintaining such a relationship rather than poisoning it could well have saved John's job.

But recall how John had been unjustly fired at Lincoln Memorial University forty-one years earlier. He had stood up for what he felt was right in the face of great personal cost. When it came to confronting organizational wrongs, he had always been uncompromising and unwilling to equivocate for the sake of expedience—just as he had been uncompromising and unequivocal in his support for his students. His attitude during the events leading to his firing was wholly in character.

A powerful force behind that firing was a deeply rooted drive for academic conformity. Even as he lowered the #MeToo boom, Porter pressed John to adhere to the norms of a rigid academic culture—to not use nicknames, to not swear, to "observe high standards of professional decorum," and to "knock and request permission to enter" colleagues' offices. Porter instructed all this, stern parent to wayward child, in that March email. He might as well have written: "You will conform. You will be just like us. You will not stand out."

John was, of course, a star, and stars by definition stand out. But stars are worth it. You see that in those student emails to the university president who ignored them.

As I left the Ann Arbor home of Lillian Back, who had hired John thirty-two years earlier, she called down to me as I reached the bottom of the long stairway from their main living quarters. She was 83 now, a petite woman with hair still damp from a shower before my arrival an hour earlier.

"This is bigger than John," she said.

I stopped and turned back to look up at her.

"They wanted to beat him down"—she pounded a fist into an open palm—"and it irks me to my core. He had to pay the price for being nontraditional."

I was unsure of what to say.

"It's always personal," she continued. "It's always personal. They wanted to get rid of him."

Epilogue

Ann Arbor, July 2019

If I did not accomplish great things, I died in their pursuit.
— Don Quixote's epitaph/Cervantes

My daughter Maya and I arrive at the Rubadeau home in Ann Arbor on the second Wednesday in July. Lily and Carol are in Milwaukee for a skating competition. It's been seven months since John's visit to Denver. Loki, the giant, white, 10-year-old Komondor, lumbers around. The big boy takes arthritis meds, and John doesn't think he'll make it another year. Mimi, a tiny white Maltese-Shi Tzu mix, is equally excited but less visually consuming. John looks great—he has lost twenty pounds since I last saw him, he tells me, though I've always considered him thin and note no obvious difference. He wears brown cargo shorts, black gym shoes with white socks, and an olive T-shirt that matches his green-brown eyes.

Pat's out shopping for family who are in town, he explains, as we walk back out to the Honda Civic hybrid in the driveway. As I loop around to the passenger side, I note two bumper stickers: one reads "Rhetoricians Eschew Obfuscation"; the other is written in maize-on-blue in a tongue I'm unfamiliar with. It's Hebrew for "Michigan," John tells me.

He drives toward campus via Pontiac Trail and honks at the house of friends who may or may not be home, en route to his favorite restaurant, Jerusalem Garden. John eats here, usually with former students, probably twice a week. It has moved around the corner since my student days to new, bigger digs completely lacking the impression that the place could collapse around you at any moment. Soon after we're seated, John excuses himself and walks through the door marked EMPLOYEES ONLY to the kitchen area to say hello to the cooks. He's friendly with them all. This is standard procedure, Pat has told me. He'll sometimes be gone long enough that she orders and is in the middle of a shawarma sandwich by the time he returns and asks her why she's eating without him.

"And he wonders why I don't like to go out all the time," she told me.

He's back sooner this time. The waiter, a bearded millennial named Mike, knows him. With a straight face, John introduces Maya as "the top 13-year-old soccer player in America." He turns to Maya. "Maya, say 'hi' to Mike."

"Hi Mike," Maya says.

John is in the middle of a diet that eschews breads, nightshade vegetables (tomatoes, eggplants, and such), corn, and other foods. "It gives you all kinds of energy and nutrients you normally don't get," John explains.

Pat has mentioned this diet.

"So he's got big mood swings, healthwise, because of food. Too much sugar, not enough protein. The diet he's theoretically on is almost all vegetables, and he doesn't eat them," she said. "Basically, he's killing himself slowly."

He exercises regularly at the UM North Campus Recreation Building, works with personal trainers ("He loves the attention," Pat says), rides an exercise bike, or, recently, shoots baskets.

"I haven't played for fifty years. I'm trying to get my shot back. I used to be able to dunk the ball with either hand—and I was white," John says. He pauses to chew on a slice of chicken.

"You were white?" I say.

"No—I was white," John says. "I was the only white guy on an all-black basketball team. The Middleton Plumbers."

I mention the *Wisconsin State Journal* team he also played on, a fact which I knew about from the box scores in the namesake papers I'd found on newspapers.com. He has no recollection.

"In those days, you could use terms like 'nigger' with those guys—your friends." He leans over toward me. "And they called me 'Honkey muffle'"

"They called you "Honkey muffle?"

John chews a bit more. "Honkey mofo."

Maya excuses herself to go to the bathroom.

"We'll be here," I tell her.

"If we're not here, we'll be back tomorrow," John says.

"We'll catch you tomorrow," I say.

Maya doesn't have to walk far before she's out of earshot in the noisy restaurant.

"Is she a pain in the ass?" John asks. He's fond of her and Lily, but this is a good question.

"Yeah. Oh, totally. Of course," I say. "She's a 13-year-old girl."

Maya returns and eats her rice but barely touches the yogurt-covered chicken.

"You don't want the chicken? It's really great," John says.

"It's way too good to be thrown away," I say.

"You can keep that unrefrigerated," John says, thinking wishfully. "When you go on a picnic, chicken stays good."

I suggest that John might take it home and eat it, but he claims that the yogurt sauce would violate his diet despite the lack of nightshades.

"You could just rinse it off," I suggest. "In the shower, like after your workout tomorrow."

"I rarely eat in the shower," John says.

We box up the chicken despite my intuiting that it's a waste of plastic-impregnated cardboard. I insist on paying the $7 tip in cash. As Mike the waiter heads off with the debit card, we resume our conversation about basketball.

"I used to have a phenomenal free-throw shot—because I got fouled a lot. I used to say to myself: 'swish, no net' or 'backboard,'" John says.

Mike the waiter comes back. "A $36 tip—that was really nice of you to do that, John" he says. He hands John, who had written the total on the tip line, the little black tray. Mike explains that he ran that as the total and is gone again.

"When I first shot free throws again like a month ago—you know how it's supposed to soar in an arc? The ball almost landed on my foot."

"Are you kidding me?" I say, laughing.

"I shit you not: I think I shot fifteen times, and I never got it even close to the rim."

Eleven tries at a bank shot standing right next to the basket yielded his first bucket in more than a half century, he continued.

"This is the guy the *Wisconsin State Journal* called 'The sharp-shooting John Rubadeau,'" I said.

"But two days ago, I was able to palm it for the first time in years," he says.

I put my hand up; he places his against mine, fingers splayed as we compare. His are a knuckle larger. Maya does the same, giggling at the even-bigger difference. With that, John stands and disappears back through the "EMPLOYEES ONLY" door to say goodbye to the guys in the kitchen.

We leave, cut through an alley, and walk through the back-door employee entrance of the place that used to be Jerusalem Garden and is now a Mexican street-food spot called Chela's. John walks through the colorful place and stops at a drink dispenser toward the front. He grabs a tiny-plastic sampler cup, pours a milky substance into it, and hands it to Maya. He then does the same with a second tiny cup which he consumes. This is, he explains, *horchata*. The manager appears; John greets him with glee.

"Isn't it great?" he asks Maya.

"Yeah!"

A muscular young man in a Chela's shirt appears.

"Kevin, you Honduran asshole!" John says. "This is my Honduran son. Take a picture."

I take a picture with my phone.

"At some point, I'm going to make you actually buy a *horchata*, ex-professor John," he tells John.

I buy Maya a *horchata*.

We return to the car and drive a couple of blocks up Liberty, turn right at what used to be a Borders bookstore, and spot a parking place in a tight space because of a woman in a State of Michigan vehicle is partially blocking it. John calls her a bitch (the windows are fortunately closed) as she finally notices and pulls up a couple of feet. I volunteer to get out and help guide him in.

"I'm an excellent parallel parker," he announces. He swings into the tight space until his right rear wheel jumps the curb.

"Oh, now you're on the curb, though," I note.

"I don't care; who gives a fuck?" John says.

John walks into the Nickels Arcade lined with boutiques and shops along a long gallery that rises to a gabled-glass skylight three stories up. I had forgotten about it entirely. He embarks on a quick-fire tour of the shops. In Arcadian Antiques, he says "Hi Rhonda" and notes the crying baby being held by Rhonda's grown daughter. "Hi, Baby," he says.

Now on to A1 Alterations, where he opens the door and leans in. "*Ni hao, Xin nian kuai le.*" he says, to the Chinese owner of the shop. This translates into "Hello, Happy New Year." It's a tight space with three-four people and a conveyor from which hangs plastic-sheathed clothing items. "I miss you guys!"

"I miss you," the proprietor says.

"I might get a part-time job here as a tailor—I'm workin' for you," John says.

"No, I'll work for you!" the proprietor says.

We walk a few steps to University Flower Shop and enter the cool, aromatic space. "*Gnädige hübsche Frau,*" John says, which roughly translates into "beautiful madame." It's a phrase widely unused by native German speakers. He then introduces me as a German speaker. "*Sprich nur Deutsch mit dieser hübschen Dame,*" John commands me. The patient florist, a native of Austria, switches tongues, and I switch with her, explaining that I was an exchange student in Oggersheim, Germany, in the mid-1980s. She comments that my accent sounds Austrian. I suggest that it's probably more American.

"He also speaks fluent Japanese," John announces with the same conviction and allegiance to truth as he did when describing Maya as the nation's top 13-year-old soccer player. And suddenly a Japanese colleague appears. I wonder for a moment if, had John said, "He speaks

216

fluent Swahili," a Bantu warrior would have appeared. "*Konnichi wa,*" the Japanese lady says, and I stumble through a description of having lived in the Sangenjaya district of Tokyo for three years that ended more than twenty years ago. She wisely switches to English and explains that she was born in Osaka. I become desperate to escape.

"Nice to meet you and thank you guys for tolerating John," I say, inching doorward.

"*Auf wiedersehen, gnädige hübsche Frau,*" John says, and we back into the gallery. There, we pause so John can demonstrate his thumb-separation illusion for Maya who masters it in eleven seconds. We exit back to State Street. We are headed to Angell Hall to check in on his old English Department haunts. But first, he stops into State Street Liquor. I'm curious as to what he's looking for, seeing as he doesn't drink.

"Yanni! Yanni! Yanni! Yanni!" he yells upon entry. "*Assalamu alaykum,* my dear-dear friend, how are you!"

Yanni, an émigré from Iraq, stands behind the counter, the more expensive bottles forming a kaleidoscopic backdrop. He wears a University of North Carolina ballcap. "Hello old friend," he says. "You still teaching or stop?"

"No, I got fired!" John says.

"Fired. Fired-fired?"

"Yeah, I sued 'em," John says, baselessly.

"Fired? In Eng-a-leesh? What kind of fire. Flame?"

John laughs. "No, no. I lost my job."

"Really? Awww," Yanni says.

A guy who looks like a professor is leaving the place and is clearly paying attention to the conversation between John and the Iraqi immigrant behind the counter. "I used to be a teacher as well," he says. "At Fordham. I didn't get fired. But it happens. You should totally get aggressive on it."

"The highest-rated professor at the University of Michigan for thirty-one years, and they fired my ass—and I didn't do anything!" John says.

"What did you teach?"

"Advanced Essay Writing."

"Go for it," the guy advises, and he's out the door.

John is here to buy lottery tickets, a long-standing habit. He takes two draws on the Mega. "Yanni, goddammit, you're looking good," he says as Yanni completes the transaction.

"Don't worry about the fire. Happen to anybody."

"No, I'm not worried at all. I didn't do anything wrong," John says.

"Don't make it like obstacle in your life, never. You did the right thing, right?"

"I did the right thing," John assures his friend.

We step back into the July sun and walk across State Street and up the steps into Angell Hall. I imagine bacteria multiplying with great fervor in the bag of yogurt chicken I'm carrying. We walk up the echoey stairs to the fourth floor, Maya running ahead. It's quiet—most students and faculty are gone for the summer. Once there, John stops to read a slogan taped to a colleague's door. "What's that say there?" he asks, unable to make it out.

"Words are the only things that last forever," I read.

"Things," John says. He clearly agrees with the sentiment, but he has never liked the word "things." It's too general, too vague for his liking—a literary cop-out. "You'd think someone would write that without using the word 'things.'"

"He doesn't like the word 'things,'" I note to Maya. I turn back to John. "How would you rewrite it?"

"'Words are the only commodity, the only thing of value, that lasts forever'—not 'thing' of value!" he says, catching himself.

"How about, 'Words are all that last forever?'"

John nods in acceptance of my edit and races again down the hallway's industrial carpeting of a purplish tinge. Maroon nameplates and heavy wooden doors interrupt yellow-white walls. Without stopping, he turns to Maya. "Hey, can you do this?" He jumps up and clicks his heels in midair. Maya can do it, but Maya isn't 79. He stops at an office and a secretary joins us. We walk together with her back down to the third floor and stop at room 3128.

The clear-plastic tray outside the room is devoid of papers or dog biscuits; a constellation of unemployed pushpins dots the door-mounted corkboard. A secretary lets us into the office that was, for years, John's three-dimensional photo gallery. Now it's a box with white walls, tiled ceiling, and carpet poured in from the hallway. The window, long blocked with photos, looks out onto a bare brick wall. A place of life now lifeless, a rainforest slashed and burned. John seems unmoved, and this comforts me. As we leave, I state the obvious, "Your office remains unoccupied."

"It'll be hard to fill it with someone of equal character. They'd have to get someone who's a child molester or something. Or a bestiality practitioner," John says. He turns to me and asks, "Did you know there's no such word as 'beastiality?'"

"I did not," I say.

John leads us out of Angell Hall and guides us through a maze that includes the Michigan League, a parking structure, and a trash-strewn alley that leads us more or less exactly to his car. On the way home, he loops around the main campus, noting the many buildings that have risen since I sat in his class. Closer to home, he stops in the neighborhood to chat to a young couple working outside. He introduces Maya, in the back seat, as the best 13-year-old soccer player in America.

"It's true," he says. "She's five-foot-seven and she's 13." He gestures toward me in the passenger seat. "He was four-foot-two when he was 13. It's just amazing."

* * *

Two days later, I leave Maya in Dearborn with her grandparents and arrive at the Rubadeau home after the lunch hour as John prepares to do some urban trapping with grandson Brody. On a low wooden fence out back, a trap baited with peanut butter on a cracker awaits an unsuspecting squirrel. Another trap on raised-bed rocks is haphazardly fortified with fraying gray duct tape. Moving to the garage, John shows me other traps, including a green cylindrical number that looks like something an infantryman might use to lob a mortar. This morning, he says, he caught a ground squirrel.

"I haven't trapped much this year," John admits. "But I've gotten three very large groundhogs. One was fourteen pounds."

As we cut across a neighbor's unfenced backyard to check a trap, Brody chases a squirrel.

"Get it get it get it!" John yells.

Brody, who is 9 and going into third grade in Shanghai, doesn't get it. His dad Jeff, Lexi's husband, is a General Motors executive there. Brody plays any infield position for his baseball team, the Shanghai Sluggers, he has told me.

Brody and I make a wide arc around a neighbor's leashed Shiba Inu, a precaution which John advises because the dog is "unfriendly." John then approaches it and gives it a nice pat. "I like dogs more than people," says a man who likes people.

We arrive at the backyard of an 89-year-old neighbor named Loumar who's dealing with a minor groundhog infestation. He's been trapping for her for probably twenty years, she guesses. John remarks that he hasn't seen her out walking. Part of it is how steep her driveway is, she tells John. Also, she's not been feeling great. A day of testing at the hospital found nothing wrong, Loumar says, "Except for I'm 89."

She changes the subject. "Catch a skunk!" she says.

"If you see any skunks, I'll catch 'em. But you gotta see 'em," John says.

"I haven't seen 'em," Loumar says.

"Have you smelled 'em?" I ask.

"Knock on wood, I haven't smelled 'em," Loumar says.

Brody interjects: "I want to beat up a squirrel."

Loumar disappears inside to find bait a skunk might appreciate. She emerges first with a hard-boiled egg, then, at John's suggestion, a hunk of cheese. "You're taking food right out of my mouth," she tells John.

"I know, You Poor Dear. My heart bleeds for you," John says. As he puts the cheese in the trap, Brody cracks the hard-boiled egg on his noggin and peels it. Once the egg's in the trap, Brody camouflages the metal cage, which is about large enough to accommodate Brody himself, with grass clippings and a lone pinecone.

Back at the house, Pat joins me in the screened-in porch. We sit at a table. Wind chimes go mad as gusts whoosh through the leaves of mature trees. Pat's portable oxygen tank puffs like a kitten's sneeze each time she inhales. Her LAM has progressed to the point that her lung capacity is less than one-third of what it should be. She's on oxygen except when she washes her face at night during which time her heart rate leaps twenty beats per minute. This disease is a slow, certain asphyxia, one she faces with heroic grace. She is thinner than I remember, her voice nearly as soft as the breeze, her eyes as beautiful as ever. We talk about unreliable oxygen companies and then John.

Pat earned her PhD in Slavic Linguistics at the end of what she joked was "the ten-year plan" in 1996, a delay largely due to her LAM treatments. The timing was not good: interest in Russian-language studies had collapsed with the Soviet Union in 1991, and Slavic departments had shrunk in kind.

She instead found work as a landscape architect's office manager. In 2000, the English Department was hiring lecturers, and Pat jumped back into academia teaching first- and second-year English classes. She liked the teaching, disliked the department politics, and dreaded her annual winter bouts with pneumonia (students tended to bull through illnesses and spread the love), a growing risk given her declining health. In late 2008, she stopped teaching.

She describes John's daily routine as up-at-ten, a workout, maybe errands, television (often CNN or MSNBC), and bed after midnight. Sometimes students come by; three or four of them call on a given day—for life advice or just to catch up. On his 79th birthday in February, he was on the phone for eight hours, she says. "I made him turn the phone off when we went to dinner." His Gmail clogged; his cell-phone voice inbox spilled over.

During his last couple of years teaching, John's student reviews stayed as superlative as ever, but he was watching more TV. "I could tell he was mentally checking out in terms of teaching. It wasn't the rush it used to be," she says.

I've talked to her several times on the phone over these last few months. She has been honest about her relationship with this man for whom, she says, "Students always take precedence over everybody else. And there's nothing I can do about that."

"And here I am, taking your time while your family's in the other room," I say.

She smiles charitably. "Why he loves me now—this is the biggest reason—we have disability plates on both cars."

"He does love you," I tell her. "When he was out in Denver, he was checking in on you constantly and leading me on wild goose chases for torrones."

The kitten sneezes; the wind chimes ring. "I know he does," Pat says. "And I do love him. But, you know, I would love him more if he showered every day."

Pat and I return inside: she to her family, I to the basement with John.

Against a wall near the bottom of the stairs, the atheist has positioned a prie-dieu, a kneeler with red velvet knee and elbow padding. A white fitball has rolled up against it. Above the prie-dieu are framed *The Michigan Daily* and other articles featuring John and a poster promoting his Golden Apple award speech of 2005, "My Life in Quotes." The space is a tongue-in-cheek shrine to himself. John remarks that he wants votive candles. Pat is not interested in votive candles.

On the opposite wall hangs a framed pencil drawing on loose-leaf paper by a former student who is now a Hollywood star. It's a convincing rendition of the bearded teacher with an anthropomorphic moon and sun looming large over his shoulders. The Moon asks, "Hey John could you write me a letter of recommendation?" The Sun chimes in, "Yeah! Me too, buddy!!"

Bags of "be bright" brand non-GMO superfood obscure short stacks of *The Passionate Papers of Fiona Pilgrim*. There's a poster of Zagreb from when it was still "Jugoslavja" and a wind-resistance Schwinn with T-shirts temporarily hanging on plastic hangars from one of its arms (he rides more or less daily while watching the little Vizio flat-screen TV on a chest of drawers).

Beyond it all is John's office with a Mac with an HP inkjet printer off to the right of the big monitor. On the wall past the monitor hang several photos, among them one of daughter Becky on the cover of a College of Saint Mary brochure. In other frames are a postcard his old friend Ron Pace sent from Egypt and an unflattering four-photo study of Ron's head at different moments during some past nap. In the

1980s, Ron's baby-furniture manufacturers'-representative business led him to a client who dreamed of starting a big-box baby-item chain. Ron sold his house and took out a loan to invest in what would quickly grow to eighty-eight Baby Superstores. The company went public in 1994; Toys "R" Us acquired it two years later and turned it into Babies "R" Us. By then, John's son Nick had joined Ron's son Derek to take over the manufacturers'-rep business based in Nashville. Most Sundays, Nick and, with time, his family had dinner at the Pace home. Nick now runs that business himself. John and Ron are still best friends.

Above all the photos hang framed quotes. Jack Porter, John's old doctor friend from Lebanon, dabbled in calligraphy as well as garden slugging, and Pat framed these quotes with scraps at the Corner Vise Frame Shop. Francis Bacon's "It is only through indignity that a man rises to dignity," reads one. Another has a quote from F. A. Birmingham's *The Writer's Craft*: "For the measure of an artist is not only his magical gift of spreading a landscape before our eyes. It is also his capacity to make us see the old landscape in a new light—to select a long familiar symbol, infuse fresh life in it, and give it immediacy and urgency of meaning." A third recites the entirety of the William Butler Yeats poem, "To a friend whose work has come to nothing."

Atop a work space above built-in cabinets, stacks of letters from students and email printouts flank an ancient Remington Standard Model 10 typewriter. I recognize it from the cover of *The Passionate Papers of Fiona Pilgrim*.

"This was my grandfather's," he points out—Florence's dad, who died before John was born. John explains how his grandfather sent four daughters to the University of Wisconsin and a son to Vienna, Austria, for medical school. "He was a very wealthy man. I never got any of that money, but this is the typewriter he used in his pharmacy."

Atop one of several stacks near the Remington I note an email from his friend and colleague Ralph Williams, written shortly after the firing. "I am hugely dismayed, John. I think of a line in Aeschylus: Sing sorrow, sorrow: but good, win out in the end."

Williams had been the sole colleague who had stood up for John. As the former English Department chair Lincoln Faller told me, "Academics, in general, are not known for their courage."

"They don't want to risk their status by getting involved in sensitive social issues within the department. The first thing people do when there's a whiff of scandal is run from it," he added.

Nearby is a draft of *Farming Circe's Acres,* John's fictionalized take on his time raising pigs in Appalachia. It's marked up in red pen in a script I remember from my own papers from thirty years before. It's easy to forget that John's dream was to be a famous writer. He is not a famous writer.

The book that emerged from this draft would be published not by Farrar, Straus and Giroux or some other storied publishing house but, rather, by Earthview Media, which I'd established a couple of years earlier to publish my first book after poor luck with traditional publishers. I gave him a spare ISBN for his magnum opus, and Bhavin Shah footed the bill to publish those 250 copies of *A Sense of Shame: Born in a State of Sin,* of which not a few remain. To paraphrase one of John's favorite quotes: in his avocation as a writer, he advanced confidently in the direction of his dreams with little tangible to show for it. His fame would, he said countless times, be posthumous. It was in his vocation as a teacher—one he stumbled into quite late in life and one that he might well have abandoned for insurance sales had that Purdue job not opened up—in which he met with a success unexpected in common hours.

From another stack, I pick up a card a student wrote in December 2014. "Thank you for helping us make that little classroom in Angell Hall into an open, full-of-life space in which nineteen unlikely people could bond. Thank you for being an open, full-of-life, quirky person with endless bits of knowledge to share. Thank you for helping us build our receptive vocabularies. Thank you for sharing your stories and bad jokes. I've learned a lot about writing in your class, and that has been amazing. I've also learned about the things I want to get out of life, and for that I'm incredibly grateful. Hugs! Nadine." The front of the card was graced with an abstract triangular design that Nadine had watercolored.

Learning about the things one wants to get out of life wasn't in John's syllabus. But few left his class without having a clearer sense of life direction than when they had arrived. Some realized that goals shaped by parental and societal expectations—ones typically involving a "safe" climb up existing career ladders into the higher echelons of respected fields (medicine, finance, law, et cetera)—weren't, in fact, their goals at all. Many changed direction and were better for it. Others, such as Vince Pagano, Marc Zeplin, Elise Yu, went on to pursue those very paths. With them, too, though, "Scratch your itch" stubbornly repeated its pings from some corner of their minds, reminding them to stay true to themselves, to do what was right for them, and to aim not just for financial gain but also, more importantly, for fulfilment as human beings.

John was, ultimately, teaching those too young to have developed a sense of their own mortality that they had just one life to live and that the career that each would choose soon after his class came to a close would largely define that life. There is no greater lesson.

As I consider Nadine's card, I can't help but be reminded of how different John was from the students he taught. He was poor; they were mostly "rich"—John's term for anyone of upper-middle-class-and-above means (which, globally speaking, is accurate). He had taken a path few students would want to take, though few of them knew much about his background—I certainly didn't. This mentor to masses, this man with the pithy maxims and the sage insights into the Secrets of Life—had, in fact, muddled through, bounced about, suffered profound tragedies and huge setbacks, and ultimately stuck around until his true calling as a teacher revealed itself. Along the way, he had penned novels that few would read—but which he loved. I wonder for a moment if comprehending all this back in the late 1980s would have led me to dismiss his wisdom. I know now that doing so would have been a grave mistake.

We all muddle through. The value of mentors is that they can share the lessons of their muddlings so we can muddle less. In John's case, those lessons sailed right past the densely settled lands of workaday worries on out to the unmappable questions of existence, ones whose mere asking moved rudders early in so many voyages of life.

We sit down, and I ask John why, rather than telling the department chair to fuck off, he didn't just apologize for saying "training bra" in public, for asking for hugs, for offering dog biscuits—even if there were nothing to apologize for. This would have been the path of least resistance, after all.

"If one is wronged, one should stand up for what's right and not let the powers that be ride roughshod over you," he said. "I stood on my basic principles. If I believe in something and am convinced that I haven't done anything wrong, I'm not going to let people push me around just because of money or politics."

He had done so at Lincoln Memorial University; he did so at Michigan. But still. "Regardless of the personal cost?" I ask. "Which in your case was getting fired?"

"Yeah..." he says. "I always thought that the love of my students would prevent that. But none of the many, many letters, the unbelivable letters." He pauses. "I just thought that the president would be a reasonable man."

Footsteps slap down the hardwood stairs. It's Isabel, his 9-year-old granddaughter via Nick, followed by her father and her Aunt Becky, who looks nowhere near thirty-seven years older than her College of Saint Mary cover shot. I see John's first wife Barbara in both of them. They have all come up from Florida (Becky) via Nashville (Nick) so Isa can spend time with her cousins, Lexi's kids Brody and Joseph, who's 12.

"This is my gay son!" John exclaims, referring to the six-foot-tall, 51-year-old heterosexual who extends his hand. We have spoken on the phone as I have with Becky too. Nick and I talk briefly about his drive north, one slowed by stops his daughter's bladder demanded every forty-five minutes. This new travel anecdote brings up one from family lore. Shortly after John had met Pat, John, Nick, and Becky joined Ron Pace and his sons Kevin and Derek on a road trip into Canada. John was as financially strapped as ever and had, at one point in the trip, tried to get the group to eat at a soup kitchen, a suggestion which Ron had vetoed. This time, they stopped at a McDonald's, where the Pace boys ordered the Quarter Pounder with cheese, fries, the whole bit.

"Becky and I got a hamburger—not the cheeseburger, because it was a nickel more—and water. No fries," Nick said. "I remember that cheese slice was five cents!"

Becky, he, and I laughed; John managed a smile. Back up the stairs they went.

* * *

John was to pick up the dogs at the groomer across town. I went along. In the Honda, I ask how things have been since he lost his job.

"It wasn't just my job. It was my life. The fuckers murdered me," he says. The air conditioner blasts in an attempt to overcome the afternoon heat.

"No, you didn't lose your life, John."

"I loved that job. It was my life."

"Yeah, but look, man. I've been around you for the better part of two days. And granted, I'm here; your family's here. But I mean, you seem like you're doing really goddamn well. Am I wrong?"

"No," he says. "It was really the best thing that ever happened to me."

This I don't believe either—while he's enjoyed freedom from correcting papers, he misses the students. And the injustice, the stain on his reputation, and the gulf between how he left and the feted nature of how he would have left on his own terms—it all grated and, in quiet moments, unexpectedly welled up into genuine anger he could do absolutely nothing about.

"They took your life in the sense that it was the way you were living for a long time. But Jesus Christ, the fact that you did what you did and made as many friends, touched so many lives, and amassed so many admirers through the process of all that teaching and all the giving you did for all those years—that has put you in a position to really, really enjoy the time you have left."

"I do have one foot in the grave."

227

"I don't mean it like that. You're in phenomenal physical shape. You clicked your goddamn heels together, you walked all over campus with us, you're tireless. I think your energy level's fantastic."

"I do have good energy. I'm very enthusiastic about life," John says. "It's all about the viewpoint. You know, people make choices—if they're gonna be happy, if they're gonna be sad. For me, I've found the perfect way to live."

"How would you describe that?"

"Well, I found my itch. I scratched it. I like people, I found a way to make a living teaching people. Helping people. Being around people. I just happen to like people. I'm a bullshitter. My dad was a bullshitter. Although he was an alcoholic, he was beloved except for in his own home. But everybody loved my dad. Everybody in Madison, Wisconsin, knew my dad."

In this college town, just about everybody knew his dad's son, and about everybody loved him, too.

When we arrive back with the freshly coiffed dogs, it's dinnertime. I intend to leave the family be, but John and Pat insist I stay and the others don't seem to mind. Grandson Joseph has helped cook up a meat sauce with spinach. We sit at the dining-room table. Next to it are three waist-high stainless-steel liquid oxygen tanks. The clear-plastic oxygen line—long enough to give Pat range around the house and down into the basement—snakes under the table and behind Pat where the giant Loki sleeps amid its loose tangle. Behind John and me is a wall-mounted, oak book stand that was salvaged decades ago from the University of Michigan math library before its move from Angell Hall. It supports an open, unabridged *American Heritage Dictionary of the English Language, Fifth Edition.*

Three of Pat and John's five offspring are here—absent are Heather (in Seattle) and Pace (in Bellingham, Washington)—plus Jeff, Joseph, Brody, and Isa. Nick, Becky and Lexi sense a good time to relay old stories for a chronicler of the life of John. First was what was known as the "pee story" in family lore.

Becky, whose wit and fire seem directly descended from her father's, takes this one. This was a road trip, and John didn't like to stop. For sustenance, they made due with baloney sandwiches with

228

Miracle Whip. The Miracle Whip jar had emptied. Nick had to go to the bathroom. Becky picks up the story. "Dad says, 'Goddammit, we're not stopping.' Nick pleads with Dad. They go back and forth. Finally, Dad says, 'Go in the jar.' He hands Nick the Miracle Whip jar. It takes a while, but Nick finally pees into the jar. He hands the jar back to Dad. Dad takes the jar—he doesn't slow down—and rolls down the window. He throws the pee out the window. Or tries to. What happens is, the pee comes flying back in the window and all over my dad."

We're all laughing now. Becky continues, "And I just lost it. I thought my dad was going to beat the shit out of me—fucking hilarious."

Nick then takes the baton for the Marshmallow Story. He's a quieter soul, an aikido personality versus his sister's karate. "There was a recipe that had mini marshmallows in it. Dad explicitly said: go to the store and buy marshmallows. I checked the recipe and saw that it said 'mini marshmallows.' We're in Lebanon, Indiana, it's winter, it's cold, and I walk to the IGA a block and a half away and buy mini marshmallows. When I get back, Dad looks at the bag and says, 'What did I ask you to buy? What are these?' I say, 'They're mini marshmallows. It's what the recipe says.' Dad says, 'What did I ask you to buy?' and I give in and say, 'Marshmallows.' Dad says, 'Go buy marshmallows'—because regular marshmallows are slightly cheaper than mini marshmallows. So I walk back to the IGA, return the mini marshmallows, buy the marshmallows, and walk back home. Then what do I do? I sit down and cut the full-sized marshmallows into mini marshmallows using scissors."

We laugh again.

These adults who were kids with such tumultuous upbringings at the hands of the bearded man stuffing green beans into his mouth beside me—these people have somehow turned out quite well-adjusted. And while Becky has told me on the phone, "My father, he is so damn weird. I'm the first to admit—he's strange," one thing is clear: despite the history, despite the quirks, not just his students love the man.

I leave after dinner and promise to be back in a couple of days. My destination: the home of Elise Yu and her husband Carl. Their

229

goldendoodle Musubi greets me at the door. Elise and Carl weren't thinking of getting a dog, but John convinced Elise she should, and she and Carl have no regrets. She and Carl walk me to the basement. Twenty-two foam-core paddlewheel photo mobiles rest partially interlocked on the basement's thick carpet. Further dozens of poster-sized, photo-crammed foam-core boards lean in thick stacks in two closets.

The paddlewheels share space with an erg rower, a case of beer and a couple of stray six packs, a golf bag, Snoopy Christmas socks, a giant teddy bear, and the box for an HP computer monitor, among other basement bric-a-brac. The paddlewheels can't be broken down. Elise and Carl are in their early thirties. I envision a child's play area with all the requisite plastic. The poignancy of these remnants will fade, and these treasures will become clutter. In a year or two or three, they will be gone.

* * *

Two days later, I swing by the Rubadeau home one last time. Pat and John are in easy chairs that flank the couch. His is a puffy dark-leather recliner with thick white stitching. The resting place of his right elbow has worn beige. Pat wears a gray long-sleeved LAM Foundation T-shirt that reads, "Can you say 'lymphangioleiomyomatosis'?"

The family visitors are out and about somewhere in town. Pat looks worn out.

"When we have company or travel, I realize how sick I am," she says.

On the wall not far from the TV hangs an orange-and-blue painted sign, its corners extended with the looping, jigsawed flourish: The Corner Vise Frame Shop.

I sit on the couch between them as countless students have. The white dogs Mimi and Loki chill on the floor, Mimi at my feet. Their vast size difference is a case study in how far selective breeding can push a species. We talk about the magnum opus. John started it in Romania, as I knew, and there wrote 616 legal-sized handwritten pages that focused on the religious side of the story. The religious satirizing of mid-20th-century America happened after he came back home "and everything was so stupid," as he puts it.

"Kind of like taking a dirty grammar book and making it into something about the #MeToo movement," Pat quips.

John nods toward Pat and says, "She worked her ass off on my books, but she never liked any of them."

"She liked *The Passionate Papers,*" I offer.

Pat adds, "Hey, I did that whole fuckin' glossary. I read the big book. Once."

"Once," John says.

"Hey," Pat says, "Arthritis." She pantomimes the massive tome crushing her lap.

"It so happens," I say, "that on this phone resides the world's only Kindle copy of *A Sense of Shame.*"

John and a former student who had ported it into a Kindle-compatible file quickly realized that the formatting was so disastrous that it couldn't be sold. And indeed, the footnotes often appear in the wrong places, and the footnotes-in-footnotes become unmanageable (and, sometimes, formatted in red). They pulled it from the Kindle store, but not before, they noted, some guy had spent $24.95 on a download. I open it up and hand my phone to John.

John quietly pokes at my phone as Pat describes how various incidents and insults had long since pulled her away from the Catholic Church, too.

"See I believe in a pantheon. A whole bunch of gods. And if there's one main god, as much as I would like it to be a woman, I don't believe it because the world's too fucked-up," she says. Her voice is soft, melodic. "But, you know, I have parking gods I pray to because I can't parallel park."

I laugh. "Does that work?"

"Yes. All the time."

John reads from my phone one of the forty satirical book-review excerpts that lead off his big book. They're part of the thirty-three pages that, thanks to Roman numerals, don't count toward the 1,110-page novel's body.

"'An exciting novel. Guaranteed to keep the reader on his toes,'" John reads. "It's from 'Narcolepsy News, Yawnkers, New York.'" He reads another faux review, this one with a literary reference to Dryden's poem *Mac Flecknoe*, then hands me back my phone. He has moved on.

It is soon time for me to leave. Pat sends John back to the upstairs bathroom to gather beard hair from a brush and put it in a Ziploc baggie. He returns with a baggie, which I take and am unsure what to do with. He promises to send my girls some on their birthdays.

"That will bother them badly," I say.

I hug Pat. John walks me outside. I realize that we haven't taken a single photo together. I line up a selfie in his front yard. When I look at the photo later, it will strike me that there's no office to add it to anymore.

I hop in my little blue rental car. John bends down to talk through the open passenger window.

"I'll need to read the manuscript twice," he says, tapping on the roof. "And don't be disappointed if nobody accepts it."

"Listen, I'm used to rejection," I say. "I'm surprised Carol didn't reject me."

He smiles at the opening.

"We all make mistakes," he says.

GRAMMAR REVIEW

Author's Note: This wasn't, in the end, a "dirty grammar book." But John did agree that, as long as we're sharing his life and teachings, we might as well also impart some of his core grammatical and writing lessons. The insights below, derived from his course pack, are his alone.

I. The key word in my approach to the study of grammar is "synergism." Hence, every error—no matter how small it may seem in and of itself—is important because of the combined effect of all the "small" errors in your writing. This is an example of the axiom, "The whole is greater than the sum of its parts."

II. What is a sentence? Sentences surround us like air. Maybe a sentence is like pornography in that, as U.S. Supreme Court Justice Potter Stewart put it back in 1964, you know it when you see it. But a sentence is not like pornography. First, sentences are less interesting than pornography (though sentences are, occasionally, used in pornography). Second, there's a concrete definition for "sentence": A sentence (S) is a group of words containing a subject (s), a verb (v), and <u>sometimes</u> an object (o), the combination of which *must make sense.* The normal word order of the English sentence is sv(o). That is, S=sv(o).

s   v   o

This is a sentence: John hit the ball.
(The construction makes sense.)

s   v   o

This is not a sentence: After John hit the ball.
(The construction does not make sense.)

The "must make sense" part doesn't mean the information in the sentence must make sense. The sentence, "His halitosis hung in the air like a flying squirrel" is perfectly acceptable, grammatically speaking. But it doesn't make sense: flying squirrels cannot hover. If they could, they'd be called "hovering squirrels." "Donald Trump was a great president" is equally nonsensical though grammatically sound.

III. As stated above, the normal word order of the English sentence is sv(o). When this word order is either (1) preceded by a clause (c) or a phrase (p)—groups of words that do not make sense—of more than three words or (2) interrupted by a c or p, then the clause or phrase is *generally* set off by a comma or by commas.

(a) c or p, sv

After he hit the ball, John ran to first base.

(b) s, c or p, v

John, after he hit the ball, ran to first base.

(c) sv, c or p

John ran, after he hit the ball, to first base.

When the c or p comes *after* the sv(o), we *generally* don't use a comma.

(d) sv c or p

John ran to first base after he hit the ball.

(Note: no comma)

However, the *one* exception to example (d) is that, when the c or p that comes after the sv(o) has an "ing" word at, or near, its beginning, we, more often than not, use a comma.

(e) sv(o), <u>ing</u> c or p

s v   c or p

John ran to first base, knocking down the first baseman as he slid into base.

(Ideally, the phrase ". . . knocking . . . base" should have been placed closer to "John" since this is what it modifies, and we always strive to place the modifying c or p as close as possible to the word or *idea* it modifies; however, for the sake of illustration, the phrase is juxtaposed to the word "base.")

(f) NB. Under "(a)" above, remember:

c or p, sv(o)—the c or p *always* modifies the first noun mentioned after the comma.

c or p   s   v

(f-1)   Entering the library, a desk was the first object I noticed.

Of course, a desk didn't enter the library. The clause "Entering the library" should have modified "I" not the desk. To correct this sentence, we rewrite it as, "Entering the library, I immediately noticed a desk."

c or p   s   v

(f-2)   After ten minutes in the microwave, I took out the rice.

Of course, the student who wrote this sentence was not in a microwave for ten minutes. The clause "After ten minutes in the microwave" should have modified

237

"rice" not "I." To correct this sentence, we rewrite it as, "After ten minutes in the microwave, the rice was taken out." (Some grammarians will object to the sentence because of the passive voice—"to be" or "to get" plus the past tense are what constitute the passive voice. See forthcoming note at "A Few Niggling Aspects about the English Language That Mildly Torment Me—All Peccadillos to Be Sure.")

c or p   s   v

(f-3)   After boiling in water, the baby was given its pacifier.

Of course, God forbid, the baby was not boiling in the water. The clause "After boiling in water" should have modified "pacifier" not "baby." To correct this sentence, we rewrite it as, "After boiling in water, the pacifier was given to the baby." (Again, an excellent employment of the passive voice.)

IV. Within a paragraph, there are three ways to structure how sentences are constructed, and, by using these three different methods, we can, for the sake of stylistic variation, alter the arrangement of our sentences within paragraphs.

(a)   s   v   o   s   v
     S.S.—John hit the ball. He ran to first base.

(b)   s   v   o   s   v
     S;S.—John hit the ball; he ran to first base.

Note that the second sentence *does not* commence with a capital letter—unless the first word after the semicolon is a proper (uppercase) noun. (A hint: Think of the semicolon as being the writer's equivalent of a mathematician's equal sign. The group of words on one side of the semicolon must be **grammatically** equal to the words on the other side: "c or p; c or p" is the same as "c or p = c or p." "S; S" is the same as "S = S."

(c)

S, **for** S	s v o s v
S, **and** S	John hit the ball, and he ran to first base.
S, **nor** S	
S, **but** S	The above sentence is punctuated correctly.
S, **or** S	
S, **yet** S	s v o v
S, **so** S*	John hit the ball, and ran to first base.

The above sentence is incorrectly punctuated; the comma does not belong because "ran to first base" is not a sentence—it lacks a subject. Rather, it is a c or p which comes at the end of the sentence. I.e., S and c or p.

S and c or p: John hit the ball and ran to first base.   ↑
(Note: no comma)

The only other times you frequently use commas are when you set off items in a series of three or more (this is called a serial comma or Oxford comma) and when you wish to indicate a pause or a change in inflection. For a more thorough discussion of the use of commas, see the eighteen rules for comma usage in the Style Manual (pp. xx-xxv of the Fourth Edition) of *The American*

---

* Note the easiest way to remember the seven coordinating conjunctions: the mnemonic acronym FANBOYS. Coordinating conjunctions, much like semicolons, are used to connect equal grammatical units.

*Heritage College Dictionary.** One additional comment here: You can't join two sentences with a comma. This is called a comma splice or a comma fault and is grammatically incorrect: John threw the ball, he ran to first base.

V. Here are some things (I loathe the word "things") you should be aware of. 1-6 are socially distinctive markers; the appearance of these errors in your prose tends to mark you as inept and suggests to your reader that if you are guilty of sloppy writing then you may also be guilty of sloppy thinking:

(1) too (also or very)
     two (the number)
     to (everything else)
(2) there (is or are)
     their (as in possession—their house)
     they're (they are)
(3) your (as in possession—your book)
     you're (you are)
(4) it's (it is)
     its (as in possession—its food)
(5) whose (as in possession—Whose book is that?)
     who's (who is—Who's there?)
(6-a) Use "a" before words or letters which begin with a consonant *sound*: a dog; a cat; a fish; a "b"; a "d."
(6-b) Use "an" before words or letters which begin with a vowel *sound*: an animal; an idiot; an "s"; an "f."
(7) Use "who" as a pronoun when you are modifying a human. Don't use "that" or "which" to refer to humans.

---

* To my mind, there is only one dictionary, and that is the Fourth Edition of *The American Heritage College Dictionary*. In addition to a wonderful Style Manual, there are 343 usage notes that are invaluable for anyone writing American English.

(8) If you don't know when to use "who" or "whom," substitute the words "he/him" *in the clause* where the "who" or "whom" appears. If "him" works better than "he" in the clause, use "whom" because "hi<u>m</u>" and "who<u>m</u>" both end in an "<u>m</u>."

he | him

(a) The man | who gave me a ride | was my brother.

The base sentence is "The man was my brother."; the clause is "…who gave me a ride…." You would say, "He gave me a ride." You wouldn't say, "Him gave me a ride." Hence, "who" is correct in this context.

he | him

(b) The man | whom you just passed | was my brother.

The base sentence is "The man was my brother." The clause is "…whom you just passed…." You couldn't say, "You just passed he." You'd have to substitute "hi<u>m</u>" for "who<u>m</u>" in "You just passed hi<u>m</u>." Hence, "who<u>m</u>" is correct in this context.

* * *

A Few Niggling Aspects about the English Language That Mildly Torment Me—All Peccadillos to Be Sure

1. I do not like it when a plural noun is followed by the words "such as," "like," or "for example," and the writer only gives one example rather than multiple ones.

    > "I eat fruits such as oranges." A minor point to be sure, but, when I see a plural noun followed by "such as," "like," or "for example," I expect multiple examples of the plural

noun "fruits": "I eat fruits such as oranges, bananas, and apples."

2. I do not like it when a writer conflates the indicative mood with the subjunctive mood. In English, there are three major moods: the **indicative** has to do with statements of fact (I am a man.); the **imperative** has to do with commands ("Open the door." The subject of an imperative sentence is generally the implied "you," as in "You open the door."); and the **subjunctive** is introduced by words such as "if," "whether," or "wish" or words that indicate doubt, uncertainty, unreality, or hypothetical situations ("Whether I be right or wrong," "If I were you," "I wish you were here"). The indicative and the subjunctive are affected by tense. E.g., we have the present indicative: "I am here," and we have the past indicative: "I was here," and we have the present perfect indicative: "I have been here," and we have the past perfect indicative: "I had been here." Similarly, we have the present subjunctive "If that be the case"; and we have the past subjunctive "If that were the case."

3. I do not like it when students constantly confuse "e.g." (*exempli gratia*) and "i.e." (*id est*). "E.g." means "for example"; "i.e." means "that is."

4. I do not like it when, in an effort to conform to the "rules" of feminist grammar rather than the historically correct grammatical rules governing the use of the English language, a person writes, "A person sings a song, but they don't realize how bad their voice is." This is a ludicrous sentence: "A" is a singular marker; "person" is a singular noun; "sings" is a singular verb; "they" and "their" are plural markers. Why not just write, "he or she doesn't" or "that person doesn't" or "that individual doesn't"?

5. I do not like it when students use a comma rather than a colon in a business letter: "Dear Todd,"—a letter to a friend; "Dear Dr. Pagano:"—a letter to a business associate.

6. I do not like it when students employ three of my most disliked words in their writing (I care not a whit about their speech.): "things," "biweekly," and "sucks."

    a. "Things"—The only "thing" (sic) about this vague, general, all-inclusive word is that it concisely conveys a clear-minded sense of absolutely nothing.

    b. "Biweekly"—Even from context, one cannot often discern meaning when this word is employed in a sentence. Does "We shall have biweekly meetings" mean we shall have meetings twice a week or every two weeks? The same applies with "bimonthly" and "biannually."

    c. "Sucks"—I mildly object to this word solely because students have no idea about its recent etymology: from about 1928 to the present, it has been used in the main to refer to fellatio. Without exception, students know that the word "fuck" has an extraordinarily negative connotation and denotation. Depending on the social circumstances, one exercises cautions when employing the word "fuck." But that is not the case, generally, with "suck."

7. I do not like it when students are afraid of using the passive voice (see **III.** f-2) because their high-school English teachers told them it should not be used. Nothing could be further (not "farther") from the truth. I like the passive voice in two particular instances:

a. For sentence variation, I like to employ the passive voice when every other sentence in a writing sample is in the active voice; the active voice is when the subject of a sentence performs the verb's action. E.g., Say you have a series of sentences in the active voice:

Present active	Present passive
I sing a song.	A song is sung.
Past active	Past passive
I sang a song.	A song was sung.
Present active	Present passive
I walk the dog.	The dog is walked.
Past active	Past passive
I walked the dog.	The dog was walked.
Present active	Present passive
I throw a ball.	A ball is thrown.
Past active	Past passive
I threw a ball.	A ball was thrown.

You can easily see how boring the active voice would be if all these sentences were in the same paragraph. (Similarly, you can also see how boring the passive voice would be if all these sentences were in the same paragraph.)

So, I like the passive voice for sentence and stylistic variation.

b. Perhaps the most important employment of the passive voice is for the person writing or speaking to use it to avoid being sued for libel (writing) or slander (speech). Consider the following:
"John reported that Todd was a liar, a thief, and a pederast"—Todd sues John.

"It was reported that Todd was a liar, a thief, and a pederast."—Todd doesn't know who reported it; ergo, he knows not whom to sue.

About the Iran-Contra scandal, then-Vice President George H. W. Bush said, "Mistakes were made." What a wonderful employment of the passive voice. No one could accuse him of lying. However, had he used the active voice—"I made mistakes." or "Our administration made mistakes."—then the talking heads would be talking about the mistakes made by the Reagan administration.

Acknowledgements

This book is the product of much help and insight from many people. I'm especially indebted to John Rubadeau, Dr. Johnson to my Boswell, who opened many doors and patiently (and also impatiently) answered countless questions about his past and present. Equally indispensable were the insights of Pat Rubadeau, whose memories and a wonderful old writeup of how she met John provided indispensable input. Pat's expert edits to this book's draft, ones she crashed through during the initial Covid-19 isolation period in the spring of 2020, contributed vastly to the quality of this effort. Becky Cammack and Nick Rubadeau's stories and photos helped me immensely also.

Others whose memories, insights, expertise, photos, and documents played vital roles in this story deserve public notice: Lillian Back, Nina Bailey, David Barringer, Barbara Bone, Jake Butt, Gary Burchett, Bonnie Campbell, Tim Cavnar, Eric Chisholm, Stephanie Combs, Marty Cosby, Gray and Mary Jean Currier, Pat and Ann Egan, Matt Elliott, Lincoln Faller, Douglas Gordon, Evan Hansen, Susannah Nichols Hansen, Kirsten Herold, Emily Higgins, Shawn Hervey-Jumper, Lucian Leon, Dave Matthews, Matt McKillip, Chris Meyer, Nanci Milam, James and Madeline Moore, Bernd Munderloh, Ron Pace, Vince Pagano, Betty and Chris Poulous, Parker Procida, Eric Rogoff, Jean Rosella, Eric Scheible, Craig Snow, Joan Spahr, Dan Varner, Claire Wood, Elise Yu, and Leona Zeplin. Their brief mentions here belie the time and effort they spent helping me amass what I needed to write this book.

Thanks also to people who were doing their jobs but who took the time to do more than they had to: Julie Laundrie, public-records custodian of the Madison, Wisconsin, Police Department; Patricia Sellinger of the University of Michigan FOIA office; and Charlene Smith, deputy clerk, Claiborne County Chancery Court in Tazewell, Tennessee. Thanks to all; errors and misrepresentations are on me.

About the Author

Todd Neff covered science and the environment for the *Daily Camera* in Boulder, Colorado, and has taught narrative nonfiction at the University of Colorado, where he was also a Ted Scripps Fellow in Environmental Journalism.

His first book, *From Jars to the Stars*, won the Colorado Book Award for History. His second book, *The Laser That's Changing the World*, tells the story of the inventors and innovators who developed lidar for self-driving cars and many other surprising uses.

Todd graduated from the University of Michigan and the Fletcher School of Law and Diplomacy at Tufts University. He lives in Denver with his wife and two daughters.

Made in the USA
Middletown, DE
07 January 2021

31090306R00146